# A Time for Governing

# A Time for Governing

## Policy Solutions from the Pages of National Affairs

Edited by Yuval Levin and Meghan Clyne

ENCOUNTER BOOKS  NEW YORK - LONDON

First American edition published in 2012 by Encounter Books,
an activity of Encounter for Culture and Education, Inc.,
a nonprofit, tax exempt corporation.
Encounter Books website address: www.encounterbooks.com

Manufactured in the United States and printed on
acid-free paper. The paper used in this publication meets
the minimum requirements of ANSI/NISO Z39.48–1992
(R 1997) (*Permanence of Paper*).

FIRST AMERICAN EDITION
Essays from this collection first appeared in *National Affairs*.

LIBRARY OF CONGRESS CATALOGING-IN-PUBLICATION DATA
A time for governing : policy solutions from the pages of National Affairs /
edited by Yuval Levin and Meghan Clyne.
p. cm.
ISBN 978-1-59403-657-6 (pbk. : alk. paper)
1. United States—Economic policy—2009- 2. United States—Social policy—21st century. 3. Decentralization in government—United States.
4. Central-local government relations—United States. I. Levin, Yuval.
II. Clyne, Meghan. III. National Affairs (Washington, D.C.)
HC106.84T56 2012
330.973—dc23
2012005720

10 9 8 7 6 5 4 3 2 1

*This book was made possible by generous support from the Hertog/Simon Fund for Policy Analysis*

# CONTENTS

CONTENTS

# INTRODUCTION

This book is a "how to" guide for addressing some of America's most pressing public-policy challenges. Though such challenges are never in short supply, today's profusion of them is exceptional—making the need for clear thinking about them exceptionally urgent.

America finds herself in the midst of a governing crisis. It has been years in the making—caused by the crumbling of large governing institutions and public programs established in the middle of the last century, as well as by the transformation of the global economic order. The great task of American public life in the coming years will be to understand these shifts and the problems they have created, and to craft policy solutions capable of addressing them.

This collection aims to help in that task. Its first two chapters articulate the nature of the problem we face, and the subsequent 16 chapters offer specific policy reforms—of the welfare state, of the tax code, of our financial and monetary systems, of education, and of state budgets and policies.

Because they were written by 19 different authors, these essays do not agree on every point; indeed, several offer proposals that are in tension with others. But all are guided by a common vision of American life: by confidence and pride in our country, by a sense that our challenge is to build on our strengths to address our weaknesses, and by the conviction that chief among those strengths are our democratic capitalism, our ideals of liberty and equality under the law, and our roots in the longstanding traditions of the West. All of these essays also reflect the concern that American government has taken on too many tasks to perform any of them effectively. Thus each chapter offers proposals that would lead to a smaller but more capable government, and to a larger and more assertive private sector.

This vision of America and this approach to addressing its foremost problems define the work of *National Affairs*, a quarterly journal launched in 2009 to help Americans think more clearly about the challenges of self-government. Each quarter, *National Affairs* publishes essays about public policy, society, culture, politics, and the world of ideas, with an eye to what thoughtful Americans ought to know, and with a special concern for domestic policy and political economy, broadly understood.

The chapters of this book have all been previously published as essays in the journal's pages. As it is all too easy, especially in times of change and challenge, to reflect on broad abstractions while ignoring the details of specific policy problems, this collection includes some of the most manifestly policy-minded articles of those we have published to date. It is a compilation of achievable policy solutions. To speak of policy solutions is not to imply that we think that policy or politics can finally "solve" any true social problem—only that some of our problems are exacerbated by poor public policy, and could be meaningfully mitigated by thoughtful reforms.

This emphasis on achievable solutions reflects an appreciation of the "how" of government—of the ways in which the means of government can shape public life just as much as its ends. Indeed, those of us who are most inclined to think seriously about the proper ends of government are too often prone to lose sight of the importance of means. This tendency is nothing new: "A good government implies two things," James Madison wrote in Federalist No. 62. "First, fidelity to the object of government, which is the happiness of the people; secondly, a knowledge of the means by which that object can be best attained. Some governments are deficient in both these qualities; most governments are deficient in the first. I scruple not to assert, that in American governments too little attention has been paid to the last."

Not much has changed on that front, but the dilemmas of this moment demand that attention be paid to the means of American government, almost as much as to its ends. We hope that this volume contributes in some modest measure to clear thinking about both, at a time when such thinking is in critical demand.

—The Editors

# 1. America's Challenge

# Beyond the Welfare State

## *Yuval Levin*

SPRING 2011

IT IS BECOMING INCREASINGLY CLEAR that we in America are living through a period of transition. One chapter of our national life is closing, and another is about to begin. We can sense this in the tense volatility of our electoral politics, as dramatic "change elections" follow closely upon one another. We can feel it in the unseemly mood of decline that has infected our public life — leaving our usually cheerful nation fretful about global competition and unsure if the next generation will be able to live as well as the present one. Perhaps above all, we can discern it in an overwhelming sense of exhaustion emanating from many of our public institutions — our creaking mid-century transportation infrastructure, our overburdened regulatory agencies struggling to keep pace with a dynamic economy, our massive entitlement system edging toward insolvency.

But these are mostly symptoms of our mounting unease. The most significant *cause* runs deeper. We have the feeling that profound and unsettling change is afoot because the vision that has dominated our political imagination for a century — the vision of the social-democratic welfare state — is drained and growing bankrupt, and it is not yet clear just what will take its place.

That vision was an answer to a question America must still confront: How shall we balance the competing aspirations of our society — aspirations to both wealth and virtue, dynamism and compassion? How can we fulfill our simultaneous desires to race ahead yet leave no one behind? The answer offered by the social-democratic ideal was a technocratic welfare state that would balance these aspirations through all-encompassing programs of social insurance. We would

YUVAL LEVIN *is the editor of* National Affairs, *and a fellow at the Ethics and Public Policy Center.*

retain a private economy, but it would be carefully managed in order to curb its ill effects, and a large portion of its output would be used by the government to address large social problems, lessen inequality, and thus also build greater social solidarity.

Of course, this vision has never been implemented in full. But it has offered a model, for good and for ill. For the left, it provided long-term goals, criteria for distinguishing progress from retreat in making short-term compromises, and a kind of definition of the just society. For the right, it was a foil to be combated and averted — an archetype of soulless, stifling bureaucratic hubris — and it helped put objections to seemingly modest individual leftward steps into a broader, more coherent context. But both ends of our politics seemed implicitly to agree that, left to its own momentum, this is where our country was headed — where history would take us if no one stood athwart it yelling stop.

It is no longer really possible to think so. All over the developed world, nations are coming to terms with the fact that the social-democratic welfare state is turning out to be untenable. The reason is partly institutional: The administrative state is dismally inefficient and unresponsive, and therefore ill-suited to our age of endless choice and variety. The reason is also partly cultural and moral: The attempt to rescue the citizen from the burdens of responsibility has undermined the family, self-reliance, and self-government. But, in practice, it is above all fiscal: The welfare state has turned out to be unaffordable, dependent as it is upon dubious economics and the demographic model of a bygone era. Sustaining existing programs of social insurance, let alone continuing to build new ones on the social-democratic model, has become increasingly difficult in recent years, and projections for the coming decades paint an impossibly grim and baleful picture. There is simply no way that Europe, Japan, or America can actually go where the economists' long-term charts now point — to debts that utterly overwhelm their productive capacities, governments that do almost nothing but support the elderly, and economies with no room for dynamism, for growth, or for youth. Some change must come, and so it will.

But fully grasping this reality will not be easy. Our attachment to the social-democratic vision means that we tend to equate its exhaustion with our own exhaustion, and so to fall into a most un-American melancholy. On the left, fear of decline is now answered only with false hope that the dream may yet be saved through clever tinkering at the edges. On

4

the right, the coming collapse of the liberal welfare state brings calls for austerity—for less of the same—which only highlight the degree to which conservatives, too, are stuck in the social-democratic mindset.

The fact is that we do not face a choice between the liberal welfare state on one hand and austerity on the other. Those are two sides of the same coin: Austerity and decline are what will come if we do not reform the welfare state. The choice we face is between that combination and a different approach to balancing our society's deepest aspirations. America still has a little time to find such an alternative. Our moment of reckoning is coming, but it is not yet here. We have perhaps a decade in which to avert it and to foster again the preconditions for growth and opportunity without forcing a great disruption in the lives of millions, if we start now.

But we do not yet know quite how. The answer will not come from the left, which is far too committed to the old vision to accept its fate and contemplate alternatives. It must therefore emerge from the right. Conservatives must produce not only arguments against the liberal welfare state but also a different vision, a different answer to the question of how we might balance our aspirations. It must be a vision that emphasizes the pursuit of economic growth, republican virtues, and social mobility over economic security, value-neutral welfare, and social equality; that redefines the safety net as a means of making the poor more independent rather than making the middle class less so; and that translates these ideals into institutional forms that suit our modern, dynamic society.

That different vision is now beginning to take shape. Slowly, bit by bit, we are starting to see what must replace our welfare state.

## A CENTURY OF TRYING

When an intelligent and charismatic liberal president was elected in the midst of the most serious economic crisis in a generation in 2008, many on the left believed they were witnessing at last the triumph of the social-democratic dream in America. The Great Recession, they thought, could finally push aside the traditional American resistance to that dream, and create a desire for security that would yield the perfect atmosphere for the advancement of their cause. An enormous expansion of the government's role in the health sector enacted a year after Obama's inauguration lent further credence to this view.

But what seemed like the long-awaited triumph of the liberal agenda in America may actually prove to be its unraveling. When historians consider it in retrospect, the economic crisis of 2008 might well be seen as having marked the beginning of the end of the social-democratic welfare state. It will have done so by making suddenly urgent what was otherwise a gradually oncoming problem. By simultaneously showing us what a terrible debt crisis might feel like, sparking a federal spending spree that much of the public very quickly deemed excessive, and making more immediate the otherwise slowly approaching collapse of our entitlement system, the events of the past few years forced many Americans to wonder whether we were not headed toward an abyss.

This conflation of short- and medium-term problems — of annual deficits with retirement liabilities, of sluggish growth with the burden of debt, of the Obama agenda with the broader social-democratic project — is in one sense an error, of course. But it is not ultimately an error. Indeed, it is a powerfully clarifying synthesis, which has given us a vision of our future: The fiscal crisis we face *is* an extended and expanded version of our deficit problem; the recession from which we are emerging *was* a preview of life under suffocating debt; the Obama agenda *does* seek incrementally to advance the larger social-democratic vision — especially on the health-care front, where that vision has seen its greatest fiscal failures. In each case, we have become more powerfully aware of the grave troubles that await us if we do not reform our welfare state — as though the frog in the pot got a glimpse of just how hot the water was about to get. This has made a growing number of Americans (though surely still not a majority) open to changing our ways while there remains a little time to do so, and has raised the possibility of gradually putting not only one program or another but the broad vision at the heart of our politics on the table.

That vision begins with the belief that capitalism, while capable of producing great prosperity, leaves a great many people profoundly insecure, and so must be both strictly controlled by a system of robust regulations and balanced off by a system of robust social insurance. From birth to death, citizens should be ensconced in a series of protections and benefits intended to shield them from the harsh edges of the market and allow them to pursue dignified, fulfilling lives: universal child care, universal health care, universal public schooling and higher education, welfare benefits for the poor, generous labor protections for workers, dexterous management of the levers of the economy to ease the cycles of boom and bust, skillful direction of public funds to spur private productivity and efficiency, and, finally, pensions for the elderly. Each component would be overseen by a competent and rational bureaucracy, and the whole would make for a system that is not only beneficent but unifying and dignifying, and that enables the pursuit of common national goals and ideals.

This system would encompass all citizens, not only the poor, in an effort to overcome some of the social consequences of the iniquities inherent in a capitalist economy. As Robert Kuttner, founding editor of the liberal *American Prospect* magazine, has put it: "In a democratic polity that also happens to be a highly unequal market economy, there is immense civic value to treating middle-class and poor people alike. A common social security program, or medical care program, or public school program, helps to create the kind of cohesion that Europe's social democrats like to call 'social solidarity' — a sense that basic humanity and citizenship in the political community require equal treatment in at least some areas of economic life."

Thus, the inequality, dislocation, and isolation caused by capitalism could be remedied together, and in a way that would also help to get the middle class invested in the system (not to say dependent on it) and help society to grow increasingly rational and enlightened under the guidance of an educated and benevolent governing class. This kind of welfare state aims not just at keeping the poor above a certain minimum level of subsistence and helping them rise, but at a new arrangement of society to be achieved by the redistribution of resources and responsibilities.

Of course these are the general outlines of a vision of society, not particular planks of a policy agenda. But that vision has acted in the background of American (and European) politics for a century, shaping policy proposals and political battles large and small.

In our country it has often had to be pursued almost in stealth, by incremental steps undertaken as events permit. The Democratic Party has never made a full-throated case for the broader vision in the way that some European social democrats have. Part of the reason is surely America's basic orientation toward government. Ours may be the only government to arise out of a distrust of government. Again and again in our history, passionate waves of resistance to authority have rattled our politics, while periods of trust in the state have been rare. The left has sought to use those rare moments—particularly the emergency of the Great Depression and the unique stretch of relative peace and prosperity of the early 1960s—to advance the welfare state where it could. Even then, however, it always faced staunch resistance, and proceeded by fits and starts—enacting one program or another in the hope of coming back for more when circumstances allowed it.

This has left us with a somewhat disjointed arrangement of welfare-state programs, tilted disproportionately toward the elderly—who are the foremost beneficiaries of our two largest entitlement programs (Social Security and Medicare) and receive more than a quarter of the benefits provided by the third largest (Medicaid). The other elements of our welfare state have taken the form of the many dozens of smaller, more targeted programs—from Head Start to public housing to the Children's Health Insurance Program—that fill out the federal government's massive entitlement and domestic discretionary budgets. All of these individual programs, large and small, fit into a broader pattern and trajectory defined by the social-democratic ideal. And because that ideal has largely functioned in the background, it has been possible to present and understand these incremental steps as mere pragmatism, while opposition to them has had to present itself as radical and ideological.

Throughout much of the 20th century, there was a sense on the left (and therefore among most of our cultural and intellectual elite) that steps along the social-democratic trajectory constituted progress—that this was where we were fated to go, however long it might take. This sense was powerfully palpable in the debate surrounding the latest major step along that path, which was taken just last year through the health-care reforms of the Patient Protection and Affordable Care Act. Throughout that debate, the word "historic" was constantly on the lips of the bill's champions, and the notion that the bill was the latest in a long line of consistent forward steps was everywhere in the air. President Obama, when signing the measure, described it as the culmination of "almost a century of trying," and said the law contained "reforms that generations of Americans have fought for and marched for and hungered to see." As House Speaker Nancy Pelosi called the final vote to a close, she used the same gavel that had been used when the House voted to enact the Medicare and Medicaid programs in 1965, to emphasize the point that these were all elements of one large project.

THE PASSING OF AN ILLUSION

But Pelosi's chosen symbol stood for more than she intended. While the enactment of the two massive health-care entitlements of the Great Society period may have represented the peak of social-democratic activism in America, those two entitlements now also represent the failure of the social-democratic vision in practice. They have grown so unwieldy and expensive as to be thoroughly unsustainable, and in the process have helped inflate costs in the broader health-care sector in ways that now imperil the nation's fiscal future. The new health-care entitlement enacted last year promises to do more of the same, and thus to place even further stress on the crumbling foundations of our welfare state.

Nearly all of the dozens of small and large programs that compose our welfare state have come to exhibit similar problems: out-of-control costs, mediocre results, harmful unintended consequences, and by now a growing sense of inadequacy and exhaustion. This combination of problems is hardly a coincidence; it runs to the heart of the social-democratic project. The three key arguments in favor of this vision of the welfare state — its rationality and efficiency, its morality and capacity for unifying society, and its economic benefits — all turn out in reality to be among its foremost failings.

First, the welfare state functions in practice through the administrative state — the network of public agencies that employ technical expertise and bureaucratic management to enforce rules and provide benefits and services. The case for such bureaucracy is a case for impartial efficiency — an argument that a rationally organized institution following strict rules and exercising power for the public good should be the most fair, economical, and convenient way to administer large programs. This approach, grounded in the Progressive faith in scientific administration, appeals to the technocratic inclinations of the modern left, but it turns out to be poorly suited to governing actual people — especially in our dynamic modern economy.

Human societies do not work by obeying orderly commands from central managers, however well meaning; they work through the erratic interplay of individual and, even more, of familial and communal decisions answering locally felt desires and needs. Designed to offer professional expert management, our bureaucratic institutions assume a society defined by its material needs and living more or less in stasis, and so they are often at a loss to contend with a people in constant motion and possessed of a seemingly infinite imagination for cultural and commercial innovation. The result is gross inefficiency — precisely the opposite of what the administrative state is intended to yield.

In our everyday experience, the bureaucratic state presents itself not as a benevolent provider and protector but as a corpulent behemoth — flabby, slow, and expressionless, unmoved by our concerns, demanding compliance with arcane and seemingly meaningless rules as it breathes musty air in our faces and sends us to the back of the line. Largely free of competition, most administrative agencies do not have to answer directly to public preferences, and so have developed in ways that make their own operations easier (or their own employees more contented) but that grow increasingly distant from the way we live.

Unresponsive ineptitude is not merely an annoyance. The sluggishness of the welfare state drains it of its moral force. The crushing weight of bureaucracy permits neither efficiency nor idealism. It thus robs us of a good part of the energy of democratic capitalism and encourages a corrosive cynicism that cannot help but undermine the moral aims of the social-democratic vision.

Worse yet, because the institutions of the welfare state are intended to be partial substitutes for traditional familial, social, religious, and cultural mediating institutions, their growth weakens the very structures that might balance our society's restless quest for prosperity and novelty and might replenish our supply of idealism.

This is the second major failing of this vision of society — a kind of spiritual failing. Under the rules of the modern welfare state, we give up a portion of the capacity to provide for ourselves and in return are freed from a portion of the obligation to discipline ourselves. Increasing economic collectivism enables increasing moral individualism, both of which leave us with less responsibility, and therefore with less grounded and meaningful lives.

Moreover, because all citizens — not only the poor — become recipients of benefits, people in the middle class come to approach their government as claimants, not as self-governing citizens, and to approach the social safety net not as a great majority of givers eager to make sure that a small minority of recipients are spared from devastating poverty but as a mass of dependents demanding what they are owed. It is hard to imagine an ethic better suited to undermining the moral basis of a free society.

Meanwhile, because public programs can never truly take the place of traditional mediating institutions, the people who most depend upon the welfare state are relegated to a moral vacuum. Rather than strengthening social bonds, the rise of the welfare state has precipitated the collapse of family and community, especially among the poor.

This was not the purpose of our welfare state, but it is among its many unintended consequences. As Irving Kristol put it in 1997, "The secular, social-democratic founders of the modern welfare state really did think that in the kind of welfare state we have today people would be more public-spirited, more high-minded, more humanly 'fulfilled.'" They were wrong about this for the same reason that their expectations of the administrative state have proven misguided — because their understanding of the human person was far too shallow and emaciated. They assumed that moral problems were functions of material problems, so that addressing the latter would resolve the former, when the opposite is more often the case. And guided by the ethic of the modern left, they imagined that traditional institutions like the family, the church, and the local association were sources of division, prejudice, and backwardness, rather than essential pillars of our moral lives. The failure of the social-democratic vision is, in this sense, fundamentally a failure of moral wisdom.

That is not to say, of course, that it did not produce positive benefits along the way. Indeed, the era in which the social-democratic vision has dominated our politics has hardly been an age of decline for America — it has been, if anything, the American century. And it has been a time of diminishing poverty and rising standards of living. But it is now becoming apparent that this was achieved by our spending our capital (economic, moral, and human) without replenishing it, and that this failure, too, is a defining characteristic of the social-democratic vision.

America's unchallenged economic prowess in the wake of the Second World War, and the resulting surge of growth and prosperity, were essential to enabling the flurry of social-democratic activism we know as the Great Society, and which continues to define the basic shape of our domestic policy. Flush with revenue and stirred by the promise of technocratic mastery, our government took on immense entitlement commitments and major social reforms in that era, and these have certainly had some of their intended consequences. But they have also struck at the roots (economic and especially moral) of our ability to sustain our strength. The collapse of the family among the poor—powerfully propelled by the ethic of social democracy and by a horrendously designed welfare system that was not improved until the mid-1990s—has vastly worsened social and economic inequality in America, and the capacity of generations to rise out of poverty. Our entitlement commitments, particularly those of the massive health-care entitlements enacted in the 1960s, stand to make ever-greater demands on our economic strength, and so to sap our potential to sustain that strength. And our system of age-based wealth transfers relies upon a demographic model that the welfare state seriously undermines, and that now bears no relation to the reality of American life. In the age of social democracy, we have failed to think generationally, and so have failed to think of the prerequisites for renewal.

These trends all come together in the third major failing of our welfare state, and the one that, more than any other, may yet bring about real change: its economic breakdown. Simply put, we cannot afford to preserve our welfare state in anything like its present form.

The heart of the problem is the heart of our welfare state: our entitlement system. Age-based wealth transfers in an aging society are obviously problematic. As Americans are living longer and having fewer children (and as the Baby Boomers retire at a rate of 10,000 people per day over the next 20 years), the ratio of workers paying taxes to retirees collecting benefits is falling precipitously—from 16 workers per retiree in 1950 to just three today, and closer to two in the coming decades. This means that even the simplest and least troubled of our age-based transfer programs—the Social Security program—is facing serious problems: Social Security ran a deficit for the first time last year, and the Congressional Budget Office estimates it will continue to do so from now on unless its structure is reformed. Add to that our exploding health-care costs—which the design of our health-care entitlements severely exacerbates—and you will begin to get a sense of the problem we confront. The trustees of Social Security and Medicare now estimate that the two programs together have an unfunded long-term liability of $46 trillion—about $30 trillion of it in Medicare. Meanwhile, Medicaid, which provides health coverage to the poor, is now nearly as expensive as Medicare—costing more than half a trillion dollars a year, and growing swiftly.

The growth of these programs threatens to swallow the federal budget. The CBO estimates that, by 2025, Medicare, Medicaid, Social

Security, and interest payments on the debt alone will consume every last cent of federal revenues, leaving all discretionary spending to be funded by borrowing. And that spending, too, has been growing by leaps and bounds recently—domestic discretionary spending has increased by 25% in just the past three years.

That explosion in discretionary spending is why our immediate budget picture is so bleak, but the fact that an entitlement crisis waits just around the corner means that there is no clear boundary any longer between our short-term and our longer-term fiscal problems. Our debt has begun to balloon, and absent major reforms, it will not stop. CBO figures show that, if current policies remain in place, the national debt will grow much faster than the economy in the coming years: A decade from now, the United States will owe nearly $20 trillion—more than three times what we owed in 2008. At that point, interest payments alone will consume about $800 billion a year—more than four times as much as they did in 2008. And the entitlement crisis will only just be getting underway.

This explosion of both discretionary and entitlement spending is like nothing our country has ever experienced, and it is why our welfare state is unsustainable. The graph below traces the national debt from 1790 through 2050, using historical figures (the solid line) and projections (marked by dashes) from the Congressional Budget Office. Previous spikes in the debt can be traced to discrete events in our history—the Civil War, the two world wars, and the Great Depression. But the spike that is now beginning, which will be worse by far than any we have seen before, is a function of the fiscal collapse of our welfare state.

*FEDERAL DEBT HELD BY THE PUBLIC, 1790-2050*

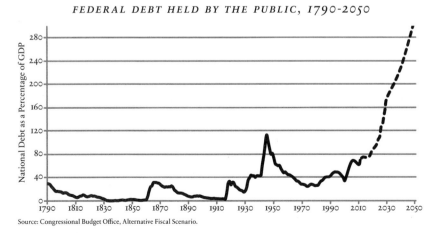

Source: Congressional Budget Office, Alternative Fiscal Scenario.

If we do not change course, by 2030, America's national debt will be nearly twice the size of the economy; by 2050, it will be roughly three times the size of the economy and will continue to grow from there. Such massive and unprecedented debt will make it impossible for America to experience anything like the growth and prosperity that marked the postwar era. Simply paying interest on this debt, let alone funding the activities of government, will require more and more borrowing, as well as cuts in other areas and major tax increases. It will also leave us exposed to tremendous risk of inflation and dependent on the goodwill of our lenders. It will leave future generations saddled with an immense burden but unable to enjoy the benefits of much of what they will be paying for, since it will make it impossible to sustain our welfare state in anything like its current form.

Japan and the nations of Western Europe are looking at similar projections. And in our country, many state governments are facing their own dire fiscal prospects as a result of similarly unsustainable retirement commitments and spending patterns. This is where the social-democratic project has gotten us. If we simply follow this trajectory, then future generations considering this chart will have no doubt as to just when the turning point came, and just which generation failed to keep its charge.

It is unimaginable that the world's foremost economic power would do this to itself by choice. And we will not. We will change course.

### DEMOCRATIC CAPITALISM

Changing course will not be easy, to be sure. It will require extraordinary sacrifices from today's young Americans, who will need to continue paying the taxes necessary to support the retirements of their parents and grandparents while denying themselves the same level of benefits so their children and grandchildren can thrive. To persuade them to make such sacrifices, our political leaders will need to offer them a plausible program of reform, and an appealing vision of American life beyond the dream of social democracy.

That vision cannot be a purist fantasy. It must be a serious answer — an answer better suited to a proper understanding of human nature and American life — to the same question that motivated the social-democratic ideal: How do we balance our aspirations to prosperity and virtue and build a thriving society that makes its wealth and promise accessible to all?

In their struggle with the left these past 60 years, conservatives have too often responded to the social-democratic vision by arguing with it in the abstract. Constitutionalism, natural rights, libertarianism, traditionalism—all offered powerful objections to the welfare state, but few viable alternatives. Conservatives have thus lacked specificity on policy, and so have been left struggling to explain themselves to the public. There have, of course, been exceptions (most notably the economic reforms of the 1980s and the welfare reforms of the 1990s). On the whole, however, conservatives have focused on the size and scope of government, but not on its proper purposes—on yelling stop, but not on where to go instead.

Now, as the social-democratic dream grows truly bankrupt and untenable, America finds itself governed by a reactionary party and a conservative party. The reactionary party, the Democratic Party, its head in the sand and its mind adrift in false nostalgia, insists that nothing is wrong, and that the welfare state requires little more than tinkering at the edges, and indeed further expansions. It lives always with the model of the Great Society in mind, and fails to grasp the ruin it threatens to bring upon the rising generation. It cannot imagine a different approach.

The conservative party, the Republican Party, still struggles for a vocabulary of resistance, and so has not taken up in earnest the vocabulary of alternatives. It calls on the spirit of the founders, but not on their genius for designing institutions; it shadowboxes Progressives who no longer exist (and whose successors, running on fumes and inertia, have nowhere near the intellectual depth to take up their case); it insists that our problem is just too much government.

But if the Republican Party is to be a truly conservative party, it will need to think its way to an agenda of conservative reform. Conservatism is reformist at its core, combining, as Edmund Burke put it, "a disposition to preserve and an ability to improve," and so responding to the changing world by means that seek to strengthen what is most essential. A conservative vision would be driven not by a desire to "fundamentally transform America" (as Barack Obama promised to do in 2008), but rather by an idea of what we want to be that is the best form of what we are. It would look to make our institutions suit us better, and so to make them serve us better and more effectively help us improve ourselves.

Our welfare state is very poorly suited to the kind of society we are—an aging society in which older people are, on the whole, wealthier than younger people. And it is very poorly suited to the kind of society we want to be—enterprising and vibrant, with a free economy, devoted to social mobility and eager to offer a hand up to the poor. A successful reform agenda would have to take account of both.

It would begin not from the assumption that capitalism is dehumanizing, but rather from the sense that too many people do not have access to capitalism's benefits. It would start not from the presumption that traditional practices and institutions must be overcome by rational administration, but rather from the firm conviction that family, church, and civil society are the means by which human beings find fulfillment and are essential counterweights to the market. It would reject the notion that universal dependence can build solidarity, and insist instead that only self-reliance, responsibility, and discipline can build mutual respect and character in a free society. It would seek to help the poor not with an empty promise of material equality but with a fervent commitment to upward mobility. It would reject the top-down bureaucratic state in favor of consumer choice and competition. It would insist on the distinction between a welfare pro-gram and a welfare state—between directed efforts to help the poor avail themselves of meaningful opportunities and a broad project to remake society along social-democratic lines.

The appeal of such a re-orientation is not that it is radical but that it is moderate—that it suits us. And for now, there is even still time to pur-sue it by moderate means—to allow today's retirees and near-retirees to receive all the benefits they have been promised as we transform our institutions going forward.

It would be folly, of course, to propose a detailed policy platform that would meet these criteria. Just as the left for a century had not a precise agenda but a general vision of what its ideal outcome would look like—a vision that could guide incremental steps and provide cri-teria for judging compromises—so the conservative vision, the ideal of democratic capitalism, can exist only in outline. But over the past half-decade, in the work of conservative scholars, intellectuals, and politicians, just such an outline has been emerging.

It would begin with a simple and predictable tax system, with a broad base and low rates, free of most of today's deductions and exclusions. The only three worth keeping in the individual tax code are the tax exemption for retirement savings (which are far preferable to universal cash benefits to retirees), a unified child tax credit (to encourage parent-hood and to offset the mistreatment of parents in the tax code), and the charitable-giving deduction (since a reduction in government's role in social welfare must be met with an increase in the role of civil society, which should be encouraged). These three exemptions are directed precisely to the needs of a modern society, and to addressing the three broad failings of the social-democratic welfare state. The corporate tax code should similarly be dramatically broadened and flattened to encourage growth, which must be the foremost goal of economic policy.

Second, essentially all government benefits—including benefits for the elderly—should be means-tested so that those in greater need receive more help and those who are not needy do not become dependent on public support. Most retirees would still receive some public benefits (and the poorest could well get more than they do now), but the design of our welfare programs would avoid creating the misimpression that they are savings programs. People who are already retired or nearly so today should be exempted from such means-testing, as they have planned for decades around the existing system; Americans below 55 or so, however, should expect public help only if they are in need once they retire. Means-testing should, to the extent possible, be designed to avoid discouraging saving and work. And private retirement savings should be strongly encouraged and incentivized, so that people who have the means would build private nest eggs with less reliance on government.

Third, we should advance a consumer-based health-care system—backed with fixed, means-tested premium supports—in which individuals purchase their own insurance in a free market regulated largely by the states. Such a system would, over time, replace today's tax exclusion for employer-based coverage (which would be converted into a flat universal tax credit for the purchase of insurance) as well as Medicare and Medicaid (which would become add-ons to that credit based on wealth, age, and health—again leaving today's retirees or near-retirees with today's benefits). This would create a single continuous system in which the poor and the old would still have heavily subsidized coverage and much of the middle class would still have moderately subsidized coverage, but everyone would make real purchasing decisions and keep the same insurance as his circumstances changed. This approach would seek to let people be active consumers, rather than passive recipients of benefits—which would be good both for the federal budget (since consumer pressure in a free market keeps costs down far better than price controls) and for the character of our nation.

Fourth, we should gradually but significantly reduce domestic discretionary spending, ending most of the discretionary Great Society programs and folding others into block grants to the states. The federal government's role in the provision of social services should be minimal, and largely limited to helping the states and the institutions of civil society better carry out their missions. It would still have some role as an investor (in infrastructure and education, above all), but this too should be strictly targeted to essential public needs that the private sector would not meet, and block-granted to the states whenever possible. Government at all levels should also look to contract its remaining functions out to the private sector where it can, both to improve efficiency and to avoid harmful conflicts between the government's obligations to the people it serves and its obligations to the people it employs—conflicts that have been rampant in our time.

Fifth, we should reduce the reach of the administrative state, paring back all but essential regulations and protections and adopting over time an ethic of keeping the playing field level rather than micromanaging market forces, and of preferring set rules (in regulation, in monetary policy, and elsewhere) to administrative discretion.

Obviously, these are only general principles and aims. And at least as important as what they contain is what they do not—what is left to the sphere of the family, religion, and civil society. Government must see itself as an ally and supporter of these crucial mediating institutions, not as a substitute for them. Its role is to sustain the preconditions for social, cultural, and economic vitality.

But these general aims offer a stark contrast to the general aims of the social-democratic vision of society—a very different understanding of what it is about capitalism that needs to be tempered and balanced, of what the sources of social solidarity really are, of the significance of responsibility and choice, and of the deepest meaning of the American experiment. They outline a government that is smaller but more effective, and gesture toward a vision of American public life that is economically sustainable and morally rich and responsible.

## MODEST MEANS TO MODEST ENDS

Champions of our welfare state view democratic capitalism as the grim reality to be overcome and social democracy as the elevated ideal to be realized. But this has it backwards. The vision of social democracy has dominated our political life for many decades, but it is failing us. Real democratic capitalism—a free society with a free economy and a commitment to help every citizen enjoy the benefits of both—is the ideal that must guide the work of American domestic policy in the coming years.

That ideal, like any ideal, will never be perfectly realized. The planks roughly sketched above are not dogmas but general guides for compromise and barter. They can help us discern steps forward from steps backward, and give us a direction to aim for. Every step in this direction, however small and unsatisfying, should be welcomed, and every step will help to ease our way to the next. Some steps (especially those involving health care and entitlements) are more urgent than others, but all point in the same direction and all can be advanced incrementally.

Even under the best of circumstances, if these policy pillars were to be fully enacted, we would still have a very sizable government, and no shortage of bureaucracy and inefficiency. There would still be plenty for Atlas to shrug about. But some of the gravest threats to our future would be addressed, and the basic orientation of our politics would be made friendlier to our deepest aspirations. Politics, after all, is not about a destination but about sustaining the conditions that allow citizens to live thriving private lives and a thriving national life. That is always a matter of adjustments and modifications in search of an arrangement of policies and institutions well suited to our character, our needs, our strengths and weaknesses, and our priorities.

Conservatives should therefore not expect to ever simply win the argument. Our challenge, rather, is to dominate the argument—to offer the vision that implicitly sets the tone for our common life. The key to doing so is the emergence of a policy-oriented conservatism, one able to make gainful compromises not because it is ambivalent about its own aims or tentative in its commitment to them but because it knows exactly what it wants—a thriving free society with a market economy, strong families, a devotion to country, and a commitment to the value of every life—and knows that this can (indeed must) be obtained gradually, by a mix of persuasion and proof. Such an approach must always remain grounded in the principles of American life—the principles of the Declaration of Independence and the Constitution, of the Western tradition and of classical liberalism. But it must also translate those principles into policy particulars. In our politics, battles over ideas are won in practice, not in theory.

Recent decades have offered some examples of such an approach—from welfare reform to the urban policing revolution—but they have been too few and far between. There are good reasons to hope that just such an approach is now emerging more broadly on the right, and good reasons to encourage and foster its emergence.

It could hardly come too soon. We need it not only because we are increasingly drowning in debt, and not only because our governing institutions are growing exhausted and out of touch with reality. We need it above all because the decline of the social-democratic welfare state risks persuading us, falsely, that America's fate is to decline along with it. On the contrary, America's fate is, as it always has been, to show the world by example how a commitment to human liberty and equality, an application of republican virtues, a belief in individual ingenuity and drive, and an unswerving devotion to helping the least among us rise can defy the cynics and the pessimists, and can make future generations proud to succeed us.

*Originally published as "Beyond the Welfare State" in the Spring 2011 issue of* National Affairs.

# Keeping America's Edge

## *Jim Manzi*

WINTER 2010

THE UNITED STATES is in a tough spot. As we dig ourselves out
from a serious financial crisis and a deep recession, our very efforts
to recover are exacerbating much more fundamental problems that our
country has let fester for too long. Beyond our short-term worries, and
behind many of today's political debates, lurks the deeper challenge of
coming to terms with America's place in the global economic order.

Our strategic situation is shaped by three inescapable realities. First
is the inherent conflict between the creative destruction involved in
free-market capitalism and the innate human propensity to avoid risk
and change. Second is ever-increasing international competition. And
third is the growing disparity in behavioral norms and social conditions
between the upper and lower income strata of American society.

These realities combine to form a daunting problem. And the task of
resolving it turns out not, by and large, to be a matter of foreign policy.
Rather, it compels us to consider how we balance economic dynamism
and growth against the unity and stability of our society. After all, we
must have continuous, rapid technological and business-model innovation to grow our economy fast enough to avoid losing power to those
who do not share America's values—and this innovation requires increasingly deregulated markets and fewer restrictions on behavior. But such
deregulation would cause significant displacement and disruption that
could seriously undermine America's social cohesion—which is not
only essential to a decent and just society, but also to producing the kind
of skilled and responsible citizens that free markets ultimately require.
Moreover, preserving the integrity of our social fabric by minimizing the
divisions that can rend society often requires government policies—to

JIM MANZI *is the founder and chairman of an applied artificial intelligence software company, and a senior fellow at the Manhattan Institute.*

reduce inequality or ensure access to jobs, education, housing, or health care—that can in turn undercut growth and prosperity. Neither innovation nor cohesion can do without the other, but neither, it seems, can avoid undermining the other.

Reconciling these competing forces is America's great challenge in the decades ahead, but will be made far more difficult by the growing bifurcation of American society. Of course, this is not a new dilemma: It has actually undergirded most of the key political-economy debates of the past 30 years. But a dysfunctional political dynamic has prevented the nation from addressing it well, and has instead given us the worst of both worlds: a ballooning welfare state that threatens future growth, along with growing socioeconomic disparities.

Both major political parties have internal factions that sit on each side of the divide between innovation and cohesion. But broadly speaking, Republicans since Ronald Reagan have been the party of innovation, and Democrats have been the party of cohesion.

Conservatives have correctly viewed the policy agenda of the left as an attempt to undo the economic reforms of the 1980s. They have therefore, as a rhetorical and political strategy, downplayed the problems of cohesion—problems like inequality, wage stagnation, worker displacement, and disparities in educational performance—to emphasize the importance of innovation and growth. Liberals, meanwhile, have correctly identified the problem of cohesion, but have generally proposed antediluvian solutions and downplayed the necessity of innovation in a competitive world. They have noted that America's economy in the immediate wake of World War II was in many ways simultaneously more regulated, more successful, and more equitable than today's economy, but mistakenly assume that by restoring greater regulation we could re-create both the equity and prosperity of that era.

The conservative view fails to acknowledge the social costs of unrestrained economic innovation—costs that have made themselves powerfully apparent in American politics throughout our history. The liberal view, meanwhile, betrays a misunderstanding of the global economic environment.

To grasp the difficulty of this moment for America, we must see more clearly the pain involved in economic innovation, the price we would pay for stifling innovation, and the daunting social obstacles that stand in the way of balancing the two.

### THE COST OF PROSPERITY

An economy built upon constant and relatively free innovation is inherently difficult to sustain in a democracy. This is not so much a matter of anti-market ideology as of the painful realities of economic change. Innovation forces change, and the pain involved tends to be felt immediately while the benefits are usually diffuse and harder to perceive in the short term.

It is therefore natural for people to organize to prevent the spread of significant innovation. The original Luddites were cotton weavers who, in the throes of Britain's Industrial Revolution, responded to their displacement by automated weaving technology directly: They smashed looms. In America, people in similar situations rarely assault property en masse, but they do form political coalitions to pass laws that restrict innovation. It is understandable that the enormous waves of innovation always sweeping over a dynamic free-market economy will arouse great unease and opposition. But for that economy to prosper, the unease and opposition must be overcome.

This dynamic is often easiest to see at a distance. Consider, for instance, our country's transition from an agricultural to an industrial economy. In 1800, America was a nation of farmers: About three-quarters of the labor force worked in agriculture. Since then, this share has been in almost continuous decline. By the eve of the Civil War, it was a little over half; by 1900 it was about one-third. Today, agriculture employs less than 3% of the work force. This has been great for consumers: Farming is now incredibly efficient, and food is cheaper and more plentiful in real terms than ever before in human history. American agriculture today is also a successful industry; in 2007, the U.S. exported over $75 billion of agricultural products, and it has maintained a positive trade surplus in food for decades. But agriculture is no longer an industry that can provide employment for very many people.

The transformation described by these statistics was not easy. It produced enormous flux in social, political, and family relationships, and the instability lasted for generations. One of the most painful things about markets is that they often make fools of our fathers: Sharp operators with an eye for trends often outperform those who carefully learn a trade and continue a tradition. And the Industrial Revolution combined material deprivation for people who had only known farming with radical uncertainty about the future for much of the country. The appeal of political resistance to such change — like that embodied by the populists and William Jennings Bryan at the turn of the 20th century — is easy to see. But their approach would have meant propping up emotionally resonant family farms while retarding the development of the industrial economy.

The industrial economy itself has witnessed a similar drama over the past 60 years. America has a very productive manufacturing sector, but that sector doesn't employ much of the population anymore. At the end of World War II, manufacturing accounted for about one-third of the American work force. Today it accounts for about one-tenth. In terms of employment, we are no longer transitioning to a service economy; we are there. Over the same period, however, manufacturing has consistently represented about 15% of rapidly growing U.S. economic output. The chart below presents the classic image of massive economic transformation.

REAL MANUFACTURING OUTPUT AND EMPLOYMENT

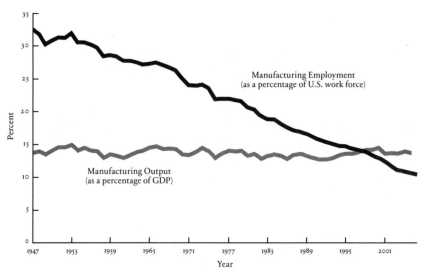

Source: Bureau of Economic Analysis; Bureau of Labor Statistics.

Ever-increasing productivity involves the use of human capital in new and constantly evolving ways. This is great for growth, but can be very hard on the people involved. It is impossible to know, moreover, what new sectors will actually be productive and how they will develop.

That is why the free play of markets with limited intrusion by the government is so essential. Almost all industrial policy ends up protecting existing institutions; this is a function of human nature and is not fixable by clever program design. As a result, industrial policy normally preserves jobs that a ruthless market would eliminate, and subsidizes the kinds of new technological developments that can be exploited by existing large firms. But these favored developments are rarely the sources of new high-wage jobs — and so such policy is more often a recipe for controlled stagnation than for continued growth. The attempt to protect ourselves from the pain of change ends up creating a sclerotic economy that, in the long run, puts everyone at greater risk.

One obvious response is to use the political process to both slow down the rate of innovation to an acceptable pace and redistribute the country's economic output in a manner designed to maintain social harmony. That way, the pain of innovation is avoided and the pain of stagnation is mitigated — especially for the middle and lower classes, who are most vulnerable to the effects of both. This is the logic of the welfare state, and the direction pursued by much of Western Europe since the Second World War.

The problem, however, is that the United States does not exist in a vacuum, and making our internal economic changes less stressful is far from our only concern. We also face external challenges, especially rising competition from abroad. And our position in the global order means we cannot afford to go easy on ourselves and constrict innovation. Quite the opposite: We need rapid growth just to keep up.

## A NATION AMONG NATIONS

American economic policy in the wake of World War II was developed by a generation of statesmen who dealt themselves a great hand of cards, and then played it brilliantly. It is hard to exaggerate the strength of America's competitive position in the world economy in September 1945: The United States accounted for an absolute majority of all global manufacturing output, had the world's most technologically advanced economy with ample supplies of natural resources, and could protect this state of affairs with an essentially invincible military that possessed a nuclear monopoly. Most of the rest of the world was in ruins, pre-industrial, or under the control of communist regimes that smothered economic initiative.

Most great powers throughout history would have reacted to such circumstances by seizing direct, long-term control over as much of the globe as possible. Instead, the United States established itself as first among equals in a loose coalition of nations that came to be known as the Free World. It also established a set of political and economic institutions and programs—the North Atlantic Treaty Organization, the Marshall Plan, the Bretton Woods system, the International Monetary Fund, the World Bank, and so forth—that encouraged rapid economic development within this coalition. Combined with the policy of containment toward the Soviet Union, this approach to geopolitics turned out to have huge strategic benefits for America.

Indeed, the fact that this strategy worked in the decades after World War II is precisely our problem today. The wealth-creation engine of the post-war world was designed in America, but available to other nations too—and so in time those that had more advanced economies before the war (predominantly Western Europe and Japan) re-industrialized to the point that, by the 1970s, they began to challenge America's position. This revived competition, along with the oil shocks of the '70s, dramatically changed the global circumstances that had allowed the United States to have it all: high rates of economic and wage growth along with a high degree of economic equality.

Ronald Reagan's solution to the '70s crisis proceeded from two diagnoses. The first was that macroeconomic pump-priming was merely creating inflation, not growth. The second was that America's economy had large untapped potential for growth, but that this potential went unrealized because of the restrictions on markets intended to promote social harmony as part of the post-war economic consensus. These included everything from price controls to government encouragement of private-sector unionization to zealous anti-trust enforcement. Reagan's strategy, therefore, was to promote sound money plus deregulation. He succeeded, and America re-emerged as the acknowledged global economic leader. Economic output per-person is now 20 to 25% higher in the U.S. than in Japan and the major European economies, and America's economy dominates the world in size and prestige.

But it is important to see that this robust growth means only that America has not lost ground in global economic competition, not that it has gained much. From 1980 through today, America's share of global output has been constant at about 21%. Europe's share, meanwhile, has been collapsing in the face of global competition — going from a little less than 40% of global production in the 1970s to about 25% today. Opting for social democracy instead of innovative capitalism, Europe has ceded this share to China (predominantly), India, and the rest of the developing world. The economic rise of the Asian heartland is the central geopolitical fact of our era, and it is safe to assume that economic and strategic competition will only increase further over the next several decades.

It is common to think of the post-war global economy as a baseline of normalcy to which we wish to return. But it seems more accurate to see that era as an anomaly: the apogee of relative global economic dominance by the West, and by the United States within the Western coalition. The hard truth is that the economic world of 1955 is gone, and even if we wanted it back — short of emerging from another global war unscathed with the rest of the world a smoking heap of rubble — we could not have it.

Yet the strategy of giving up and opting out of this international economic competition in order to focus on quality of life is simply not feasible for the United States. Europeans can get away with it only because they benefit from the external military protection America provides; we, however, have no similar guardian to turn to. We do not live in a Kantian world of perpetual commercial peace. Were America to retreat from global competition, sooner or later those who oppose our values would become strong enough to take away our wealth and freedom.

### A HOUSE DIVIDED

If the pain of innovation calls for some mitigation of its effects, but the demands of global competition require that we not unduly stifle innovation, clearly some balance must be found. Our effort to strike such equilibrium, however, is made far more difficult by the internal deterioration of our society — which harms both our ability to compete and our capacity for social cohesion.

Of the many social and cultural changes that have rocked American society over the past half-century, the most relevant to the state of our political economy today may be the growing bifurcation of America. Increasingly, our country is segregated into high-income groups with a tendency to bourgeois norms, and low-income groups experiencing profound social breakdown.

This breakdown did not happen overnight. Longstanding academic and *avant garde* attacks on traditional social norms exploded into a political and popular movement identified with the left in the 1960s. In the '70s, American attitudes and behavior began to change on a mass scale. This cultural shift naturally stimulated a response in defense of tradition from the right. At the time, it was often characterized as a call for "law and order"—but this pushback also incorporated resistance to evolving sexual mores and gender roles, to racial equality, and to the decriminalization of drugs and other activities previously considered anti-social.

This resistance movement—which in a sense came to power with the Nixon administration—was clearly concerned with questions of social cohesion and stability, even to the point of implementing highly interventionist economic policies directed to such concerns. (The wage and price controls it imposed on much of the economy are proof enough of that.) But others on the right disagreed, arguing that the natural ally of traditional morality was libertarian economics, and vice versa, because long-term economic success rested on a foundation of traditional cultural mores. An important part of Ronald Reagan's political genius was his determination to unite social and economic conservatives behind this integrated vision, making them key components of a governing coalition by the time he became president in 1980.

But while conservatives could make a strong case for the notion that cultural stability and cohesion were essential to economic growth, most preferred to ignore the opposite side of the coin: the worry that economic dynamism was harmful to social cohesion. And in the 1990s, a neutral observer could have been forgiven for believing that, despite the economic successes of the 1980s, the cultural foundations of democratic capitalism were collapsing. Crime rates, illegitimacy, drug use, and many other measures of social dysfunction were all on the rise, seemingly without limit.

Fortunately, starting later in that decade and continuing through today, America seems to have renormalized to some degree. Many of these trends—particularly the spike in crime—reversed course.

The new normal, however, is different from the old normal. To begin with, certain strands of the old bourgeois consensus have frayed, and others have simply disappeared, at least for some parts of the population. The wealthier and better-educated segments of our society, for example, have re-established the primacy of stable families and revived their intolerance of crime and public disorder. But they have combined this return to tradition with very non-traditional attitudes about sex, masculinity, and overt piety.

More important, while affluent and educated Americans are returning to the traditional family model, the poor and less-educated are not. The gap between rich and poor today is also a gap in cultural norms and mores to a degree unparalleled in our modern experience. The overall divorce rate, for example, exploded in the 1970s, but has since returned to just about its 1960 level for those with a college education. For the less educated, however, the rate has continued to climb—and women without high-school diplomas are now about three times as likely to divorce within ten years of their first marriage as their college-educated counterparts.

Child-rearing has seen a similar split. In 1965, almost no mothers with any level of education reported that they had never been married. Today, this still holds true for mothers who have finished college: Only 3% have never been married. But that figure stands in stark contrast with the nearly 25% of mothers without high-school diplomas who say that they have never been married. In fact, last year, about 40% of *all* American births occurred out of wedlock. And about 70% of African-American children—as well as most Hispanic children—are born to unmarried mothers. But this situation obtains for low-wage, non-college-educated whites as well: It is estimated that about 70% of children born to non-Hispanic white women with no more than a high-school education and income below $20,000 per year were born out of wedlock.

The level of family disruption in America is enormous compared to almost every other country in the developed world. Of course, out-of-wedlock births are as common in many European countries as they are in the United States. But the estimated percentage of 15-year-olds living with both of their biological parents is far lower in the United States than in Western Europe, because unmarried European parents are much more likely to raise children together. It is hard to exaggerate the chaotic conditions under which something like a third of American children are being raised—or to overstate the negative impact this disorder has on their academic achievement, social skills, and character formation. There are certainly heroic exceptions, but the sad fact is that most of these children could not possibly compete with their foreign counterparts.

As the lower classes in America experience these alarming regressions, wealthier and better-educated Americans have managed to re-create a great deal of the lifestyle of the old WASP ascendancy—if with different justifications for it. Political correctness serves the same basic function for this cohort that "good manners" did for an earlier elite; environmental-ism increasingly stands in for the ethic of controlling impulses so as to live within limits; and an expensive, competitive school culture—from pre-K play groups up through graduate school—socializes the new elite for con-structive competition among peers. These Americans have even re-created the old WASP aesthetic preference for the antique, authentic, and pseudo-utilitarian at the expense of vulgar displays of wealth. In many cases, they live in literally the same homes as the previous upper class.

Such behavior enables multi-generational success in a capitalist economy, and will serve the new elite well. But what remains to be seen is whether this new upper class will have the nerve, wit, and sense of pur-pose that led the old WASP elite to develop a social matrix that offered broadly shared prosperity to generations of Americans.

Their task will be made very difficult by the growing bifurcation of social norms in America. A welfare state can best perform its basic function—buffering the human consequences of the market, with-out unduly hampering its effectiveness—where enough widely shared social capital exists to guide the behavior of most people in a bourgeois direction. Because the economic incentives the welfare state creates push people toward short-term indolence, free riding, and self-absorption, it requires some pre-existing norms that will balance off these incentives, and it thus consumes the kind of social capital it needs to operate (just as a free market can consume the social capital produced by traditional morality, which it relies on.)

Post-war America had much more widely shared bourgeois norms, and so was better able to contend with the negative side effects of the welfare state. Today's American underclass, however, is increasingly developing in the absence of such norms—to a large degree as the result of the welfare state itself. Meanwhile, the need for innovation and the pressures of a global economy only continue to reinforce the causes of our social bifurcation.

## INEQUALITY AS SYMPTOM

Perhaps the best illustration of these pressures—to innovate and deregu-late without coming apart at the seams—is found in widening economic inequalities. It has often been noted that American society has become increasingly unequal in economic terms over the past 30 years. As Federal Reserve chairman Ben Bernanke noted in a 2007 speech, "the share of income received by households in the top fifth of the income distribution, after taxes have been paid and government transfers have been received, rose from 42% in 1979 to 50% in 2004, while the share of income received by those in the bottom fifth of the distribution declined from 7% to 5%. The share of after-tax income garnered by the households in the top 1% of the income distribution increased from 8% in 1979 to 14% in 2004." A typical senior partner in a high-end investment-banking, corporate-law, or management-consulting firm can now expect to make upwards of $1 million per year. In the stratosphere of the economy, the increases in wealth have been mind-boggling: Even after the recent market meltdowns, there are about 30 times as many American billionaires today as there were in 1982.

The growth in inequality that began in the 1970s was driven by the social and economic forces outlined earlier. In 1970, "non-distributive services" (finance, professional services, health care, and so on) became for the first time a larger part of the private economy than goods-producing industries. This shift to services tended to enhance the prospects of the cognitive elite at the expense of traditional industrial workers. At the same time, as we have seen, the combination of changes in cultural mores and the growth of social programs began to disassemble the traditional family—ultimately leading to a class-based divide in family structure, which privileges the better-educated Americans already reaping the benefits of the shifting economy. The social capital transmitted by intact families has therefore become a more and more relevant source of competitive advantage.

Two exogenous shocks were also important. First, American domestic production of oil peaked in 1971; oil imports doubled between 1970 and 1975; and OPEC was able to drive large price increases. This oil shock was directly regressive, but it also tended to disproportionately harm those industries that were the source of high-wage union jobs. Second, the percentage of the U.S. population born abroad—which had reached its historical minimum in 1970—began to rise rapidly as mass immigration resumed after a multi-decade hiatus. This development increased inequality further by introducing a large low-income group to the population, and by intensifying wage competition among lower-skill workers.

The Reagan economic revolution exacerbated the problem. Its success resulted, in part, from forcing extremely painful restructuring on industry after industry. One critical consequence of this restructuring was a new compensation paradigm—one that relies on markets rather than on corporate diktats, regulation, or historical norms to set pay. This new regime also accepts a much higher degree of income disparity based on market-denominated performance, and it expects that most people will exploit the resulting demand for talent by moving from company to company many times during a career. Growing inequality was a price we paid for the economic growth needed to recover from the '70s slump and to retain our global position.

Rising inequality would have been easier to swallow had it been merely a statistical artifact of rapid growth in prosperity that substantially benefited the middle class and maintained social mobility. But this was not the case. Over the same period in which inequality has grown, wages have been stagnating for large swaths of the middle class, and income mobility has been declining.

Evaluating the real change in economic circumstances of a typical American family over the past 30 years is extremely complex. To begin with, the typical family is smaller than it was three decades ago. Further, how we adjust for inflation has an enormous impact on any comparative calculations. Finally, family budgets must increasingly account for previously unpaid work—like child care, or attending to sick relatives.

Despite these complicating factors, a few trends still emerge rather clearly. First, average living standards have continued to rise since 1980. Second, the real hourly wages for a typical non-supervisory job have not increased very much over this period. Third, this wage stagnation is at least partly explained by the rising costs of health care—which, because of the American system of employer-based health insurance, are usually deducted implicitly from what workers see as wages. Fourth, personal indebtedness has risen dramatically over the same period and accelerated rapidly during the past decade—so that at least some of the increased consumption was simply borrowed. And last, income mobility—the likelihood of an individual moving up the relative income distribution—appears to have declined slightly over the past three decades, according to multiple studies by the Federal Reserve Banks of Boston and Chicago.

Furthermore, the divisive effects of this cluster of trends—rising income inequality and reduced income mobility, some degree of middle-class wage stagnation, increased personal debt, and increased class stratification of stable social behavior—are only intensified by climbing rates of assortative mating and residential segregation, as well as an increasingly crude and corrosive popular culture combined with the technology-driven fragmentation of mass media.

So economic inequality is likely to cause problems with social cohesion—but far more important, it is a symptom of our deeper problem. As the unsustainable high tide of post-war American dominance has slowly ebbed, many—perhaps most—of our country's workers appear unable to compete internationally at the level required to maintain anything like their current standard of living. And a shrinking elite portion of the American population, itself a shrinking fraction of the world population, cannot indefinitely maintain our global position.

We are between a rock and a hard place. If we reverse the market-based reforms that have allowed us to prosper, we will cede global economic share; but if we let inequality and its underlying causes grow unchecked, we will hollow out the middle class—threatening social cohesion, and eventually surrendering our international position anyway. This, and not some world-is-flat happy talk, is what the challenge of globalization means for America. But unfortunately, by a combination of carelessness and design, we appear now to be embracing a counterproductive response to this daunting dilemma.

### TOWARD SOCIAL DEMOCRACY

The past year, spanning the final months of the Bush administration and the opening months of the Obama administration, has produced a stunning transformation of American political economy. The first major initiative of the new president and Congress was the artfully labeled stimulus bill, which will have the federal government spend nearly $800 billion over the next ten years—less than 15% of it in fiscal year 2009. More than a short-term emergency measure, the stimulus represents a medium-term transformation of the character of federal spending—and government action—in America.

Only about 5% of the money appropriated is intended to fund things like roads and bridges. The legislation is instead dominated by outright social spending: increases in food-stamp benefits and unemployment benefits; various direct and special-purpose spending relabeled as tax credits for renewable-energy programs; increased funding for the Department of Health and Human Services; and increased school-based financial assistance, housing assistance, and other direct benefits. The objective effect of the bill is to shift the balance of U.S. government spending away from defense and public safety, and toward social-welfare programs. Because the amount of spending involved is so enormous, this will be a dramatic material shift—not a merely symbolic gesture.

Meanwhile, the federal government has also intervened aggressively in both the financial and industrial sectors of the economy in order to produce specific desired outcomes for particular corporations. It has nationalized America's largest auto company (General Motors) and intervened in the bankruptcy proceeding of the third-largest auto company (Chrysler), privileging labor unions at the expense of bondholders. It has, in effect, nationalized what was America's largest insurance company (American International Group) and largest bank (Citigroup), and appears to have exerted extra-legal financial pressure on what was the second-largest bank (Bank of America) to get it to purchase the country's largest securities company (Merrill Lynch). The implicit government guarantees provided to home-loan giants Fannie Mae and Freddie Mac have been called in, and the federal government is now the largest de facto lender in the residential real-estate market. The government has selected the CEOs and is setting compensation at major automotive and financial companies across the country.

On top of these interventions in finance and commerce, the administration and congressional Democrats are also pursuing both a new climate and energy strategy and large-scale health-care reform. Their agenda would place the government at the center of these two vital sectors of the economy, sacrificing some economic vitality for public control. The latter program would also create an enormous new federal entitlement.

All told, finance, insurance, real estate, automobiles, energy, and health care account for about one-third of the U.S. economy. Reconfiguring these industries to conform to political calculations, and not market-driven decisions, is likely to transform American economic life. And the fiscal consequences of the spending involved will be enormous. The federal budget deficit for 2009 was about 11% of gross domestic product, which is far higher than any the United States has experienced since World War II. This deficit spending is the real stimulus. Something like 10% of all the economic demand in the United States is supported by government borrowing from the future, which is essential to propping up the current "recovery." Even more important, the Congressional

Budget Office projects that existing laws will now lock in a structural budget deficit of more than 3% of GDP every year for the foreseeable future. And this assumes we will escape the current global economic situation without further financial catastrophe (and that America won't be forced into a war or other unanticipated major contingency over the next several decades). The CBO states flatly that this long-term budget path is "unsustainable."

The basic character of America's financial position is changing before our eyes. One year ago, federal government debt held by the public was 41% of GDP. Today, it is about 54% of GDP. The CBO projects that it will approach 70% of GDP by 2020, which is a level not seen since the immediate aftermath of World War II. Unless expenditures are reduced or taxes are raised, this debt will continue to accumulate indefinitely—until we reach the point at which we can no longer find enough lenders to simply roll it over. At that moment, Americans will face exactly three choices: raise taxes, default on debt, or devalue the currency. The most likely outcome is higher taxes, probably including a value-added tax (VAT)—essentially the equivalent of a national sales tax—as it would be hard to find another method that could collect enough revenue to keep our debt under control.

Seen together, these initiatives—shifting government spending away from defense and public safety toward social programs; deeper direct involvement of the government in the operation of large corporations across a substantial portion of the economy; energy rationing in the name of managing climate change; more direct government control of health-care provision; and higher tax rates that probably include a VAT—point in a clear direction. The end result would be an America much closer to the European model of a social-welfare state, which prioritizes cohesion over innovation.

Of course, the European model is not an inherently terrible way to organize human society. It is, however, a model very poorly suited to America's current strategic situation, and would leave us in a far worse position to deal with the challenge of balancing innovation and cohesion. We do not have the luxury of drowning our sorrows in borrowed money while watching our power and influence wane.

America's challenge is more serious than that: How do we continue to increase the market orientation of the American economy, while helping more Americans participate in it more fully?

## A NEW APPROACH

It won't be easy. But along with taking steps to better balance America's government finances and reform our entitlement system, several preliminary ideas can help guide our thinking as we confront, at last, the reality of America's circumstances.

To begin with, we must unwind some recent errors that fail to take account of these circumstances. Most obviously, government ownership of industrial assets is almost a guarantee that the painful decisions required for international competitiveness will not be made. When it comes to the auto industry, for instance, we need to take the loss and move on. As soon as possible, the government should announce a structured program to sell off the equity it holds in GM. Similarly, the federal government should relinquish direct control of banks and insurance companies. One virtue of the slow rollout of spending under the stimulus bill, moreover, is that most of it can be stopped — and should be. Any programs that have been temporarily increased under the terms of the law should be forced back down to pre-stimulus levels, and attempts to make these changes permanent should be resisted in the absence of a sustainable fiscal regime. Avoiding economically extravagant cap-and-trade legislation and, to the extent possible, a government takeover of health insurance would also help us avoid unforced errors.

Second, the financial crisis has demonstrated obvious systemic problems of poor regulation and under-regulation of some aspects of the financial sector that must be addressed, though for at least a decade prior to the crisis, over-regulation, lawsuits, and aggressive government prosecution seriously damaged the competitiveness of other parts of America's financial system. Since 1995 the U.S. share of total equity capital raised in the world's top ten economies has declined from 41% to 28%. We do not want the systemic risks of under-regulation, but we should also be careful not to overcompensate for them.

Regulation to avoid systemic risk must therefore proceed from a clear understanding of its causes. In the recent crisis, the reason the government has been forced to prop up financial institutions isn't that they are too big to fail, but rather that they are too *interconnected* to fail. For example, a series of complex and unregulated financial obligations meant that the failure of Lehman Brothers — a mid-size investment bank — threatened to crash the entire U.S. banking system.

As we work to adapt our regulatory structure to fit the 21st century, we should therefore adopt a modernized version of a New Deal-era innovation: focus on creating walls that contain busts, rather than on applying brakes that hold back the entire system. Our reforms should establish "tiers" of financial activities of increasing risk, volatility, and complexity that are open to any investor—and somewhere within this framework, almost any non-coercive transaction should be legally permitted. The tiers should then be compartmentalized, however, so that a bust in a higher-risk tier doesn't propagate to lower-risk tiers. And while the government should provide guarantees such as deposit insurance in the low-risk tiers, it should unsparingly permit failure in the higher-risk tiers. Such reform would provide the benefits of better capital allocation, continued market innovation, and stability. It would address some of the problems of cohesion by allowing more Americans to participate in our market system without being as exposed—or unwittingly exposed—to the brutal effects of market collapses. It would also help get the government out of the banking business and preserve America's position as the global leader in financial services without turning our financial sector into a time bomb.

Third, over the coming decades, we should seek to deregulate public schools. It would be foolish to imagine that we can simply educate everyone in America to be globally competitive. In a nation where about 40% of births occur outside of wedlock, many children will be left behind. Nonetheless, schools remain one of our primary policy instruments for enhancing both social mobility and our competitive position. They are essential to the task of balancing innovation and cohesion. To function effectively, though, America's schools need to be improved dramatically. Our basic model of public schooling—accepting raw material in the form of five-year-olds, and then adding value through a series of processing steps to produce educated graduates 12 (or more) years later—reflects the vision of the old industrial economy. This worked well in an earlier era, but improvements that might have kept this model up to date have been stalled for decades. We now need a new vision for schools that looks a lot more like Silicon Valley than Detroit: decentralized, entrepreneurial, and flexible.

For a generation, many on the right have argued for school choice—especially through the use of vouchers—as the primary means of achieving this vision. Their approach, however, has been both too doctrinaire and too artificial. If school choice ever becomes more than tinker-toy demonstration projects, taxpayers will appropriately demand that a range of controls and requirements be imposed on the schools they are ultimately funding. At that point, what would be the difference between such "private" schools and "public" schools that were allowed greater flexibility in hiring, curriculum, and student acceptance, and had to compete for students in order to capture funding? Little beyond the label.

We should pursue the creation of a real marketplace among ever more deregulated publicly financed schools—a market in which funding follows students, and far broader discretion is permitted to those who actually teach and manage in our schools. There are real-world examples of such systems that work well today—both Sweden and the Netherlands, for instance, have implemented this kind of plan at the national level.

Fourth, we should reconceptualize immigration as recruiting. Assimilating immigrants is a demonstrated core capability of America's political economy—and it is one we should take advantage of. A robust-yet-reasonable amount of immigration is healthy for America. It is a continuing source of vitality—and, in combination with birth rates around the replacement level, creates a sustainable rate of overall population growth and age-demographic balance. But unfortunately, the manner in which we have actually handled immigration since the 1970s has yielded large-scale legal and illegal immigration of a low-skilled population from Latin America. It is hard to imagine a more damaging way to expose and inflame the fault lines of America's political economy: We have chosen a strategy that provides low-wage gardeners and nannies for the elite, low-cost home improvement and fresh produce for the middle class, and fierce wage competition for the working class.

Instead, we should think of immigration as an opportunity to improve our stock of human capital. Once we have re-established control of our southern border, and as we preserve our commitment to political asylum, we should also set up recruiting offices looking for the best possible talent everywhere: from Mexico City to Beijing to Helsinki to Calcutta. Australia and Canada have demonstrated the practicality of skills-based immigration policies for many years. We should improve upon their example by using testing and other methods to apply a basic tenet of all human capital-intensive organizations managing for the long-term: Always pick talent over skill. It would be great for America as a whole to have, say, 500,000 smart, motivated people move here each year with the intention of becoming citizens.

### FACING THE FUTURE

These broad proposals are, of course, mostly ways to stop digging our hole even deeper. At the moment, that would be no small achievement—since we are moving toward a model of social democracy that is likely to dim our long-term prospects.

But more important than these particular steps is the imperative to see our problem clearly, and to shape our political and economic arguments around it in the coming years. An America that wants to keep its global edge cannot afford to neglect the necessity of innovation and growth, or to ignore the necessity of social cohesion and stability. For the moment, the former of these is in special need of defense—since the party in power seems inclined to sacrifice economic dynamism for its vision of social justice. Eventually, however, the challenge of sustaining the moral fabric and social unity of America may prove the more difficult problem. Strong families—and the commitments and habits they teach—are essential to both a market economy and a working democracy. More than ever before, the health of America's social institutions must be a priority for all those concerned about our country's future—and especially those who would champion innovation and free markets.

Balancing economic innovation and social cohesion is the challenge of every free nation today—but it is a particularly pressing challenge for the special nation that holds in its hands so much of the fate of democracy and capitalism in our world.

*Originally published as "Keeping America's Edge" in the Winter 2010 issue of* National Affairs.

# 11. Reforming the Welfare State

# How to Replace Obamacare

## *James C. Capretta and Robert E. Moffit*

SPRING 2012

W HEN THE PATIENT PROTECTION AND AFFORDABLE CARE ACT (commonly known as "Obamacare") was signed into law in the spring
of 2010, congressional opponents vowed that the fight was not over. The
most disastrous features of the new law would not take effect until 2014,
leaving time for a concerted campaign to avert catastrophe. The way to
spend that time, these opponents argued, was working to "repeal and
replace" the law that Congress had just enacted.

The "repeal and replace" formulation quickly caught on, but it was
not without its critics. That Obamacare should be "repealed" was obvious, given how strenuously conservatives and many independents
objected to the new law. But "replace"? Hammering out the details of
a new health-care law might easily stir controversy and sow discord,
thereby undermining the push for "repeal."

This concern is not unfounded. But repeal will not be enough, for a
simple reason: Although Obamacare would worsen many of the problems with our system of health-care financing, that system clearly *does*
call out for serious reform. Despite the widespread public antipathy toward the new health-care law, simply reverting to the pre-Obamacare
status quo would be viewed by many Americans, perhaps even most, as
unacceptable. After all, a repeal-only approach would leave many of the
most grievous flaws in our system of financing health care unaddressed.
Chief among them would be steadily rising health-care costs, driven
by the same misguided government policies that so evidently demand
reform.

JAMES C. CAPRETTA *is a visiting fellow at the American Enterprise Institute and a fellow
at the Ethics and Public Policy Center.*

ROBERT E. MOFFIT *is a senior fellow in the Center for Policy Innovation at the Heritage
Foundation.*

If the problems that are today obvious to the public had been addressed by market-oriented policies over the past few decades, there would have been no political opening through which to ram Obamacare. Instead, these problems were allowed to fester; by 2009, they had become so acute that there was strong sentiment, even among some business-oriented conservatives, that "something had to be done." And as the 2010 congressional debate over Obamacare reached its climax, this sentiment—that some action, even an imperfect one, would be better than nothing—likely played a large role in enabling the health-care law to pass.

This history suggests that, now that Obamacare is with us, the law cannot be reversed without a credible proposal for what should take its place. Those reforms must account for both the strengths and the weaknesses of our health-care system, and must solve the problems that contributed to the demand for Obamacare in the first place. There is room for debate about the particulars of these reforms, and different components of our health-care system will call for different kinds of fixes. What any effective solution must involve, however, is the creation of a true market in health coverage—one that drives efficiency through competition, and places health-care decisions in the hands of consumers and taxpayers, where they belong.

### WHAT NEEDS FIXING

America's health-care system has important strengths that must not be overlooked. Most notable among these are an openness to medical innovation that is absent from more centrally planned systems and a network of clinics and hospitals capable of offering the most advanced care found anywhere in the world. The vast majority of Americans (almost 80%) have ready access to this high level of care through third-party insurance arrangements, obtaining coverage from their employers or from federal programs like Medicare and Medicaid. Another 10% have individually purchased coverage.

But for all its considerable strengths, the system suffers from pervasive weaknesses as well. The most serious of these is rapidly rising costs. According to the Congressional Budget Office, between 1975 and 2005, annual per-person health spending in the United States rose, on average, 2 percentage points faster than per-person economic growth. In other words, the escalation of health costs has far outpaced the rise in our national income. This has left more and more people unable to afford insurance, and it now poses significant problems for government budgets: Both federal and state governments spend an enormous amount on health care, but government's revenue base for taxation grows along with the economy, not with health-care costs. So as government spending on health care has surged, tax collection has not kept pace—yielding the primary driver of today's deficits and mounting debt.

Of course, government health-care programs and policies are largely responsible for these rising costs in the first place. To begin, the design of Medicare is terribly flawed: Because the program pays providers of care based on the volume of their services, it creates a massive incentive for inefficiency and overuse. And because Medicare is the biggest payer in most health-care markets in America, that incentive badly distorts the economics of the entire sector. Furthermore, the Medicaid program inflates costs by (among other policies) having states control how the program is run while the federal government pays most of the bills. The result is that neither party has both the incentive and ability to keep costs in check.

The third driver is the tax exclusion for employer-provided insurance: The federal government does not count the amount that employers spend on health insurance for their employees toward workers' taxable income. This tax exclusion inflates costs by effectively rewarding higher-premium plans and by encouraging employer-purchased insurance, thereby preventing a real consumer market in coverage. The people who use the insurance (workers) are not the people who buy it (employers); many Americans thus have no idea how much is spent for the health care they receive. As a result, there is no clear relationship between cost and value, without which there can be no real prices, no real incentives for efficiency and quality, and thus no limitations on the growth of costs.

But while the cost explosion is clearly the greatest problem with America's health-care system (and the cause of most of its other problems), costs are not always the focus of the public debate. The most politically salient problem is often the lack of secure insurance coverage for many millions of Americans, and the related problem of insuring Americans with pre-existing and expensive medical conditions. This concern—that if these Americans lost their insurance they might not be able to find affordable coverage again—is of course related to the high cost of care, which has made it more difficult to provide affordable coverage for everyone, including the sickest among us. But the problem of providing stable insurance to people with pre-existing conditions is also driven by factors unrelated to costs. Foremost among these is the heavy reliance on employer-sponsored insurance that is not owned by workers, and therefore not portable when workers move from job to job or leave the work force.

Proponents of Obamacare like to create the impression that there are tens of millions of Americans trapped by their pre-existing conditions, sick and stuck with lousy insurance and no options. In truth, the vast majority of working Americans have good and secure coverage today, including many millions of people with expensive health conditions. Thanks in part to protections enacted into federal law in 1996 (through the Health Insurance Portability and Accountability Act, or HIPAA), a person who remains continuously insured as he moves from job to job is protected against inflated premiums and coverage exclusions stemming from a health condition. Thus only a very small percentage of Americans face the pre-existing condition dilemma.

But a small percentage of our large population is still a lot of people. There is no denying that cracks in the system exist, and that many Americans fall through them. This is particularly true of people who need to move from job-based coverage into the individual market. Here the 1996 law is entirely inadequate: People who leave the work force and need to buy insurance on their own can face sky-high premiums for weak coverage just because they happen to suffer from a health condition over which they often have little control. Though the number of families in such circumstances is relatively small, it is large enough that many Americans are personally acquainted with people facing these unpleasant realities. This experience is enough to shape public opinion; surveys show that roughly four out of five Americans support provisions in Obamacare that require insurers to sell their products to all comers at the same rates without regard to health status.

The Obama administration is trying to channel this desire to fix the problem of covering pre-existing conditions into a case for retaining the entire Obamacare edifice. Starting in the middle of 2009, the president and his top aides took to calling their plan "insurance reform," as if the law's most important elements were simply new rules designed to protect hapless consumers from unscrupulous insurance companies.

This is, of course, a gross mischaracterization of what Obamacare actually does. Among other features, the law implements a massive expansion of taxpayer obligations. It adds two new entitlement programs at an expense of at least $1 trillion over a decade. In that same period, it raises taxes by more than $500 billion. It cuts Medicare payments to those providing medical services by roughly $500 billion, and sets up an unaccountable board — the Independent Payment Advisory Board — to enforce new caps on future Medicare growth through specific payment cuts to Medicare providers. Most egregiously, it puts the federal government in command of the health sector, giving bureaucrats immense new power to decide matters ranging from what services must be covered in every American's insurance plan to how doctors and hospitals organize themselves and do business.

Obamacare is thus far more than "insurance reform." But it is revealing that this is how the administration hopes the law will be perceived by average Americans. Obamacare's opponents should take note of the appeal of this idea: Our nation does need real insurance reform, but it can be implemented in ways that address the problems with our health-care system instead of exacerbating them.

PILLARS OF REFORM

To be credible, the replacement for Obamacare must address in a plausible way the genuine problems with our system of financing health care. Pre-eminent among these are the explosion in costs, the rising numbers of uninsured, and the challenge of covering Americans with pre-existing conditions.

The good news for Obamacare opponents is that much of the work of building such a plan has already been done. A small but persistent band of reformers and economists has spent many years promoting and refining the elements of a market-based approach to remedying what ails American health care. These ideas have animated scores of plans released by various organizations, including some proposed after Obamacare's enactment. And while these plans differ in their details, they share a core set of seven principles that should form the basis of any proposal for replacing Obamacare.

The first crucial component of any serious reform must be a "defined contribution" approach to the public financing of health care — the essential prerequisite for a functioning marketplace that imposes cost and quality discipline. In most sectors of our economy, the normal dynamics of supply and demand keep costs in check and reward suppliers that find innovative ways to deliver more for less. As described above, however, this is not the case in the health-care sector, principally because the federal government has completely distorted consumer incentives.

For market forces to work, consumers must be cost-conscious. Those who decide to consume goods or services must face tradeoffs that require them to prioritize the various uses of their money. In the health sector, there is virtually no cost consciousness on the part of consumers: The vast majority of Americans get their insurance through their employers or through Medicare or Medicaid. In each case, as noted above, the federal subsidy grows as the cost of insurance grows, thereby undermining the incentive to keep costs low. When an employer decides to provide a more generous health-benefit plan to his employees, the U.S. Treasury pays for a good portion of the added costs, because health insurance is a tax-free fringe benefit for workers. When a doctor orders more tests or procedures of dubious clinical value for a patient enrolled in Medicare, it is mainly taxpayers who pick up the tab. And when states pile more people into Medicaid, it is again taxpayers—federal and state—who shoulder the cost. With this kind of subsidy structure, it is not at all surprising that cost escalation throughout the health system has been rapid.

A replacement program for Obamacare must therefore move American health care away from open-ended government subsidies and tax breaks, and toward a defined-contribution system. Under this approach, health coverage would be provided through competing insurance plans; government's involvement would come through the provision of a fixed financial contribution toward the purchase of insurance by each beneficiary. That subsidy would not vary based on a person's insurance plan, giving Americans every incentive to shop for good value in their health coverage and to get the most for their defined-contribution dollars.

In the context of employer plans, this approach would mean moving away from the unlimited tax break that is conferred on employer-paid premiums, and instead providing directly to workers a fixed tax credit that would offset the cost of enrollment in the private insurance plans of their choice. Workers selecting more expensive insurance plans would pay for the added premiums out of their own pockets. Those choosing low-premium, high-value plans would pocket the savings, enabling them to offset additional health expenses if they wished to do so. This system would not only be more efficient: It would also be a far more equitable way to provide health benefits through the tax code. American taxpayers would get a break for health coverage as individuals, irrespective of their employment status or the generosity of the health plan provided by their employers.

In the context of Medicare and Medicaid, meanwhile, the government would similarly provide a fixed (though of course far more generous) level of support, sometimes called "premium support," that would guarantee insurance coverage to beneficiaries but would allow them to choose among competing options and encourage them to seek out the best value for their money (as discussed at greater length below).

The second pillar of reform should be personal responsibility and continuous-coverage protection. Obamacare attempts to address the challenge of covering people with pre-existing conditions with heavy-handed mandates, especially the requirement that all Americans enroll in government-approved insurance plans (the so-called "individual mandate"). A replacement program for Obamacare should come at the problem from the opposite direction, with government forsaking coercion and instead extending a new commitment to the American people: If you stay continuously enrolled in health insurance, with at least catastrophic coverage, you will never again face the prospect of high premiums associated with developing a costly health condition.

For this commitment to become a reality, some changes would have to be made to both federal law and state insurance regulation. (These proposed changes are discussed in more detail in the next chapter.) To begin, the federal government would need to close the gaps in protection that emerge when people move from employer-sponsored plans to the individual market regulated by the states. This problem could be remedied by amending the 1996 HIPAA law to allow workers to move directly from group to individual insurance without first having to pay out of pocket for the (lengthy) extension of their employer-based plans through so-called "COBRA" coverage. In 1985, the Consolidated Omnibus Budget Reconciliation Act (or COBRA) allowed workers who lose their jobs to remain on their employers' health-insurance plans for months, provided they pay the full premium cost themselves (usually a significant expense). HIPAA then required workers eligible for this COBRA option to exercise it before they could be given any protection in the individual insurance markets regulated by the states. Since hardly any workers follow this prescribed course, they enter the individual market with no protections from pre-existing condition exclusions. That would change if workers were protected when they moved directly from group to individual insurance plans.

Next, states would need to amend their regulations of the individual and small-business insurance markets to require insurers to sell coverage to customers who have remained continuously covered. These new regulations would also have to require that such coverage be made available at standard rates—that is, at rates that apply without regard to differences in health status (age and geographic adjustments would be permitted).

Because some workers who leave job-based plans for the individual market could be quite sick, a credible Obamacare replacement plan would also need to include a new approach to covering the high insurance costs for these Americans. Different proposals have offered different mechanisms, but all would move the burden away from the sick patients themselves to a larger and broader pool of people, either through regulation or through a direct government program such as a high-risk pool. For people who have not been continuously insured, these protections generally would not apply. States could continue to allow insurers to charge higher premiums to these individuals based on their respective health risks. There would thus be a very strong incentive for all Americans to remain continuously covered. (At the time of enactment, it would make sense to give those Americans who were not in continuous coverage the opportunity to come into the new system without penalty and to secure this new protection.)

This approach would achieve the goal of providing realistic and affordable options for people with pre-existing conditions, but without imposing the misguided, overbearing, and counter-productive architecture of Obamacare—and in a way that encourages a competitive insurance market and an innovative health sector rather than undermining them.

The third pillar of reform must be a genuine partnership with the states. Under Obamacare, states are treated as mere functionaries in a new centrally planned and federally managed system. The law gives state officials a take-it-or-leave-it choice: They can implement and administer the new policies under Obamacare—such as state-level insurance exchanges—to the letter, without any deviation or adjustment, incurring the extra costs of these new programs along the way. Or state governments can refuse this managerial responsibility and instead have the federal government come in and operate the exchanges and other new components of the law on the states' behalf. But in neither case are the states afforded any independence or flexibility, any room to adapt the requirements imposed by Obamacare to the particular circumstances of their populations, or to innovate to achieve greater quality or efficiency.

A replacement plan must be true to the Constitution and reflect a genuine federalist philosophy. Any program to address the problems in American health care will entail some degree of national policy, but it can still leave ample room for state initiative and encourage state-level solutions. There is good reason to allow such discretion: States vary significantly in their demographics, their economic profiles, their infrastructure, their levels of employment and poverty, their Medicaid enrollments, and their numbers of uninsured. There is wide disparity among states in the costs of uncompensated care, the scope of employment-based health insurance, and the condition of individual health-insurance markets. States differ markedly in the range of their health-care problems and in their capacities to cope with them.

Moreover, states can be powerful engines of policy innovation and experimentation in health-care reform, insurance-market reform, and tort and medical-malpractice reform, as well as in the financing and delivery of care in safety-net programs. In recent decades, a number of states have attempted their own solutions to our health-care financing crisis. But because that financing crisis is driven by deformed federal policies, all that these states have been able to do is try to mitigate the effects of Washington's mistakes. A reform that addressed those mistakes directly at the national level could then free the states to address the problems of health-care financing in the ways that best suit their needs.

To respect federalism and reap its benefits, nothing in an Obamacare replacement agenda should compel state adoption, instead leaving the participation of state governments completely voluntary. Those states that do participate in any federal initiative should be given meaningful control over the most important components of regulation, especially the power to design and operate their own health-insurance markets (within minimal federal standards). Such deference to state authority would mean allowing states to retain full control over matters like what coverage to require in health insurance and how to facilitate consumer enrollment in qualified plans. Crucially, no Obamacare replacement program should include a federal requirement that states set up health-insurance exchanges that could later become instruments of excessive regulatory control. Rather, states should be given two tasks: informing consumers of their insurance options, and easing their enrollment into the plans they choose by cooperating with the federal government to facilitate the payment of credits and vouchers directly to private insurers. *How* states perform these critical tasks should be left entirely up to them.

Defined-contribution financial support, protection for Americans who remain continuously enrolled in insurance plans, and genuine federalism are the essential overall concepts that must define any serious health-care reform. But policymakers will also need to apply these principles to the transformation of today's funding and financing mechanisms: the tax exclusion for employer-provided health coverage, and the Medicaid and Medicare systems.

### TAX REFORM AND HEALTH REFORM

The fourth pillar of a real reform agenda would therefore address the tax treatment of employer-sponsored plans. Today's arrangement is somewhat counterintuitive: Because the tax exclusion for health-care premiums is open-ended, workers and employers have an incentive to make health benefits a disproportionately large share of total compensation. And because employers obtain and manage health plans for their workers, there is far too much distance between those who purchase care and those who consume it. The key decisions in American health care thus rest not with patients and doctors, but rather with employers, managed-care executives, and government officials — a structure that has prevented the emergence of a properly functioning marketplace. Individuals and families rarely have a property right in their health-insurance policies and rarely control the terms and conditions of coverage (as they do with auto, life, or home owner's insurance). Health insurance is rarely portable in any real sense of the term, as workers cannot remain enrolled in the same insurance plans when they switch jobs.

Federal tax policy is at the root of these market malfunctions, and has caused a host of related problems. These include higher health-care costs, the absence of continuous and secure coverage, a lack of transparency in health-care financing, discrimination against lower-income workers and favoritism toward higher-income workers, and a playing field tilted decidedly in favor of group health insurance and against individually purchased coverage. Among economists, including some of President Obama's advisors, there is an overwhelming consensus that reform of health-insurance markets must begin with a major change in the federal tax treatment of health insurance.

The most plausible way to implement such a change would be to transform today's tax exclusion for employer-provided insurance into a standard tax credit that would extend to all Americans, regardless of employment status, which they could then use to purchase the private coverage of their choice. As to how such a consumer-controlled federal tax credit would be designed, policymakers have a variety of options from which to choose. For instance, in its 2011 "Saving the American Dream" plan, the Heritage Foundation proposed replacing today's unlimited tax break with a new, non-refundable tax credit that would be phased out for the wealthiest citizens. Another approach would be to limit the credit to some pre-determined level of insurance coverage. Because the credit amount would not be increased for workers selecting more expensive insurance plans, those choosing such plans would pay the difference while those opting for plans with lower premiums would not be penalized (with a diminished tax benefit) for economizing.

One such proposal was offered during the 2008 presidential campaign by Senator John McCain, who suggested a universal program of refundable tax credits that would be payable to all households. In 2007, President George W. Bush proposed replacing today's tax treatment of insurance with a universal deduction for health-insurance premiums that would be available to people in employer-sponsored plans, as well as to those in the individual market. In both cases, the value of these credits and deductions would increase over time by some measure of inflation—ensuring that they would keep pace with fluctuations in the cost of living, while also ensuring that government's costs would remain predictable and manageable.

In all of these formulations, the essential common element is a move toward consumer control. Individuals would become active, cost-conscious consumers looking for value in the health-care marketplace. This shift would, in turn, create tremendous incentives for those delivering medical services to find better and less expensive ways of caring for patients and keeping them well.

For the purposes of implementing tax-based health-care reform, it would make sense to bifurcate the market for employer-based coverage into small and large employers. For smaller employers (for instance, those with fewer than 200 employees), there is reason to move quickly to change the tax treatment of job-based insurance: Many small businesses do not even offer coverage today, so a reform that substituted tax credits for today's tax preference would immediately help millions of working Americans get better coverage than they now have. Indeed, the availability of a credit or deduction would likely reduce the number of uninsured Americans by a significant measure. Consumers wouldn't want to leave the credit money on the table, and insurers would be eager to provide them with ways to spend it. Insurance companies would thus have every reason to design minimal plans (including, at the very least, catastrophic coverage) with prices roughly equal to the amount of the credit or deduction, and consumers who might otherwise not buy coverage would have every reason to purchase those plans. Moreover, the insurance marketplace for small-business workers tends to be volatile, with workers passing in and out of coverage frequently as they change jobs or leave the work force. Moving toward a tax-credit system would give these workers the chance to sign up for insurance that they would own and keep, even as their life circumstances changed.

On the other hand, many tens of millions of Americans are now signed up with good and stable large-employer plans. Although these workers see a need for reform, they do not want to lose the coverage they have today. For both political and practical reasons, it would make sense to leave these people where they are, in their large-employer plans, as the reforms in the other parts of the marketplace are implemented and refined. The advantages of these changes—including the expansion of personal and portable health insurance, lower-cost health coverage, and higher take-home pay—would, over time, become evident to workers in large-employer plans. The key, however, is that the decision to change coverage would rest not with government but with workers and employers, who would be under no obligation to change the terms of employees' benefit plans. The only modification that should be pursued immediately is the placement of an upper limit on the amount of employer-paid premiums eligible for the existing federal tax break; this would level the playing field somewhat between the existing tax benefit and the new tax credit. Under this proposal, premiums paid by employers above the upper limit would be counted as taxable compensation to workers. This would give both employers and employees a stronger incentive than they have today to move toward low-premium, high-value plans.

An important additional detail of such a reform plan would apply to people who are eligible for a federal tax credit (or perhaps a Medicaid voucher) and yet still do not sign up for coverage. For these people, one option would be to establish an automatic-enrollment program in which states assign people on a random basis to a series of state-approved private plans. The insurers offering these default options would be allowed to adjust the up-front deductibles as necessary to ensure that the premiums for the insurance plans do not exceed the credits enrollees are eligible to receive. The aim would be to make sure that people who are placed in an insurance plan by default pay no additional premiums out of their own pockets. Those automatically enrolled could switch out of their default plans into other insurance plans at any time (subject to state rules governing enrollment periods); if they had moral or other reasons for not carrying insurance coverage, they would be free to drop out of insurance enrollment altogether.

Such a default enrollment program could be an important feature of a credible replacement plan, allowing millions of Americans to leave the ranks of the uninsured and to secure continuous-coverage protection without the coercion of Obamacare's mandates. This flexibility would likely be a very attractive selling point for a consensus replacement proposal.

### IMPROVING HEALTH CARE FOR THE VULNERABLE

The fifth key component of a genuine health-care reform plan must be an overhaul of Medicaid. Medicaid is actually three separate programs: health insurance for lower-income working-age adults and their children, health and long-term care for the non-elderly with severe disabilities, and long-term care for the frail elderly. For the purposes of replacing Obamacare, the relevant program to change is insurance coverage for working-age adults and children; the other parts will need reform as well, but should be addressed in a separate legislative effort.

Medicaid coverage for working-age adults and children has its roots in welfare. Starting in 1965, women with low incomes, along with their dependent children, were given cash support through a federal-state program (known as Aid to Families with Dependent Children until 1996, and then transformed into the Temporary Assistance for Needy Families program), and provided with medical coverage through Medicaid. Over the years, Medicaid has been modified many times by federal and state statutes, but the program still retains its welfare-based characteristics. Most troubling among these is the program's tendency to discourage recipients from securing better-paying jobs, since Medicaid coverage is not integrated with our employment-based system of insurance. For instance, if a woman on Medicaid were to accept a higher-paying job, she might lose her Medicaid insurance without being offered insurance through her place of employment. The result could therefore be a net reduction in her overall financial well-being.

Furthermore, because Medicaid pays exceedingly low fees to care providers, the program does not always offer high-quality coverage. Not surprisingly, as states have pushed physician-reimbursement levels well below the actual costs of caring for Medicaid patients, many doctors have responded by severely restricting the number of Medicaid patients they will see. The result for people on Medicaid is often a lack of accessible quality health care, precisely what the program is supposed to provide.

In replacing Obamacare, policymakers should move lower-income people out of the limited sphere of Medicaid options and into the same private health-insurance markets in which their fellow citizens purchase coverage. This change would afford these patients greater access to doctors and specialists, and would reduce the disincentive to higher-paying work.

There is more than one way to accomplish this objective. In the Heritage Foundation proposal noted above, for instance, existing financing for acute care provided through Medicaid and the State Children's Health Insurance Program would be transformed into a large pool of funding to be re-allocated to current beneficiaries and other low-income Americans in the form of a federal health-care subsidy (the equivalent of a "refundable tax credit") for private insurance. If they wished, state governments could provide their own support on top of this federal aid. Benefits under such a plan would be means-tested, with the lowest-income Americans receiving the most generous level of assistance and subsidies being gradually reduced for those with higher incomes as they became eligible for federal tax credits for coverage. (Because the credit in the Heritage plan is non-refundable, people would not be eligible for it until they earned enough to pay federal income taxes.)

A similar approach would give Medicaid recipients the same federal tax credit that workers would receive in a reformed marketplace for health insurance. The federal government could then convert Medicaid into a per-person allotment to the states, funded through a block grant, that would supplement the base credit for a state's low-income residents. The federal allotment to the states would be set so that, when combined with the federal support for the base tax credits or vouchers for the Medicaid-eligible population, total federal spending on the Medicaid population in a state would equal the amount that would have been spent under pre-Obamacare Medicaid. After the first year, the federal allotment to the states could be set to grow commensurate with the economy or some other reasonable measure of inflation. States would not be required to reform Medicaid in this manner; if they did, though, they would have far greater freedom to run the program according to their own priorities instead of in response to federal dictates.

The same move toward market incentives and efficiency should also characterize our approach to Medicare reform in the wake of Obamacare's repeal. The sixth pillar of a replacement plan must therefore be a premium-support reform of Medicare.

It is hard to overstate the importance of such a reform to the larger goals of controlling costs and improving quality and access to coverage. Of all the changes that are necessary to bring more cost discipline to health care, moving Medicare toward a defined-contribution structure, and away from today's open-ended defined-benefit structure, is certainly the most vital. Medicare is the largest payer for services in most markets; the system of hospital and physician care in most communities has been built up around Medicare's financial incentives.

Today, the program's dominant fee-for-service structure provides all the wrong incentives. All of the various suppliers of medical services for Medicare patients — the diagnostic labs, the physicians, the hospitals, the outpatient clinics, the nursing homes, and many others — can bill the program separately whenever they render a service to a patient. Absent Medicare's incentives, they might well consolidate and coordinate to reduce overhead and streamline care, providing higher-quality services at lower cost. Thanks to Medicare, however, these organizations can sustain themselves financially without having to affiliate with any of the other service providers. The result is extreme fragmentation and lack of coordination, which permeates the entire health-care system to the detriment of patient care.

As long as Medicare continues to operate as it does today, the way doctors and hospitals are organized will not change and will, in most markets, remain excessively costly and inefficient. This will soon prove disastrous for the federal budget: The first wave of the huge Baby Boom generation, 77 million strong, is beginning to retire. Between 2010 and 2030, Medicare's enrollment is projected to increase from 47 million to more than 80 million beneficiaries, while the ratio of workers to beneficiaries will decline from 3.7-to-1 today to 2.4-to-1 in 2030.

Obamacare's "solution" for Medicare will exacerbate the problem, not solve it. The law claims to yield $575 billion in savings over ten years through Medicare payment cuts, but those cuts won't bring more efficiency to the program. They are simply across-the-board price controls that will shift costs off of the federal balance sheets and onto non-Medicare patients (whose costs would rise to make up the difference), while also driving willing suppliers out of the marketplace. Moreover, Obamacare has imposed, for the first time in Medicare's history, a hard cap on the growth of Medicare spending, tying it to the rate of inflation and subsequently to growth in the general economy. This would, in effect, amount to a global budget for Medicare, analogous in some ways to the tough budgetary caps characteristic of single-payer health programs. To make matters worse, this cap would be enforced in accordance with the decisions of a new Independent Payment Advisory Board—a group of 15 appointed experts whose decisions would be automatically implemented unless Congress actively rejected them.

It is worth noting that, under the statute, the IPAB's authority is confined to selective Medicare payment reductions (that is, to reducing the fees paid per service in an otherwise unreformed system), and would not extend to any changes in benefit design, beneficiary payment, or the structure of the program itself. Thus there is no prospect that the IPAB will implement reforms capable of making Medicare more efficient. The board can enforce the hard cap on Medicare spending only in the same way budget cuts have always been imposed by Congress in Medicare: through price controls that exacerbate the inefficiencies in how health care is delivered to patients.

The alternative to this disastrous, top-down, micromanaged approach is to convert Medicare into a premium-support program. While such a reform should try to capture the bulk of the huge Baby Boom generation, it should also be carefully phased in, applying only to future enrollees. A transition to a new premium-support model should exempt from the changes people who are currently in the Medicare program and those very close to retiring (for instance, the plan offered by Republican congressman Paul Ryan and Democratic senator Ron Wyden would start with Americans who are 55 today, and so will enter the program in ten years).

In lieu of today's open-ended benefit, a premium-support system would allow new beneficiaries (after the transition) to decide how to use a fixed-dollar contribution provided by Medicare. Each beneficiary would choose from a menu of approved insurance plans. If a beneficiary's premium for his chosen plan was higher than the Medicare contribution, he would pay the difference out of his own pocket. If he chose a less expensive plan, he would pay lower premiums and keep the savings. This structure would provide a powerful incentive for the program's participants to find high-value plans that charge low premiums for quality care, and therefore for insurers to offer such plans.

With cost-conscious consumers looking for the best value for their money, cost-cutting innovations would be rewarded, not punished as they are today. Physicians and hospitals would have strong financial incentives to re-organize themselves to increase productivity and efficiency in order to capture a larger share of what would become a highly competitive marketplace. This is the only way to slow the growth of health-care costs without harming the quality of care.

While Medicare reform is absolutely essential to restraining cost escalation and to improving the affordability of health care for all Americans, it need not be enacted in the same legislation as an Obamacare replacement program. This is true especially because a replacement program would be focused primarily on providing an alternative vision of insurance coverage for working-age Americans, not retirees. Still, the reform of Medicare suggested here is entirely consistent with, and in fact reinforces, the rest of the reforms proposed above. It is up to the sponsors of replacement legislation to decide whether moving one or two pieces of health-care legislation through Congress at a time would be more likely to result in enactment.

### FISCAL RESPONSIBILITY, FOR A CHANGE

Finally, as a key criticism of Obamacare is the danger it poses to federal finances, the seventh pillar of a serious health-care reform plan must be the full offset of all new costs through spending cuts.

If past experience is any guide, Obamacare's new entitlement and massive expansions of Medicaid could cost several times more than the official estimate (about $1 trillion over a decade). Moreover, Obamacare's sponsors resorted to a series of gimmicks and budgetary sleights of hand to make it seem as if the legislation would actually improve, rather than worsen, the long-term budget outlook. But while repealing Obamacare would avert these costs, a credible replacement program would certainly entail some expenses of its own. These would result especially from the subsidization of coverage—whether through the tax credit for the purchase of private insurance, the additional support for many lower-wage workers, or the support for Americans who enter the insurance pool with pre-existing conditions.

To be sure, some of the new costs from a replacement program would be offset by the savings reaped from other components of the reform package. For example, placing an upper limit on the tax break for employer-paid premiums in the large-employer market would generate substantial revenue, partially offsetting the cost of extending credits to Americans in the small-business and individual marketplaces. The reforms of Medicaid, too, would help, ensuring that future federal costs would grow at a more moderate pace than is expected under current law.

Even so, additional spending reductions will be necessary to fully offset the added budgetary burden of replacement legislation. The spending reductions chosen should be real cuts, not budget gimmicks, and should be of sufficient magnitude to ensure that the legislation results in a net decline in federal spending, taxes, and future budget deficits.

The first place to look for such cuts is within existing health-entitlement spending. For instance, both Medicare and Medicaid subsidize hospitals for caring for the uninsured and underinsured. These subsidies could be cut back substantially or eliminated altogether in a replacement program, since that program would extend insurance protection to millions of uninsured people, thus allowing tens of billions of dollars in savings from these indirect means of support. In addition, the Medicare fee-for-service program should be modified to reduce costs even during the window that precedes the full transition to a premium-support program for new entrants. Such changes could include gradually increasing the retirement age, as well as adjusting the rules for supplementary insurance coverage so that seniors have an incentive to responsibly restrain their health-care spending. Policymakers might also consider using some type of means test, adjusting the level of Medicare subsidies or premiums based on income, in order to ensure that taxpayer dollars are not providing needlessly generous benefits to the very wealthy.

## A HISTORIC OPPORTUNITY

The enactment of Obamacare has created a political opening for a credible alternative to the health-care status quo. But it would be foolish to assume that opening will last very long; once it has closed, it is not likely to appear again.

Obamacare is deeply unpopular because it is based on a bureaucratic, government-centered vision of American health care. The entire program is rooted in an expansion of federal power and everything that entails: massive new entitlements, additional dependence on government, tax hikes that hinder economic growth, and federal micromanagement of health care that produces a sharp decline in the quality of American medicine. This is exactly what voters do *not* want in a proposal to reform the nation's health-care system.

But voters do want a better system, with more security and with affordable and reliable coverage and care. Conservatives thus have a rare opportunity to advance their vision of reform. It will entail some controversy and political risk, which cannot be avoided in a policy arena as complex as health care. But the policy and political upsides are well worth the effort. A market-driven alternative can beat Obamacare on every metric that matters. It will be less costly to taxpayers, more flexible in meeting the diverse needs of citizens, less bureaucratic, and consistent with the Constitution and our values.

Some might observe that if this kind of program had been advanced by conservatives ten years ago, Obamacare might have been avoided in the first place. Perhaps. But it is still not too late to avert disaster: Americans are hungry for a credible alternative to Obamacare, one that carries much less risk for future taxpayers and does not give government control over the delivery of medical care. Now is the time to offer it to them.

*Originally published as "How to Replace Obamacare" in the Spring 2012 issue of* National Affairs.

# How to Cover Pre-existing Conditions

## James C. Capretta and Tom Miller

SUMMER 2010

T HE HEALTH-CARE LEGISLATION enacted this spring followed more than a year of heated, rancorous debate. But rather than subdue the public's passions, the bill's passage has only stoked them. Opposition to the new law remains very high, and Republicans have made clear their intention to push for its repeal if they gain control of Congress and the White House in 2010 and 2012.

For their part, President Obama and other champions of the legislation insist that public attitudes will soon change. More Americans will come to appreciate the law, they argue, once people have a better grasp of its benefits. And foremost among these benefits is the law's prohibition of "pre-existing condition" exclusions in health insurance — which would prevent insurance companies from denying coverage to customers with serious medical problems.

Like most of the health-care bill's major provisions, this ban will not take full effect until 2014. But the mere prospect of finally addressing the "pre-existing condition problem" is held up as an enormous selling point of the law. At long last, the bill's advocates claim, America has a solution to a profound failing of our current system — a solution that will eliminate a source of worry for millions, and that opponents would not dare undo. Indeed, while describing the plight of a young woman in the audience at a rally he attended in April, Obama told the crowd: "If [opponents of the law] want to look at Lauren Gallagher in the eye and tell her they plan to take away her father's ability to get health insurance... they can run on that platform."

The president's dramatic talents notwithstanding, the choice he presents is a false one. We do not face an either-or showdown between

JAMES C. CAPRETTA is a fellow at the Ethics and Public Policy Center.
TOM MILLER is a resident fellow at the American Enterprise Institute.

cruelly denying sick people treatment and a massive new federal health-insurance entitlement. The problem of covering Americans with pre-existing conditions is certainly real, but the notion that the only way to solve it is through a massive transformation of America's health-care system — one that will increase costs, raise taxes, displace millions of the happily insured, create a new entitlement, and undermine our private insurance sector — is simply wrong.

The case for repealing the newly enacted law, then, is not that there are no problems to solve in American health care. Rather, it is that there are far better solutions available.

### THE PRE-EXISTING DILEMMA

The challenge of covering people with pre-existing conditions is a function of the way our health-insurance system has evolved over many years — and especially of the fact that it is largely employer-based, voluntary, and distorted by complex subsidies and regulations that favor some insurance purchasers over others.

Since most working Americans get health insurance as a benefit of employment, losing or changing jobs often means losing or changing insurance coverage. As a result, most people are not continuously covered by the same plan throughout their lives. If they move directly from one employer-sponsored health plan to another, the disruption is usually not a problem (for reasons laid out below). But whenever someone, by choice or necessity, leaves employer-sponsored insurance to purchase health insurance on his own, the switch in coverage can present several challenges.

In a voluntary individual insurance market, insurers must have some means of preventing large mismatches between the premiums they take in and the claims they will likely need to pay out. The classic form of such a mismatch is the case of a consumer who waits until he is sick to purchase or enroll in an individual insurance plan. If an insurer offers coverage to such a person without pricing the expected costs of the enrollee's illness into the premium, the expense of paying out medical claims will almost certainly exceed the premiums collected. The practice will also encourage other people not to buy insurance until they need to draw on it — a problem known as "adverse selection." Why pay for insurance when you're healthy if you can buy it for the same price when you get sick? It would be the equivalent of purchasing auto insurance only after you've totaled your car—and insurers would obviously go bankrupt if this were their business model.

Insurers selling directly to individual consumers use two practices to prevent widespread adverse selection. First, they try to take into account the health status of prospective customers when determining their premiums (a process called "underwriting," by which they consider an applicant's age and other demographic factors and, in certain cases, medical history). Second, in some instances, they deny coverage of pre-existing conditions for a set period of time after a customer enrolls, so that if he buys insurance (or changes insurers) only after he has already been diagnosed with a costly condition, he cannot immediately use the new coverage to pay for medical claims associated with his existing ailment. Taken together, these two practices have led to the pre-existing condition problem: People who are sick can find themselves without health-care coverage, and without the ability to secure coverage at an affordable price, sometimes through no fault of their own.

From the rhetoric of some politicians, one might think this dilemma lies at the very core of America's health-care crisis. But in fact, the problem is relatively contained. Senior citizens can get health-care coverage through Medicare; the poor have Medicaid; and most Americans who have employer-based coverage do not run across the "pre-existing condition problem." It primarily affects a subgroup of sick, working-age Americans—those who do not receive health coverage from their employers, do not qualify for Medicaid, and are not able to buy coverage in the individual market because their health conditions make their premiums too high (or cause insurers to reject them altogether).

Pre-existing conditions are not much of an issue in the (vastly larger) employer-based insurance market for several reasons. First, job-based plans are implicitly "community rated" products—meaning that everyone who is covered by the same plan is charged more or less the same price. Underwriting of individual patients is therefore minimal, as insurers sell group plans to firms based on the risk profile of the entire work force. (The high costs of caring for some workers with diabetes, for instance, are balanced by the relatively low costs associated with their more healthy co-workers.) Risk levels in employer plans are also somewhat contained by the plans' very nature, in that only relatively healthy people are likely to show up to work regularly, stay employed, and gain access to job-related insurance benefits.

Of course, these techniques for spreading risk do not always work perfectly. Some smaller firms may have fewer workers across whom an occasional high-cost risk might be spread; in some industries—like automobile manufacturing or coal mining—the balance between new "healthy" workers and older "unhealthy" ones may be unfavorably tipped by demographic and economic factors. Even within larger firms, there is evidence that employers sometimes reduce cash wages to adjust for the cost of insuring some workers (particularly older and more obese ones) whose actual health-care expenses are likely to be much higher than average. Still, on the whole, the sick and the healthy pay roughly the same premiums in job-based plans. And insurers see it as a sustainable business practice, because selling to a group allows for the balancing of high and low risks.

Moreover, in 1996, Congress provided an important protection to workers by making it unlawful for employer-sponsored plans to impose exclusions on pre-existing conditions for workers in continuous group insurance coverage. This means that if a person stays covered by job-based plans long enough (usually six months), he can move from one job to another without fear of losing insurance protection, or of having to wait longer than other new hires before gaining coverage for ailments he may have developed. If a new hire maintained insurance in his old job, his new employer's plan must cover him—even if the worker has developed an expensive medical condition.

In theory, this law—called the Health Insurance Portability and Accountability Act (or HIPAA)—also provided "portability" rights to people moving from job-based plans to individually owned coverage. The law gave state governments a few options for meeting this mandate: They could establish high-risk pools (which, as discussed below, is the approach most states have followed); they could require that all individual-market health insurers within their states offer insurance to all eligible individuals, without any limits on coverage of pre-existing medical conditions; or they could use their regulatory powers to create a mix of rules that would have similar results. But unfortunately, none of these approaches has worked well enough, and today many people still end up falling through the cracks.

The problem starts with HIPAA's requirement that a worker first exhaust his right to temporary continuous coverage under his former employer's plan (through a federal program called COBRA, which lets workers keep buying into their employers' insurance plans, generally for up to 18 months after leaving their jobs) before he can enter the individual insurance market without a pre-existing condition exclusion. Many workers are not aware of this requirement (though employers must advise them of it in a written notice); even if they are, the premiums required to stay in an employer's plan through COBRA are often too high for them to pay. This is because COBRA premiums must cover both the employer and employee share of costs, and generally provide more expensive comprehensive benefits than individual-market alternatives. And unlike premiums paid in employer-based plans, these COBRA premiums do not receive any tax advantage—making them more expensive still. As a result, many workers facing this fully loaded "sticker shock" price choose not to pay the premiums, simply hoping for the best until they can find new jobs (and new coverage). In so doing, they inadvertently waive their HIPAA rights—leaving themselves vulnerable to exclusions and high costs for pre-existing conditions when they try to buy insurance on their own.

But even if a sick person abides by HIPAA's requirements and remains continuously insured—thereby protecting himself from pre-existing condition exclusions in the individual market—nothing in current federal law prevents insurers from charging him more than they charge healthy people. Insurers are prohibited only from denying coverage for a pre-existing condition altogether; it is quite permissible, however, for insurance providers to charge unaffordable premiums (unless an individual state's laws happen to prevent or restrict the practice), thus achieving essentially the same outcome.

Likewise, current law and regulations provide no premium protections for persons moving *between* individual insurance policies. A healthy worker who leaves an employer plan for the individual market might find an affordable plan at first—but if he ever wanted to switch insurers (or was forced to by, say, moving to a new state), he would face the risk of having his premium recalculated based on a new assessment of his health.

Of course, the fact that the problem of pre-existing condition coverage is limited almost entirely to the individual market does not mean that it pervades that market. In 2008, at the request of the U.S. Department of Health and Human Services, health economists Mark Pauly and Bradley Herring examined how people with chronic health conditions, and thus high anticipated health-care expenses, actually fared when seeking insurance in the individual market. Pauly and Herring found little, if any, evidence that enrollees in poor health generally paid higher premiums for individual insurance. Nor did they find that the onset of chronic conditions is necessarily associated with increased premiums in subsequent years. Existing "guaranteed renewability" requirements in federal and state law already prevent insurers from continuously reclassifying people (and the premiums they pay) based on health risks. And most private insurers already provided such protection as standard business practice before they were legally required to do so.

But even if the exclusions and prohibitive premiums caused by pre-existing conditions are not a universal problem in the individual insurance market, they clearly affect many Americans. Estimates range from 2 to 4 million, out of a total population of about 260 million people under the age of 65. More important than the sheer number, however, is the fact that many Americans know someone who has faced this situation directly, and fear that they could find themselves in the same boat—which explains the strong public support for changing the way insurance companies treat pre-existing conditions.

Most people find it unacceptable that responsible fellow citizens who have tried to stay insured throughout their lives can suddenly find themselves sick and unable to get adequate coverage. On the other hand, insurers clearly need some way of aligning premiums and risks in order to stay financially solvent. And because the smaller individual market now often operates as a last resort for those lacking better insurance options through employers, insurers must plan for the risk that people seeking individual coverage are doing so because they believe they will need substantial medical attention.

Of course, insurers have incentives to avoid excessive underwriting. For one thing, screening is expensive. For another, if insurers screen too aggressively, they will lose customers whose care would not in fact have been very costly. Insurance companies balance the benefits of screening against these costs in the individual market no less than in others: Indeed, the most extensive research in this area, by Pauly and Herring, has demonstrated that there is already a great deal of pooling of health risks in the individual market. But some people clearly still cannot get covered.

The question is what should be done for them. The most effective solution would be not heavy-handed regulation, but rather a new insurance marketplace built around truly portable, individually owned insurance. If households, not firms, chose and controlled their own insurance plans, people would no longer face the risks that come with changing coverage based on new employment arrangements. By carrying the same insurance plan from one job to the next (or even through periods with no job at all), individuals would keep their coverage even as their health status changed. Moreover, insurers would have strong incentives to do what they could to keep their enrollees healthy, knowing full well that some of them could be enrolled for many years. That is how health insurance is supposed to work.

But moving to true insurance portability will not be easy. It will require fundamental reform of the tax treatment of health insurance in order to level the playing field between plans owned by employers and those owned by individuals, as well as a reworking of some current insurance regulations. For now, both reforms face long political odds. And even if these changes were to happen, we would still need some way of covering people who already suffer from costly health conditions (and so could not easily buy their own portable insurance, even once a new system got up and running).

Short of such a transformation, then, what can be done to help people shut out by the current system? Some states have attempted to address the problem by imposing price controls on health-insurance premiums — requiring insurers to sell to all comers, regardless of their health status (a rule called "guaranteed issue") and at standard rates ("community rating"). But this has only caused insurers to increase the premiums they charge everyone else — even young, healthy customers — in order to make up for the losses associated with the enrollment of these more expensive cases at below-cost premiums. And when premiums rise for younger and healthier customers in a voluntary marketplace, a significant number of these people — weighing the low risk of an expensive illness against the high cost of buying health insurance — will drop out of coverage altogether. The pool of enrollees thus becomes older and less healthy, further driving up premium costs for the enrollees who remain. The resulting vicious cycle triggered by excessive regulation can cause so many consumers and insurers to flee that the entire market can collapse. This is what happened in Washington state and Kentucky when such reforms were tried in the 1990s, before they had to be "repealed and replaced."

The new federal health-care legislation, meanwhile, aims to solve the "pre-existing" problem by dramatically transforming our entire health-care system — even though most insured Americans are quite happy with the coverage they have—and by creating an enormous and expensive system of regulations and entitlements. Obamacare thus creates an even greater risk of system collapse—in this case, with taxpayers picking up the pieces.

As so often happens, though, the model for a promising national solution has begun to emerge from the states. Across the country, state policymakers have turned to an approach that does not require a fundamental transformation of the insurance marketplace: the creation of high-risk pools. Unfortunately, these state-level efforts have not been sufficiently ambitious or adequately funded; they would also be badly undermined by the new federal health-care law. But if that law is in fact repealed, reformers concerned about the problem of pre-existing conditions should champion a system of robust, well-funded high-risk pools as a smart and effective solution.

## PROMISE AND SHORTCOMINGS

High-risk pools are basically a policy mechanism for bridging the gap between the high cost of providing insurance to patients with predictably expensive pre-existing health conditions and the comparatively low premiums those patients can afford. In most states that have established such programs, the pool is a highly regulated, independent non-profit entity that functions as an insurance program, offering a selection of health-benefit plans. The work of managing benefits and interacting with customers (such as the collection of premiums and the payment of claims) is usually contracted out to participating private insurance companies. In other states, the risk-pool program is run more directly by the state health or insurance department (which, again, contracts out most key management functions to private insurers).

People who try to get insurance and are denied, or who receive only unaffordable coverage offers, may apply to participate in the high-risk pool program; the program's administrators then determine each applicant's eligibility. Common eligibility criteria in the states include one or more of the following: having been rejected for coverage, based on health reasons, by private insurers; having been refused coverage except at rates exceeding the subsidized premium offered in the high-risk pool; having received private coverage offers, but only with restrictive riders or pre-existing condition limitations; the existence of particular medical conditions (like HIV/AIDS, cancer, or diabetes) presumed to result in rejection by health insurers; or being a dependent of a person eligible for high-risk pool coverage. The pools also often cover people who, having maintained continuous coverage under HIPAA rules, need to find new insurance arrangements in the individual market.

Because everyone in the pool has, by definition, a high-risk profile, average claim costs are necessarily quite high. But eligible individuals' premiums are capped at various levels above standard rates; beyond those caps, premium payments are fully subsidized from various public revenue sources. The idea is that people will pay only the premiums they can afford, and the difference between those payments and the real cost of insurance will be made up by taxpayers.

In theory, such pools should not only help provide coverage for people with pre-existing conditions, but should also help lower premium costs in the rest of the insurance marketplace. This is because the uncertainty involved in covering the least healthy consumers would be removed from the cost structure financed by normal premium payments. When that is done, premiums go down and become more attractive for lower-risk customers, thus further expanding the pool of premium payers (and again lowering costs for everyone else).

The first high-risk pools were instituted in Minnesota and Connecticut back in 1976; today, 35 states operate some version of the plans. In 2008, approximately 200,000 people were enrolled in state high-risk pools; the average length of enrollment was three years (about 20 to 25% of enrollees leave each year), and the average age of those enrolled was 49. The premium costs that enrollees in these high-risk pools must pay are generally capped at levels between 125% and 150% of standard market rates (although some states—like Texas and South Carolina—go up to 200% or higher, while others—like Minnesota—cap them even below 125% for some categories of beneficiaries).

Premium revenue contributed by enrollees amounted to just over half (54%) of total high-risk pool funding in 2008; the rest came from a combination of assessments on private insurance carriers (23.2%), state general revenues (5%), state tobacco taxes (2.2%), and federal grants (1.7%). (A total of about $286 million has been awarded to states to establish new high-risk pools or subsidize existing ones under a federal program in operation since 2002.) The less transparent categories of "other assessments" (7.4%) and "other" (6.3%) comprised the rest of the funding sources.

Although high-risk pools have helped hundreds of thousands of Americans, they have nonetheless fallen far short of meeting the needs they are meant to address. In addition to the large differences among the state plans in terms of eligibility rules, benefit design, premium prices, subsidies, and financing, there are also huge discrepancies when it comes to effectiveness.

The pools" main shortcoming in every instance, though, is the large mismatch between the number of people who need them and the amount of money made available to subsidize them. Just how many people might face pre-existing condition exclusions and might benefit from high-risk pools is not a simple question, but several serious attempts have been made in recent years to arrive at a reliable figure.

In a 2001 survey by the Department of Health and Human Services, respondents were asked if they had "ever been denied health insurance because of poor health." The data collected indicate that about 2 million people might be eligible for enrollment in high-risk pools.

In a different study, using 2006 data, the Government Accountability Office determined roughly the percentage of uninsured individuals who had at least one chronic health condition, and then applied it to census estimates of the average number of uninsured people in each state with an existing high-risk pool. (The aim was to get a sense of how many more people might be covered by such pools if they were available to all who needed them.) The GAO concluded that as many as 4 million Americans could be covered by more generously funded high-risk pools—20 times the number now covered.

More recently, University of Pennsylvania health economist Mark Pauly looked at data about the number of people with chronic health conditions whose expected medical expenses are more than twice the national average. He first estimated the total nationwide high-risk group at around 4% of the under-65 population, excluding people receiving Medicaid—a number in the low millions. But Pauly ultimately concluded that the number of people who were both high-risk and looking for coverage in the individual market at any given point was far lower—on the order of tens of thousands.

Regardless of the particular sources or estimating methods, however, it is clear that the demand for premium assistance among those with high expected health costs far exceeds the state high-risk pools' current financial capacity.

Assuming that the higher ranges of these estimates are correct, what would it cost to use high-risk pools to cover between 2 and 4 million people? For an initial assessment, it might be best to start with the 2008 average subsidized cost of $4,341 per pool enrollee—the amount states contributed to their programs beyond the premiums paid by enrollees. If we assume that as many as 4 million more people might need (and seek) high-risk pool coverage, the annual cost of public subsidies could be as high as $17 billion. Other variables might include whether the new enrollees are likely to be somewhat less costly than current ones (since their situations might be less dire); whether benefits and cost-sharing levels are more or less generous than under current high-risk pool coverage; and whether additional income-based subsidies for enrollees are included. All of this suggests a rough estimate of between $15 and $20 billion per year for a comprehensive set of high-risk pool programs.

Given that cost, and the fiscal stresses most state governments are feeling these days, it is not surprising that state-based pools have been underfunded and closed off to many potential beneficiaries. Indeed, the most common complaint about high-risk pools has been that their coverage remains too expensive and too limited. Most state pools offer comprehensive insurance benefits (of the sort that most people in employer-based coverage receive), generally with 20% co-insurance, although they tend to impose higher deductibles (and some have lower lifetime-coverage limits) than private insurers. Furthermore, to control costs, all current state high-risk pools actually impose pre-existing condition exclusion periods—ranging from two months to one year—for enrollees who forfeited (or never accrued) portability rights under HIPAA. Facing fiscal pressures, many states are also not particularly aggressive in trying to boost high-risk pool enrollment through advertising and outreach to potential enrollees; nor have they been eager to pay commissions as generous as those paid by private insurers to insurance agents who bring in customers.

In short, the lack of adequate financing still leaves millions of potential high-risk beneficiaries with inferior options—and sometimes no options—for health-care coverage. So while high-risk pools offer a plausible and promising conceptual model for covering people with pre-existing conditions, their real-life implementation has (at least to date) left much room for improvement.

Champions of pro-market health-care reform should therefore urge states to properly design and operate high-risk pools, and should call on the federal government to properly fund them. Such pools would offer an effective, yet far less expensive and intrusive, approach to the problem of covering pre-existing conditions than the tack taken by the new health-care law. And very soon—well before its most important provisions take effect in 2014—that law will put pre-existing conditions and risk pools front and center in our national health-care debate.

### OBAMACARE'S SHALLOW POOLS

High-risk pools have tended not to be popular with liberal health-care reformers, who would prefer instead deep government involvement in the inner workings of the insurance system. The health-care plan Barack Obama offered when he ran for president in 2008 therefore made no room for the pools, and Obama-campaign surrogates were critical, if not dismissive, of Senator John McCain's proposal to use such pools as part of a broader reform of the health-care system.

President Obama and congressional Democrats remained disdainful of high-risk pools when they began to develop their health-care legislation last year, relying instead on mandates and subsidies for private insurance—along with a substantial expansion of Medicaid—to move toward universal insurance coverage. Unfortunately, their approach to addressing the needs of people with pre-existing conditions is modeled on one that has failed in several state efforts in recent decades: The new law includes an outright ban on insurers' excluding pre-existing conditions from coverage, and on insurers' requiring people with higher health risks to pay higher premiums (older enrollees would still pay more than younger ones, up to a point).

But the new federal law does differ from previous state efforts in one important way: Starting in 2014, health-insurance coverage will no longer be voluntary; every American must either carry insurance or pay a fine. In theory, mandating insurance enrollment should prevent the young and healthy from fleeing the marketplace when their premiums are increased to cover higher-cost cases (thus preventing any regulation-induced meltdown of private insurance markets). But many industry experts argue that the insurance mandate—which charges a penalty of less than $1,000 for failing to purchase insurance that could cost several times that much—will not work as planned, because too many young and healthy people will choose to stay out of the system. For them, it will still make financial sense to go without coverage. The Obama plan could therefore bring about the same cycle that eventually doomed state initiatives in the past.

Furthermore, as part of a legislative ploy to mask Obamacare's full cost and to keep the 10-year Congressional Budget Office score below $1 trillion, the new insurance system will not go into effect until 2014. But to sell the bill to the public, Democrats knew they had to offer something on the pre-existing condition front in the interim. To fill the gap, they turned to the very mechanism they had long derided: high-risk pools. The bill requires that high-risk pools for people with pre-existing conditions be established within three months of the law's enactment (meaning they must begin by the end of June), and operate until January 1, 2014, when the new insurance rules and subsidies would go into effect.

It is clear from the language of the legislation that these high-risk pool provisions were crudely cobbled together as an afterthought to Obamacare's other, more sweeping reforms. Little press or public attention was paid to them either before or after the bill passed. As a result, these provisions are likely to exacerbate the problems faced by states and patients, rather than resolve them.

To begin with, the notion that the new high-risk pools can be up and running effectively within a mere 90 days is sheer fantasy. Although the secretary of Health and Human Services has the authority to contract with existing state-based pools, the requirements for their eligibility as federal partners under the new law will be difficult to meet. As many as 20 states object to participating in the new law's high-risk pool program, including a dozen states already operating their own high-risk pools (which would be required to undergo significant changes). But the alternative — setting up one or more entirely separate, federally managed high-risk pools that would exist for less than four years — would be unnecessarily costly and redundant (even *if* it could be done quickly and competently, which is a pretty big "if").

Moreover, the law prohibits the high-risk pools from imposing *any* pre-existing condition exclusions from coverage. Eligible individuals cannot be charged premiums that exceed the standard non-group insurance rate in each state — a significant departure from the practice of all current state-based high-risk pools (which, to one degree or another, charge higher-than-standard rates). Age-based premium rating will be more constrained than it is under state high-risk plans today, and insurers in the new risk pools will be required to pay at least 65% of the costs of covered medical treatments and procedures (clashing with some states' established practices, which require patients to pay for a greater portion of their own treatments). In effect, the new law would impose on the high-risk pools many of the restrictions it will place on insurance coverage, benefits, and premiums in the new health exchanges to be established in 2014 — but three and a half years before the latter are fully drafted and implemented.

The law also grossly underfunds the high-risk pools it requires, authorizing a total of only $5 billion for three and a half years of operation. The bill tries to get around its own tight purse strings by authorizing the newly mandated risk pools to "stop taking applications for participation in the program…to comply with the funding limitation" when the money runs out; it also vaguely empowers the HHS secretary to make "such adjustments as are necessary" to eliminate any deficit in the program during any fiscal year. In addition, the law suppresses potential demand for new high-risk pool coverage by limiting eligibility to people who have already been uninsured for six months. Merely having a pre-existing condition, and being turned down for coverage because of it, will not suffice. Nor can one gain admission to the new pools if one is already enrolled in an existing state high-risk pool but facing higher premiums with greater cost-sharing. After all, people in these circumstances are not "uninsured."

In other words, then, the secretary of Health and Human Services is first authorized to determine which pre-existing conditions make a potential enrollee eligible for federal high-risk pool coverage — and then, as budget funds run short, is required to figure out how to avoid actually providing that person with the promised health-care coverage. The results are easy to foresee: waiting periods, benefit limits, and rationing of care — all the practices for which the new law's champions like to attack the private insurance industry.

The administration's own cost estimates reflect the degree to which optimistic promises are out of step with harsh reality. In April, the chief actuary of the Department of Health and Human Services released a cost projection for the new program, predicting that the $5 billion the law allocates for three and a half years of high-risk pools will in fact be exhausted in the program's first or second year. The actuary estimates that only 375,000 people shut out of insurance elsewhere will obtain health-care coverage through the high-risk pools — a number that falls far short of the 2 to 4 million people in the targeted population. One can therefore expect that, soon after the program is launched, it will be short of funds and forced to turn applicants away.

This coming failure of Obamacare's high-risk pool component will put the question of pre-existing conditions at the heart of the continuing health-care debate. For opponents of the new law, it will be crucial to show the public that the failure of the temporary high-risk pool is a function of its careless design, but not an indictment of the fundamental concept. They must show the public that the solution to our enduring "pre-existing" problem is a well-designed and well-funded system of state high-risk pools — not the new law's massive and misguided transformation of American health care.

### THE REAL SOLUTION

What would a well-designed system of high-risk pools look like? Its guiding principle is straightforward enough: Americans who stay in continuous insurance coverage should not be penalized for developing costly health conditions. Any system capable of upholding this principle would need to incorporate several key components.

First, it would require Congress to fix several of the flaws in HIPAA noted above. Workers leaving job-based plans for the individual market should be able to do so without being penalized for failing to exhaust their COBRA rights. If a worker moves directly from an employer-provided plan to an individual policy, he should not be denied coverage based on a pre-existing condition.

Second, there should be limits (imposed by states, based on broader federal guidelines) on underwriting for people who move from the employer-based market to the individual market. This could be achieved by, for instance, capping the premiums charged to high-risk customers at some fixed level above their standard rates, regardless of income, and then having the government provide supplemental subsidies to the poor on a sliding scale. Another option is to take income as well as risk into account when setting the premium caps — so that if two people have the same risk level, the wealthier of the two will pay higher premiums. The aim of both ideas is to allow insurers to take higher health risks into account when calculating premiums, while also ensuring that people with expensive health conditions are not completely priced out of the market. (Identifying people at very high risks could also help insurers to better tailor health-care interventions in order to encourage these customers to change their behavior and lower their risks over time.)

Of course, limiting premiums this way will mean that the gap between a customer's contribution and the actual cost of insuring him must be bridged with taxpayer dollars through high-risk pool programs in the states. If these programs are to function properly, they must therefore be well funded—somewhere in the range of $15 to $20 billion per year. This funding should come in the form of a capped annual appropriation to the states from Congress. Making high-risk pools an open-ended entitlement—like, say, Medicaid—would create the same problems of runaway costs that are likely to plague the whole of the Democrats' health-reform plan. It is therefore better to set initially generous, but still firmly limited, annual appropriations; only after the program has undergone the necessary trial and error of implementation and practice—thus providing a better sense of the pools' actual needs and costs—should lawmakers re-examine the funding commitments.

Third, the risk pools themselves must be structured properly to prevent participating private insurers from dumping unwanted (but not truly high-risk) customers into the public-subsidy system. If an insurer believes that an applicant's health status argues for charging him a premium higher than, say, 1.5 times the standard rate, the insurer should be allowed to direct the customer to the high-risk pool program in his state. The job of determining eligibility for the subsidy should be contracted out by the state to a neutral third party with experience in medical-insurance underwriting, with private insurers collaborating to determine in advance the criteria for high-risk selection. If the third party finds no basis for designating the applicant an unusually high risk, the insurer seeking the evaluation would be required to take the applicant at no more than the maximum rate of (in this example) 1.5 times the standard premium. (And if the insurer makes failed claims too often, it would pay additional penalty fees to the state—thus discouraging so-called "risk dumping.") But if the insurer's application is deemed valid, the state would subsidize the individual's high premium in its high-risk pool program, taking into account the enrollee's income and other resources.

Fourth, insurers participating in the individual market would need to offer coverage without a new risk assessment to anyone who has maintained an individual policy for some minimum period when he applies for a new one. This would mean that market entrants would face a risk evaluation only once; they would then have the right to renew their policies at the same rate class from any licensed insurer.

Finally, when these reforms are first implemented, there will need to be a one-time open-season enrollment period to allow people who have fallen through the cracks over the years to re-establish their rights by maintaining continuous coverage. Those who have forfeited their coverage would get just one chance to become insured under the new rules (though perhaps at higher rates than those who had not forfeited their rights); once the enrollment window closed, everyone would know that people who remain continuously insured are protected, and that those who choose not to become insured have taken a risk.

### A BETTER WAY

This approach to covering pre-existing conditions would not be inexpensive, of course. But its price tag would be tiny compared to the recent health-care bill's. And using high-risk pools to cover people who are uninsured because of pre-existing medical conditions would not cede all power over our health-care system to bureaucrats in Washington. Nor would it disrupt insurance arrangements that are working well for the vast majority of Americans. It would leave in place the many protections already available to people in the much larger employer-based insurance market. Indeed, it would likely ease cost pressures on many Americans who are currently insured—by properly funding high-risk individuals who are now pushing insurance premiums up for everyone.

The many advantages of high-risk pools create an opening for opponents of Obama's approach. Critics should seize the chance to present a coherent case to the public for replacing the deeply flawed new law—advancing in its place a series of targeted, incremental solutions to the specific problems plaguing our health-care system.

The challenge of covering Americans with pre-existing conditions offers the earliest, and perhaps best, proving ground for their case. It is a challenge that those who oppose Obamacare's overreach should embrace—not a vulnerability that should scare them away from the cause of repeal.

*Originally published as "How to Cover Pre-existing Conditions" in the Summer 2010 issue of* National Affairs.

# How to Fix Medicare

## *Avik Roy*

SUMMER 2011

A T THE HEART OF AMERICA'S FISCAL CRISIS is the looming collapse of our entitlement system. And the primary cause of that looming collapse is the explosion of costs in Medicare, the federal program that provides health insurance to every American over 65. Without major reforms of the program, there is simply no way for us to address the federal deficit, contain the national debt, or save Medicare itself from collapse.

Medicare's woes are partly demographic. In 2030, when the last of the Baby Boomers retires, there will be 77 million people on Medicare, up from 47 million today. But there will be fewer working people funding the benefits of this much larger retiree population: In 2030, there will be 2.3 workers per retiree, compared to 3.4 today and about 4 when the program was created.

But a bigger part of Medicare's troubles is the rapid inflation of health-care costs. In 2010, the per capita cost of providing health-care services in America increased by 6.1%, according to Standard & Poor's, while overall inflation increased by only 1.5%. Over the past decade, health-care inflation has risen 48%, while inflation in the broader economy has increased by only 26%, according to the Department of Labor.

Providing an increasingly expensive service to a rapidly growing population while drawing on a fast-declining pool of taxpayers is, of course, a recipe for fiscal doom. The Congressional Budget Office now projects that the Medicare program will be effectively bankrupt in 2021, and its continuing growth will increasingly burden the federal budget, sinking the nation deeper into debt. The program's trustees report that its unfunded long-term liability — the gap between the benefits that will

*AVIK ROY is a health-care analyst at Monness, Crespi, Hardt & Co. in New York, and serves on the Board of Policy Advisors of the Heartland Institute.*

need to be paid out and the revenues available to pay for them over the coming decades — is more than $30 trillion.

It is simply not possible to address this problem only by increasing the taxes that fund Medicare. Medicare spending is growing at a much faster rate than the economy (and therefore faster than the tax base). As Andrew Rettenmaier and Thomas Saving have shown, Medicare payroll taxes would need to quadruple today in order to cover the program's unfunded liabilities; alternatively, income-tax rates would need to increase by 57%. And even this would be sufficient only if we made the generous, but dubious, assumption that dramatic tax increases would not retard future economic growth (and thereby future tax revenues).

Another solution must be found, and soon. If Washington fixes Medicare only after a debt-driven economic disruption, the likely outcome will involve draconian across-the-board cuts in benefits to retirees, painful rationing of medical services, and restricted access to doctors and hospitals. In such a scenario, the wealthy will be affected the least, as they will be the ones most able to purchase supplemental insurance to address their needs. It will be the poorest, and the sickest, of Medicare's enrollees who will get left behind.

If Medicare reform is urgent for the sake of our most vulnerable retirees, it is also necessary for the sake of our health-care system. By subsidizing the massive over-utilization of health-care resources, and by underpaying doctors and physicians (who must pass on the costs to patients with private insurance), Medicare drives up the cost of health care not only for the elderly but for everyone. Rising costs, in turn, make health care unaffordable for tens of millions of middle-class Americans. And these problems will only get worse as the elderly become a larger share of the population.

An effective reform of the program would have to both restructure the way Medicare itself works and help to restrain the growth of health-care costs more generally. That seems like a monumental task, but ironically the poor design of Medicare actually makes that task more achievable, by making the key problems with the program readily apparent and addressable.

Legislators have understandably been reluctant to take on the task of reform, given that Medicare is popular with its recipients and that those recipients are a large and powerful constituency. But if Medicare reforms seem politically difficult now, they will be nearly impossible when the elderly population reaches 80 million. We can be certain that the retirees of the future, too, will vote in large numbers.

The time to take up meaningful Medicare reform must therefore be now. By considering the history and design of the program, as well as the reasons why past efforts to fix it have failed, we can better see our way toward a politically plausible and economically sustainable set of solutions.

### WHAT IS MEDICARE?

We Americans have lived with Medicare for 45 years, so such a program may seem to us a standard component of modern government. But it is worth remembering that ours is the only developed country that makes age-based distinctions in its provision of government health coverage.

In many other countries, state-funded health insurance began with the poor, and was gradually extended up the income ladder. But in mid-20th-century America, there was still a significant stigma attached to being "on the dole," and income tests were considered demeaning.

Policymakers who sought an expanded role for government in health care thus believed that starting with the elderly would be more politically palatable. After all, the elderly were a far more sympathetic group in the public's eyes: Older Americans had less opportunity to earn their own money in order to fund their health care, and were therefore generally poorer than other Americans (along with being less healthy). Being both relatively poor and relatively unhealthy, they were in turn also less likely to have health insurance. And policymakers believed that the model of Social Security as a "self-financed" program for the elderly, paid for with a dedicated payroll tax, could easily be extended to health insurance.

For many years, however, federal health-care initiatives were successfully opposed by a coalition of Republicans and conservative Democrats, as well as by the organized force of American doctors, who feared that socialized medicine would restrict their freedom to serve their patients as they thought best. But this dynamic shifted dramatically in 1964, when Barry Goldwater challenged Lyndon Johnson for the presidency.

The 1964 election, which many on the right fondly recall as the dawn of modern conservatism, was in fact the greatest victory for the left in American history. Democrats gained 36 seats in the House of Representatives — giving them an astonishing 155-seat majority — and increased their already huge Senate majority by two seats, nudging them up to a 36-seat majority. (By comparison, the substantial Democratic majorities held after the 2008 election were merely 79 seats in the House and 20 seats in the Senate.) Even taking conservative-leaning Democrats into account, liberals were utterly in control of Washington in 1965. Suddenly, Democrats found themselves with a mandate to enact far-reaching reforms, and they did not waste the opportunity.

The very first bill of the 1965 congressional session—H.R. 1 in the House and S 1 in the Senate—was titled "Hospital Insurance for the Aged through Social Security." The focus on hospital insurance reflected the fact that hospitalization costs represented the greatest financial burden on the elderly at the time. As the so-called "Medi-care" bill zipped through Congress, Republican leaders, still reeling and disoriented from their painful defeat, criticized the proposal from the *left*, arguing that the legislation was inadequate because it covered neither physician services nor prescription drugs.

They proposed instead a more comprehensive but voluntary plan, comparable to the one that was at the time administered by Aetna for federal employees. But Democrats were perfectly happy to accommodate these objections within their more ambitious non-voluntary program, and the final bill included a new entitlement composed of two Medicare programs for the elderly—Part A and Part B—along with a separate health-care entitlement for the poor called Medicaid.

Medicare Part A covered hospital expenses—60 days of hospital care after the beneficiary paid a deductible of $40 and an additional 30 days of hospital expenses for which the beneficiary would pay $10 per day. The program would be financed through a payroll tax similar to the one that paid for Social Security, though at a lower rate—a flat rate that was originally 0.7%, half of which was paid by the employee and half by the employer. Part B provided coverage for outpatient physician and nursing services, outpatient diagnostic services, medical equipment, and drugs administered by physicians (but not prescription drugs purchased by the patient). Unlike Part A, Part B would be funded by premiums from retirees, along with federal subsidies equal to those premiums.

These two parts of Medicare still constitute the bulk of the program today, and they have not changed all that much—though the deductibles have of course grown with inflation. This year, Part A covers 60 days of hospital care with a total deductible of $1,132, an additional 30 days with a deductible of $283 per day, 60 more days at $566 per day, and then all costs beyond that period. These figures would suggest some significant cost-sharing after the first two months in a hospital, but, as we shall see, the great majority of seniors have private supplemental insurance coverage that leaves them with essentially no deductible costs for Medicare at all. The payroll tax that still funds this program is now 2.9% — still shared equally between employer and employee — though the health-care law enacted last year stands to increase the employee share for wealthier workers (those earning over $200,000) by a further 0.9% starting in 2013.

Part B is also much as it was at the outset, covering physician services, outpatient care, and medical equipment. Seniors today pay a $162 deductible for such services, in addition to 20% of all costs beyond the deductible for most services — though again, supplemental insurance often covers that amount for them. In 1982, a third component was added — which came to be known as Medicare Part C, and later Medicare Advantage — under which seniors have the option of allowing private insurers to manage their Part A and Part B benefits (as discussed below). And in 2003, President George W. Bush and Congress added a prescription-drug benefit, known as Medicare Part D, in which seniors choose from a menu of approved private coverage options for drugs. Parts A and B of the program, however, remain by far its most significant and most expensive components (accounting for roughly 90% of its costs), and are the keys to Medicare's fiscal woes.

The cost overruns started very early, and were in large part an unintended function of Medicare's original design. The fact that Part B included coverage of physician services outside of hospitals meant that the great bulk of American doctors would come to interact with this new federal program — since older Americans are the ones who most frequently visit most doctors. In an effort to avoid a fight with the American Medical Association over this transformation in the lives of the nation's physicians, Medicare's designers opted not to specify any particular limits on physician-reimbursement rates. Instead, the legislation stated that doctors were to be paid according to so-called "usual, customary, and reasonable" rates — a vague reference to a system of determining payment rates that a few Blue Shield plans had been trying out in the 1960s.

The law provided no specific definition of "usual, customary, and reasonable," and essentially no guidance regarding how such a definition should be arrived at by Medicare's administrators. Medicare would pay health-care providers on a per-service basis — creating a major incentive to provide more services to patients in order to tap into this massive new source of funds — and the fee per service was left largely undefined. The program was thus launched with no clear plan for keeping its costs under control, and it included no real incentives for doctors, patients, or administrators to do so themselves.

GROWTH IN MEDICARE EXPENDITURES, RELATIVE TO 1968 LEVELS

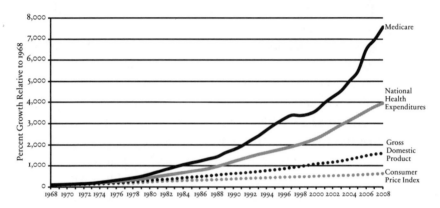

The consequences were immediate and dramatic. The annual growth of physician fees in America went from 3.8% in 1965 to 7.8% in 1966. In that same first year of Medicare's existence, hospital costs increased by 21.9%; over the subsequent five years, they grew by an average of 14% each year. These figures flummoxed government forecasters, who had projected that growth in hospital costs would actually *slow* after the enactment of Medicare. Instead, costs continued to grow rapidly. When Medicare was enacted, the staff of the House Ways and Means Committee (which was responsible for estimating the program's costs and effects, since the Congressional Budget Office had yet to be created) projected that its cost would grow from under $5 billion in its first year to $12 billion in 1990 — accounting for inflation — because they expected that hospital-cost growth would not exceed wage growth from 1975 onward. Instead, Medicare expenditures grew at roughly 2.4 times the rate of inflation over that period, and in 1990 reached not $12 billion but $110 billion. By 2000, the program cost $219 billion. Last year, it cost just over $520 billion. According to the Congressional Budget Office, if Medicare is not reformed, by 2020 it will cost about a trillion dollars a year.

Health-care costs beyond Medicare have also exploded in this period, and without question that has helped to drive Medicare's growth. But Medicare spending has increased faster than overall inflation in the health sector, and appears in many respects to have driven that inflation.

So what happened? Why have Medicare's costs gotten so out of control?

### PUSHING COSTS UP

The largest driver of Medicare cost inflation is the fact that retirees bear little of the expense for their own care. As a result, seniors have no incentive to avoid unnecessary or overpriced treatments. Rettenmaier and Saving have shown that, between 1960 and 1985, growth in health expenditures was highest in those categories of spending in which consumer cost-sharing was lowest (such as hospital care), and lowest where consumers were most responsible for their own expenses (like prescription drugs, which were not covered by Medicare during that period).

The same holds true for all consumers of health care—not just the elderly. Medicaid and the system of employer-based health insurance both provide a great deal of first-dollar insurance coverage, meaning that consumers do not pay directly for services they receive and therefore have no clear sense of relative costs and values. In 1960, individuals paid directly for 52% of national health expenditures, but by 2008 that share had declined to just 12%. Americans are shielded from the real costs of their health care; as a result, it costs too much.

| Cost-Sharing and Health-Care Spending Growth, 1960-1985 | | |
|---|---|---|
| Spending Category | Percent Paid by Consumers | Percent Real Per Capita Spending Growth |
| Hospital Care | 10.5% | 286% |
| Physician Services | 42.8% | 259% |
| Prescription Drugs | 79.9% | 74% |

Source: Rettenmaier and Saving, *The Diagnosis and Treatment of Medicare*, 2007.

In theory, Medicare does include some cost-sharing provisions, especially for physician payments under Part B. But over time, private insurance companies began to realize that Medicare's design allowed them to provide seniors with supplemental coverage to pay for the deductible and co-insurance requirements of the program—a good deal for insurers (for whom costs are finite and low), as well as for the seniors who purchase such plans (and are thereby freed from any direct cost for health care). Today, almost 90% of seniors have supplemental coverage plans, which means in effect that they have unlimited health coverage for a low and fixed cost, and thereby every incentive to seek generous, and even unneeded, care.

Combined with the fact that Medicare generally pays health-care providers on a per-service basis rather than on a per-patient or per-outcome basis, this means that Medicare creates an enormous incentive for everyone involved to provide *more* services to seniors. Volume, more than the cost of individual services, has been Medicare's fiscal downfall. And, as discussed below, reformers trying to fix the program's finances — from the 1970s through the health-care bill enacted last year — have sought to do so through price controls that reduce the amount the program pays for each service provided, which actually creates an even greater incentive for physicians and hospitals to provide a greater *number* of services to make up the lost revenue.

In a detailed study of this phenomenon conducted in 2007, the Congressional Budget Office found that, between 1997 and 2005, the fees paid by Medicare for individual physician services actually declined by 5%, but the total amount spent on such services by the program increased by an astonishing 35% — because of enormous growth in volume.

Beyond the skewed incentives it creates, Medicare also inflates costs as a result of its byzantine structure, which hampers efficiency. Many people wrongly believe that Medicare is more efficient than private insurance; that view was often stated by champions of Obamacare during the debate preceding the law's enactment. These advocates argued that Medicare's administrative costs — the money it spends on expenses other than patient care — are just 3% of total costs, compared to 15% to 20% in the case of private, employer-sponsored insurance. But these figures are highly misleading, for several reasons.

First, other government agencies help administer the Medicare program. The Internal Revenue Service collects the taxes that fund the program; the Social Security Administration helps collect some of the premiums paid by beneficiaries (which are deducted from Social Security checks); the Department of Health and Human Services helps to manage accounting, auditing, and fraud issues and pays for marketing costs, building costs, and more. Private insurers obviously don't have this kind of outside or off-budget help. Medicare's administration is also tax-exempt, whereas insurers must pay state excise taxes on the premiums they charge; the tax is counted as an administrative cost. In addition, Medicare's massive size leads to economies of scale that private insurers could also achieve, if not exceed, were they equally large.

But most important, because Medicare patients are older, they are substantially sicker than the average insured patient—driving up the denominator of such calculations significantly. For example: If two patients cost $30 each to manage, but the first requires $100 of health expenditures and the second, much sicker patient requires $1,000, the first patient's insurance will have an administrative-cost ratio of 30%, but the second's will have a ratio of only 3%. This hardly means the second patient's insurance is more efficient—administratively, the patients are identical. Instead, the more favorable figure is produced by the second patient's more severe illness.

A more accurate measure of overhead would therefore be the administrative costs per patient, rather than per dollar of medical expenses. And by that measure, even with all the administrative advantages Medicare has over private coverage, the program's administrative costs are actually significantly *higher* than those of private insurers. In 2005, for example, private insurers spent $453 per beneficiary on administrative costs, compared to $509 for Medicare.

Medicare's fragmentary, piecemeal character leads to other problems as well. The static nature of government benefits means that Medicare remains largely stuck in the health-care models of 1965, even though considerable innovation in health insurance has taken place since then. For instance, retirees pay almost nothing for inpatient hospitalization costs in the first two months, but do pay more for outpatient physician care. As a result, the elderly have an incentive to seek expensive hospital care when less expensive outpatient care might suffice. By law, traditional Medicare is not allowed to steer patients to more cost-efficient hospitals and doctors, the way private plans can.

As already noted, repeated attempts at reducing the growth of Medicare spending have taken the form of price controls to restrict fees paid for individual services. These controls, by paying relatively more for certain diagnoses than for others, incentivize doctors to game the system instead of providing optimal care. Overall, Medicare pays doctors and hospitals about 80% of what they receive from private insurers; many providers overcharge younger patients with private insurance in order to make up the difference.

As a result of such price controls and of the program's tangled web of rules and requirements, doctors are increasingly dropping out of the Medicare program. According to a 2008 survey from the Center for Studying Health System Change, more than one-quarter of all physicians actively restrict the number of Medicare patients in their practices. The American Academy of Family Physicians says that 13% of its members did not accept Medicare patients at all in 2009 — up from 8% in 2008 and 6% in 2004.

PHYSICIANS WHO ACCEPT NO NEW PATIENTS,
BY FORM OF INSURANCE

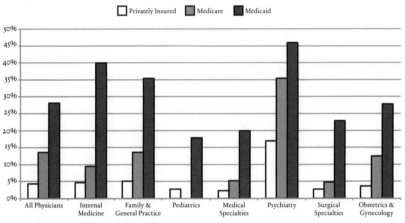

Source: Center for Studying Health System Change, 2008 Health Tracking Study Physician Survey.

If Medicare continues to cut physician reimbursements without fundamental reform, it will become even more difficult for retirees to find doctors who will see them. This problem has been apparent for years in the Medicaid program, which restricts physician payments even more severely than Medicare in most states. Studies show that many Medicaid patients fare worse in terms of basic health outcomes than those with no insurance at all. But thanks to last year's health-care law, Medicare payment rates are set to fall *below* those of Medicaid in the latter part of this decade, according to Medicare's chief actuary, Richard Foster. Unless the program is reformed to rely less on such price controls, Medicare patients will find it increasingly difficult to get care.

Without a doubt, the growth of the retiree population is also an important source of stress on Medicare's finances. That growth is driven by two factors: the aging of the Baby Boomers, and increasing life expectancy. When Medicare was enacted in 1965, the average life expectancy at birth was 70.2 years. In other words, it was anticipated that Medicare would cover an average person's health expenditures for the last 5.2 years of his life. In 2010, the average American lived to the age of 78.4; Medicare thus covered the last 13.4 years of his life — a 158% increase in the coverage period. The U.S. Census Bureau projects that, in the coming decades, American life expectancy will continue to elongate by approximately one year for every eight years that pass.

Of course, unlike the growth of costs due to the incentive structure of Medicare, the extension of life expectancies is not bad news. The overall story of Medicare is not entirely bad, either. The program has provided the elderly with health insurance for more than four decades. Seniors rely on it and like it; the program is extremely popular. But along the way, it has done grave damage to our broader health-care sector — contributing to an unsustainable inflation of costs that puts the program itself in jeopardy, and that makes it harder for younger Americans to afford insurance for themselves and their families.

Today, the program's finances are completely out of control. And the illusion of pre-funded benefits — the notion that Americans pay into the system while they work and then merely withdraw the funds they put in when they retire — no longer bears any relation to reality. According to calculations published earlier this year by Eugene Steuerle and Stephanie Rennane of the Urban Institute, the average two-earner married couple retiring in 2010 had paid $109,000 in Medicare taxes while working, but will receive $343,000 in benefits during retirement. A similar couple retiring in 2030 will have paid $167,000 in taxes and will receive $530,000 in benefits. Medicare is simply a massive (and growing) transfer of resources from younger to older Americans. And since the elderly are no longer the poorest Americans — on the contrary; Americans over the age of 65 are now significantly wealthier than younger Americans — that often means that Medicare is a transfer of resources from poorer to wealthier Americans. The illusion of an earned benefit, like the illusion of Medicare as a self-sustaining program, must be overcome if we are to address Medicare's woes.

Clearly, it is well past time to save Medicare from itself. But how?

### FAILED FIXES

Because the problem of cost overruns became apparent so soon after Medicare's enactment, almost every president after Lyndon Johnson tried his hand at restraining the program's growing expense. In 1972, under Richard Nixon, Congress allowed for the creation of Medicare health-maintenance organizations, in the hope that private managed care might help keep down the program's costs. Consumers had little incentive to use them, however, and the experiment was a failure. Nixon's other Medicare adjustment undermined his efforts: He also expanded Medicare to include people under 65 who qualified for Social Security disability benefits and had received them for two years, which of course only further swelled Medicare's budget.

In 1977, under Jimmy Carter, the Health Care Financing Administration was created to more efficiently administer Medicare and Medicaid, setting the programs apart from Social Security. In 1983, under Ronald Reagan, HCFA imposed a "prospective payment system" whereby hospitals and physicians would be reimbursed at a set rate for a specific diagnosis—Medicare's first price controls.

But after a few years, hospitals and physicians grew wise to the new system, and found ways to shift patients from poorly paying "diagnosis-related groups" to higher-paying ones—a practice called "upcoding." So in 1988, a team led by William Hsiao, an economist at the Harvard School of Public Health, proposed a new system of price controls for Medicare called the Resource-Based Relative Value Scale, or RBRVS. Hsiao invented a complex formula that combined the time, effort, judgment, skill, and stress of addressing a specific medical problem (the "physician work" factor) with local medical-practice costs and related considerations. The formula was adopted by Congress as part of the 1989 budget deal in an effort to manage Medicare's costs. But few of Hsiao's factors had anything to do with the way in which economies normally price goods and services, and the RBRVS system did little to improve the economic value of health-care decisions, or Medicare's finances.

Also in 1988, Congress passed the short-lived Medicare Catastrophic Coverage Act, which expanded Medicare Part A to cover an unlimited number of hospital days, eliminated the daily co-insurance requirement for stays longer than 30 days, and provided a benefit for outpatient prescription drugs, among numerous other perks. President Reagan had insisted that the MCCA be deficit-neutral; it therefore incorporated a means-tested supplemental premium of up to $800 to pay for these extra benefits. But that supplemental premium proved to be extremely unpopular with retirees, and the entire law was repealed in 1989.

The next major push for Medicare reform began in the mid-1990s. The new Republican Congress proposed reducing projected Medicare spending by $270 billion, along with a package of tax cuts; President Clinton accused Republicans of fleecing Medicare to aid the wealthy, and counter-proposed $128 billion in reductions with no tax cuts.

Eventually, in 1997, the two sides produced the Balanced Budget Act, which included an important Medicare reform. The law created the Sustainable Growth Rate, a formula that tied physician reimbursements to GDP growth as a way of keeping costs under control. While the SGR may have helped to hold down costs in the short term — Medicare expenditures were essentially flat in 1998 and '99 — by 2001, those costs had resumed their historical growth rate. The 1997 law would thus have required significant cuts in doctor fees, but doctors protested, and Congress began passing so-called "doc fix" legislation to increase physician reimbursements above their SGR-mandated levels — essentially ignoring the law's requirement on an annual basis almost every year since 2003. As a result of politics and interest-group concerns (not to mention the basic economics of health care), price controls have thus proven a thoroughly inadequate means of holding down Medicare costs.

Unfortunately, Obamacare only doubles down on this failed approach. Like prior attempts to limit costs through price controls, the new law simply caps annual Medicare growth but fails to fundamentally transform the system to allow it to live within such caps. Starting in 2015, per capita Medicare spending growth will be limited to a fixed rate set between the general rate of inflation and health-care-cost inflation. Then, starting in 2018, that rate will be set permanently at per capita GDP growth plus one percentage point—a rate far lower than Medicare's growth in recent decades. And just how will costs be kept within these boundaries? The law establishes a board of experts—the 15-member Independent Payment Advisory Board—that will be charged with making the necessary changes to Medicare's payment rates and practices. But the board is prohibited from requiring greater cost-sharing by Medicare recipients, and from changing the basic "fee-for-service" structure of the program. So it cannot pursue market-based reforms. All it can do is tweak the program's price controls, in the hope that just the right mix of cuts in payments to doctors and hospitals will cause those doctors and hospitals to become more efficient.

This is exactly the approach that has failed to control prices in the past, and the one that Congress has had to override each year through the "doc fix." It simply pays doctors less and less for the same services without giving them any incentive to improve their efficiency or productivity by changing how they work. There is no reason to imagine this oft-failed approach will succeed this time around. Indeed, in May, the Medicare program's own actuary explained why he expects Obamacare's price controls to fail:

> By the end of the long-range projection period, Medicare prices for hospital, skilled nursing facility, home health, hospice, ambulatory surgical center, diagnostic laboratory, and many other services [under the new law] would be less than half of their level under the prior law. Medicare prices would be considerably below the current relative level of Medicaid prices, which have already led to access problems for Medicaid enrollees, and far below the levels paid by private health insurance. Well before that point, Congress would have to intervene to prevent the withdrawal of providers from the Medicare market and the severe problems with beneficiary access to care that would result. Overriding the productivity adjustments, as Congress has done repeatedly in the case of physician payment rates, would lead to far higher costs for Medicare in the long range than those projected under current law.

Medicare's future under Obamacare thus looks much like its past — only worse.

### MARKET REFORMS

But if price controls have been a failure, most attempts at market-oriented reforms have not fared much better. In 1982, Congress introduced Medicare Part C, which allows private insurers to administer Medicare plans at 95% of the combined cost of Part A and Part B. The idea was that these private plans could save money because they would integrate Part A and Part B coverage into a single benefit package, and would thus be managed more efficiently by private entities. Part C was popular with retirees; enrollment grew at 30% a year in the mid-1990s, peaking at 16% of Medicare enrollees in 1999. But unfortunately, this system strongly incentivized private plans to "cherry-pick" younger and healthier retirees, leaving the rest to traditional Medicare — thereby raising, rather than reducing, overall costs (because the larger traditional Medicare program still dominated the health-care market, and so its higher costs meant higher health-care costs overall).

Things changed in 1997, when the Balanced Budget Act introduced a more sophisticated risk-adjustment system so as to curtail cherry-picking. As a result, insurers started to drop out of Part C (since their costs were going to rise), and enrollment stalled. It turned out that, for beneficiaries of equivalent health and age, private plans were slightly *more* costly than traditional Medicare, because the fragmented community of private insurers lacked the government's market power to negotiate lower rates. The fact that private insurers had to compete in the same market with traditional Medicare put them at an immense disadvantage, yet Medicare's market advantage did not make it any more efficient or cost-effective.

This problem was revisited in 2003, when President Bush signed the Medicare Modernization Act. The MMA increased reimbursements to private insurers in order to compensate for their lack of market power; by 2009, Part C plans (rechristened "Medicare Advantage" plans) were paid 14% more per patient on average than traditional Medicare. In return, private insurers reduced premiums. These changes increased the popularity of privately-managed Medicare plans; by 2010, Medicare Advantage enrolled 11 million retirees, or nearly 25% of all Medicare participants. But again, they did not significantly reduce costs, as they were still playing in a field dominated by a highly inefficient fee-for-service Medicare program.

Market-based reforms cannot have their desired effect—introducing meaningful competition and consumer pressures to bring down costs—as long as this traditional fee-for-service structure of Medicare remains the dominant force in the market, because providers still have a powerful incentive to conform their behavior to Medicare's inefficient design. For a market reform to work, it seems, it has to be comprehensive—either replacing traditional Medicare or turning it into just one option among many. Today's reformers would be wise to keep this lesson in mind.

The most successful cost-control experiment in Medicare—the relatively new prescription-drug component called Part D—has been proving this point. The Part D benefit, added in 2003, is a so-called "premium support" program. Seniors are given a set amount of money to apply toward their choice of plan, selected from a menu of private prescription-drug coverage options. If they prefer a more expensive plan, they can make up the difference themselves. Because this premium-support program is the only source of prescription-drug funding in Medicare, it is able to bring real market forces to bear.

The program also contains a further cost-control mechanism that has come to be known as the "donut hole," by which recipients are required to pay for all drug costs above a certain minimum level and below a ceiling—a design intended to simultaneously make seniors sensitive to prices yet shield them from catastrophic costs. In 2009, the donut hole required retirees to pay 100% of prescription-drug costs above $2,700 and below $6,154, in order to discourage unnecessary spending. (Obamacare would eliminate this element of the program as well—sparing seniors from the donut hole, but thereby also shielding them from market forces that can help restrain costs.)

These two market-based elements have indeed kept costs down for this component of Medicare. While Medicare Part D has provided drug coverage to most Medicare recipients and is very popular with seniors, it has so far come in more than 30% *below* the original cost expectations of the Congressional Budget Office. In a recent report, the actuary of Medicare projects that Part D's cost over its first decade will likely be more than 40% below those original estimates.

Some market-based reforms, then, can work. The premium-support model of Medicare Part D has been a great success. But its application has been limited, and overall Medicare costs continue to climb.

PREMIUM SUPPORT

Could there be a way to apply the lessons of this "premium support" and cost-sharing approach to the broader program? The history of failed reform efforts includes one intriguing twist that suggests there just might be.

In 1997, as a result of the Balanced Budget Act, Congress organized the National Bipartisan Commission on the Future of Medicare, under the leadership of Democratic senator John Breaux and Republican representative Bill Thomas. The commission's final recommendation, supported by members of both parties, was that Medicare should be converted to a "market-based Premium Support model" similar to the one used in the Federal Employees Health Benefits Program.

Under the commission's proposed system, retirees would have been able to choose between private health plans and a traditional government-run fee-for-service plan (a consolidation of Medicare Parts A, B, and C). Thus traditional Medicare would have become one option among many, competing for business. Regardless of what option they chose, beneficiaries would have been expected to pay a premium equal to 12% of per capita health costs, but would have paid no premium at all if they bought a plan that was at least 15% cheaper than the average one. In addition, the commission recommended increasing the Medicare eligibility age from 65 to 67, in harmony with Social Security.

After the commission made its proposal, President Clinton made a counter-proposal, shaped in large part by his Treasury secretary, Lawrence Summers. He proposed "managed competition" for Medicare, in which private insurers would have engaged in competitive bidding for health coverage of the elderly. Retirees who chose plans that cost less than the average bid would have retained three-fourths of the savings. Clinton also proposed new subsidies to encourage employers to retain private-sector health coverage for their retirees, taking some of the burden off of Medicare.

These two sets of proposals were, in many ways, quite compatible. Indeed, according to historian Steven Gillon, President Clinton and House Speaker Newt Gingrich, along with several prominent Senate Democrats, were close in 1997 to a historic agreement for reforming Medicare along these lines. But after the Monica Lewinsky scandal erupted in early 1998, Clinton was focused on defending himself from impeachment, and this required currying the favor of ideological Democrats over pragmatic ones. Thus no serious effort was made to bridge the various reform proposals, and Medicare's problems went unresolved.

Even though it went by the wayside, the basic structure of the Breaux-Thomas commission's proposal — transforming Medicare into a premium-support system in which retirees have a pre-set benefit they can use toward the purchase of approved private insurance plans — remains the most plausible approach to addressing Medicare's immense and growing problems. A number of reform proposals offered in the years since the commission's report have followed its lead in general terms, though always with particular tweaks or additions.

The most prominent, and surely the most important, of these is the 2012 budget resolution recently passed (by the Republican majority on a party-line vote) in the House of Representatives. Proposed by House Budget Committee chairman Paul Ryan, the budget included a plan to transform Medicare into a premium-support system beginning in 2022.

This would mean that all current retirees, as well as people who will retire by that year, would be left in the existing Medicare system (unless he chooses to, no American now over the age of 55 would be transitioned into the system of premium support); a new structure, however, would be established for new retirees from 2022 onward.

Rather than pay all providers a set fee directly, this approach would let retirees use the money (in the form of a premium-support payment that would start at current Medicare rates and grow with overall inflation) to choose insurance plans from a menu of private coverage options. To participate, private insurers would have to agree to accept all Medicare recipients, to charge the same premiums to all beneficiaries of the same age, and to provide at least a minimum benefits package required by the Office of Personnel Management (which runs the Federal Employee Health Benefit Plan), with the idea of providing all seniors with guaranteed affordable comprehensive coverage.

The level of premium support would increase with age, and poor seniors and those in the worst health would also get significantly greater support, while the wealthiest would receive less and so need to use more of their own money to buy coverage. And the premium-support model would not be a small experiment overshadowed by traditional Medicare (and thus unable to really change the way insurers and providers do business): It would be the core of the new Medicare system, and the means by which seniors would be guaranteed coverage.

This approach, then, would work like the Medicare prescription-drug benefit (and like the health-insurance program made available to federal employees). Insurers and providers would need to compete for seniors' dollars, and to do so they would be free to find innovative ways to offer better quality at lower costs. That's how markets produce efficiency: by letting sellers find ways to offer buyers what they want at prices they are willing to pay.

Although the precise effect of this approach on overall health-care costs is difficult to predict, there is no question that such a reform would dramatically improve Medicare's fiscal prospects and reduce the burdens it would place on the broader federal budget.

### FIXING MEDICARE

Something like the Ryan approach will be crucial to the future of Medicare. The program is set to go bankrupt in a decade, and seems past the point of small fixes or yet another tweak to the price-control formula (as proposed under Obamacare). A broader reform must come. Medicare's history, its importance to the seniors who depend on it, and the nature of its fiscal problems suggest that such a reform must take account of six factors.

First, we must remember that Medicare's primary achievement—protecting economically vulnerable retirees—is a salutary one, the preservation of which must be the cornerstone of reform. We must also promise current and soon-to-be retirees that their benefits will not change. As many have suggested (and as the Ryan budget proposes), reforms should be implemented only for future enrollees age 55 or younger, in order to allow for a gradual transition into a reformed system, and to preserve benefits for those who have long planned their retirements around the existing system.

Second, we must appreciate the power of cost-sharing. When patients are aware of the costs of their care, and assume partial responsibility for higher expenditures, they are more likely to make sensible decisions about whether to pursue treatment. This can do much more to curb health-care cost inflation than can crude price controls or benefit cuts. As discussed above, from 2003 to 2010, Medicare's prescription-drug benefit contained significant cost-sharing provisions, in plans administered entirely by private insurers, and the program came in under budget as a result. Most important, so long as Medicare remains in its current form, the role of supplemental "Medigap" plans must be seriously re-examined. These plans do much to undermine value-oriented health-care consumption by shielding seniors from all cost-sharing.

Third, we must introduce means-testing into Medicare. Some conservatives, because of their aversion to wealth redistribution, have opposed means tests; some liberals have opposed them because they fear that Medicare will lose political support if its benefits are not uniform. Both of these arguments fail to stand up to scrutiny. If we raise taxes to bridge our enormous deficits instead of reducing Medicare spending, those taxes will fall disproportionately on the wealthy and discourage economic growth. Spending less is a better solution, because taxes cannot be increased as quickly as Medicare expenditures will rise. As to Medicare's political support, the explosive growth of Medicaid shows that welfare programs can have just as much support as entitlements do. Either way, the political concerns of the left and right pale in comparison to the fiscal crisis we now face.

Fourth, we should index the Medicare retirement age to life expectancy, as tabulated by the Census Bureau each year. This would ensure that the program is not exposed to increases—expected or unexpected—in American longevity. Once again, the Bipartisan Medicare Commission of the late 1990s offered a framework for thinking about how to adjust the eligibility age for Medicare. Improving our age-dependency ratio—the number of retirees per worker—must come in part through normalizing our retirement age, inducing more middle-aged people to remain in the work force, and from restoring the tax subsidies (eliminated by Obamacare) that encourage employers to maintain private health coverage for retirees.

Fifth, we must address the substantial problem of Medicare fraud. It is estimated that $60 to $100 billion of annual Medicare spending—between 8% and 13% of the total—is fraudulent. Medicare processes over one billion claims per year, and is required by law to reimburse claims within 15 to 30 days. This makes it almost impossible to prevent criminal activity. Private administration of the program would do much to incentivize the development of more thorough auditing practices.

Finally, Medicare must evolve into a system in which individuals can shop for value in insurance plans. They already have the ability to do this with Medicare Parts C and D, but not with A and B. As discussed above, the Breaux-Thomas commission proposed a premium-support system in which Medicare would subsidize retirees in purchasing insurance. The Ryan budget suggested a similar approach, as did the deficit-reduction task force of the Bipartisan Policy Center, headed by former Republican senator Pete Domenici and former Congressional Budget Office director Alice Rivlin, a Democrat, earlier this year. Some of the specifics of their plans differed, of course, but they shared the conviction that a transition to premium support is essential to Medicare's future.

### MEDICARE IN CONTEXT

Important as these reforms of the structure of Medicare would be, an enduring solution to Medicare's problems would also require a reform of the broader health-care system.

Until our whole system moves in the direction of an individual market for health insurance, we will have no voluntary mechanism by which to encourage Americans to shop for value in health care. If overall health spending for Americans below the age of 65 continues to rise at a much faster pace than inflation (because of the perverse incentives of the employer-based insurance system and of Medicaid), Medicare's expenditures will rise with it.

Addressing this problem would require reforming and integrating Medicare, Medicaid, the employer-sponsored system, and the individual market (and would therefore require replacing Obamacare with a very different set of health-care reforms well beyond Medicare). It would involve addressing the runaway costs of defensive medicine and medical-malpractice litigation. Such changes would of course be extremely difficult to undertake, as the heated ongoing health-care debate amply demonstrates. But a meaningful and effective reform of Medicare could offer a plausible first step along such a path—addressing some of the most significant causes of the cost-inflation problem, and offering proof that sensible market-based reforms can work.

This moment in our politics—when our long-term fiscal situation has suddenly captured public attention—might just offer the opportunity to attempt such a step. It is an opportunity we must not allow to slip by.

*Originally published as "Saving Medicare from Itself" in the Summer 2011 issue of* National Affairs.

# How to Fix Medicaid

## *John Hood*

SUMMER 2010

T HE SWEEPING HEALTH-CARE LEGISLATION enacted this spring is many things. It is a vast expansion of federal power. It is a budget-busting entitlement. It is a regulatory nightmare. But to a far greater degree than its advocates have acknowledged, it is also a massive expansion of Medicaid. This means that, under the new law, a hugely expensive program already deep in crisis would not only continue essentially unreformed: It would be put at the very center of America's health-care system.

Medicaid is a joint federal-state program of health coverage for the poor. Its exact rules and practices vary from state to state; generally speaking, however, it is open to people with low incomes (below or just above the federal poverty level) and with some additional compelling condition of need — like being a parent, or having a serious disability. With these eligibility restrictions in place, Medicaid already covers 60 million Americans and accounts for 16 cents of every dollar spent on medical services in the United States.

Under Obamacare, though, people with household incomes up to 133% of the federal poverty level (about $14,400 for individuals, or $29,300 for a family of four) will be eligible for Medicaid regardless of whether they meet any of the other conditions of need. As a result of these loosened eligibility requirements, the bill's proponents expect some 16 million more Americans to sign up for Medicaid between 2014 (when the new rules go into effect) and 2019. This enormous increase in the Medicaid rolls represents about half of Obamacare's projected reduction in the number of uninsured Americans.

On paper, this Medicaid expansion also accounts for about half of the Congressional Budget Office's $940 billion cost projection over the

JOHN HOOD *is president of the John Locke Foundation, a state-policy think tank based in North Carolina, and the author of, among other books,* Investor Politics.

new law's first 10 years. But the effects of expanding Medicaid — one of the most expensive, unwieldy, and perverse creations of American government — will almost certainly be much larger, more extensive, and more dramatic than the CBO's computations suggest.

It is likely, for instance, that far more than 16 million additional people will sign up for Medicaid. As a result of the new eligibility rules, many Americans who are now insured through their employers — but who nonetheless have incomes below the new threshold — will suddenly be eligible for essentially free health care from the government. Many of their employers, as small businesses, will be exempt from any penalties for dropping their employees' coverage. These workers will thus be "crowded out" of private coverage into Medicaid, vastly increasing public costs.

Although there are no hard estimates of the anticipated crowd-out effect of the new law, past experience with Medicaid expansions provides plenty of reasons to be concerned. For example, the National Center for Policy Analysis estimates that of every tax dollar spent on Medicaid expansions during the 1990s, at least half went to new enrollees who dropped their private health plans to join the program, rather than to previously uninsured people. For the related State Children's Health Insurance Program established in the late 1990s, the crowd-out effect averaged about 60%.

Obamacare will therefore put Medicaid increasingly at the heart of our health-care system. For reformers truly interested in "bending the cost curve," this is very bad news: The flaws of the existing Medicaid program — and the extraordinary strain they place on the nation's finances — are high among the reasons why health-care reform is needed in the first place. And Obamacare's exacerbation of those flaws is high among the reasons why the new law will need to be rolled back, and why any serious alternative proposal for improving our health-care system must include Medicaid reform.

### THE BOTTOM LAYER

The slapdash way in which a huge and unwieldy expansion of Medicaid became the centerpiece of Obamacare is very much in line with the entitlement's pedigree. From the outset, the story of Medicaid has been one of carelessness, poor planning, and ill-conceived policy design.

The story begins in 1934, when President Franklin Roosevelt appointed a commission to fashion sweeping social-welfare legislation that he intended to champion the following year. The commission's final report proposed the programs that would become Social Security and Aid to Families with Dependent Children, as well as a national health-insurance plan resembling programs that, by then, had already been adopted in several European countries.

But Roosevelt decided that the commission's policy ambitions exceeded his political appetite, and so he left the health-care component out of the 1935 Social Security Act. Still, advocates in and out of government kept pushing. In 1937, another Roosevelt-administration commission outlined a long-term strategy for enacting a "comprehensive National Health Program"; this initiative would have included federal health and disability insurance funded by payroll taxes, as well as federal support for hospitals and federal aid for state medical-assistance programs. Roosevelt did not act on those proposals, but each of them would, in one form or another, become federal law in the course of the following 30 years.

During the 1940s and '50s, a succession of liberal politicians championed national health-insurance legislation only to see their proposals wilt under the glare of unsympathetic voters (and the American Medical Association). So advocates adopted a more incremental strategy. In 1956, Congress and the Eisenhower administration added disability benefits to Social Security. And in 1960, two congressional Democrats—Arkansas representative Wilbur Mills and Oklahoma senator Robert Kerr—teamed up to pitch a federal bailout of failing state programs that provided relief to destitute seniors and people with severe physical or mental disabilities. Unlike calls for universal health care, the Kerr-Mills proposal built on what most lawmakers had long considered to be a legitimate role for government (albeit one that belonged at the state level): to secure housing, sustenance, and basic care for a small group of clearly infirm people whose needs far exceeded their families' resources (and who might otherwise populate street corners or prisons). Mills in particular saw the 1960 legislation as a way to head off any broader, more intrusive federal legislation on health care. He was, of course, mistaken: The program created a precedent for federal bailouts of state relief programs, but without actually appropriating much money for them. Emboldened, hospitals and state governments pushed for more.

In 1964, after resounding Democratic electoral victories, President Lyndon Johnson decided it was time to enact the health-care proposals that had been left out of the Social Security Act nearly 30 years earlier. As the debate began, there were three significant ideas on the table. The main Democratic bill, which reporters soon dubbed "Medi-care," proposed a universal, government-run health plan for senior citizens, to be funded by payroll taxes. A Republican bill that earned the less elegant nickname "Better-care" proposed a voluntary health plan for seniors that would have been funded by a combination of premiums and general tax revenues. A third, bipartisan bill was called "Elder-care" and, unlike previous legislative efforts, had the backing of the American Medical Association; it sought to strengthen the Kerr-Mills system of federal grants to state programs caring for the indigent, the disabled, and poor seniors in nursing homes.

By this time, Wilbur Mills had become chairman of the House Ways and Means Committee, which made him central to the process of crafting the final bill. He decided to take that process behind closed doors and to fashion what came to be called the "three-layer cake" — an amalgam of the three bills. The Democratic bill became Medicare Part A, which provides hospitalization insurance. The Republican bill mutated into Medicare Part B, covering physician charges but retaining only a semblance of voluntary participation and patient premiums. Elder-care morphed into Medicaid — attracting the least legislative attention of the three proposals, and serving primarily to satisfy insistent demands for greater federal support for state health-care programs tending to the poorest of the poor. Compared to the other two components of the legislation, Medicaid was almost an afterthought.

This lack of planning and careful attention certainly revealed itself in the program's haphazard design. Unlike the two parts of Medicare, Medicaid is a joint federal-state undertaking: Each state administers its own Medicaid system, though it must follow broad federal guidelines for the program's design and operation. Funding responsibilities are shared by the federal government and the states in accordance with a formula based largely on the scope of poverty within each state; wealthier states, like Connecticut and Colorado, receive a 50% federal share, while poorer states receive significantly larger federal subsidies. (The largest share this year is Mississippi's, at 74.7%.)

Wilbur Mills and other early champions of the program denied that Medicaid was intended to be another large entitlement; they saw it merely as a safety net for the poorest and most helpless Americans. But it didn't take long for state politicians and lawyers to figure out how to maximize the participation of the able-bodied poor, and for financial advisors to juggle the assets of middle-class seniors so that Medicaid would pay for their nursing-home bills. The sloppiness of the legislation—including the many loopholes it opened up—made out-of-control costs inevitable.

### A BALLOONING ENTITLEMENT

The sheer scope of the Medicaid program today would have shocked its designers. Politicians, analysts, and the media tend to focus their attention on the controversial management, rapid growth, and shaky finances of Medicare—and yet Medicaid enrolls more people than Medicare, spends almost as much on hospital and doctor payments, and presents the government and health providers with at least as many fiscal and managerial headaches.

Medicaid is also projected to grow more rapidly than Medicare—and was even before the passage of Obamacare. In fact, if it hadn't been for the Bush administration's Medicare expansion in 2003, Medicaid would probably already be the country's most expensive health-care entitlement. According to the Department of Health and Human Services, Medicare expenditures will be about $516 billion in 2010, while Medicaid (including the State Children's Health Insurance Program) will cost $436 billion (to be shared by states and the federal Treasury).

Many factors have contributed to Medicaid's astonishing growth rate. At its inception in 1965, the program cost state and federal taxpayers

*MEDICAID SPENDING 1965-2010*

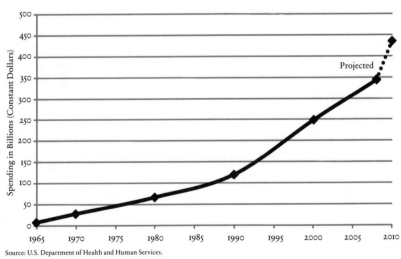

Source: U.S. Department of Health and Human Services.

only $1.3 billion, or about $9 billion in today's dollars. Projected to increase only modestly, annual Medicaid spending (combined state and federal) in fact exploded—to $29 billion in 1970, $68 billion in 1980, $121 billion in 1990, and $250 billion in 2000 (all in 2010 dollars). Obviously, the growth in the cost of health care more generally has outpaced that of most other goods and services during the same period. But in most years since 1965, Medicaid spending has grown faster than either private health spending or Medicare spending.

One reason for this cost explosion has been Medicaid's repeated expansions of eligibility and benefits—expansions that are encouraged by the program's matching-funds design. Under the current system, federal policymakers establish general guidelines, while state policymakers set the specific provisions of their own Medicaid programs. Often, county-level officials are responsible for the actual implementation and enforcement of eligibility and benefit rules.

This shared funding and administration of Medicaid has created a host of perverse incentives, especially for policymakers at the state and local levels. They reap all the political benefits of more generous coverage or looser eligibility rules, but pay only a fraction of the financial cost of such largesse, since the federal government picks up most of the tab. And during downturns and times of lean budgets, state lawmakers will bear the entire political burden if they allow steep eligibility cuts—but will reap only a portion of the fiscal benefits, since most of the cost savings will accrue to the federal government. State and local officials are thus more inclined to spend lavishly on Medicaid than on programs funded entirely by the state.

Moreover, because of both historical accident and the program's design, Medicaid has ended up paying for a very large share of the most expensive of all medical services. From 1960 to 1990, the fastest-growing category of health-care spending was long-term care: stays in nursing homes and home-health visits for elderly and disabled patients. Since 1990, increases in nursing-home spending have moderated some, but the cost of home-based health care has skyrocketed.

Nearly all Americans over the age of 65 are enrolled in Medicare to cover routine doctor visits, hospitalizations, drugs, and other medical services. But Medicare does not cover long-term care or nursing-home stays. For seniors with low incomes, though, Medicaid does pay for such costs: Indeed, it is the single largest payer of nursing-home bills in America (covering 43% of all costs). It also pays one-third of all home-based health-care bills—a number that is projected to grow to one-half by the end of the decade. Thus, as America's population has aged, Medicaid has bloated.

Finally, because Medicaid is, in principle, a means-tested program of public assistance, its design makes it extremely difficult to introduce cost-saving incentives that motivate recipients to think and act like consumers. Federal laws and policies restrict how much cost-sharing states can impose on recipients. And while some states have conducted promising experiments with financial incentives—such as cash accounts managed by recipients—any state's room to maneuver is limited by federal law. Medicaid has also been plagued for years by fraudulent enrollments and claims; such abuse is exacerbated by the fact that the program involves a class of claimants who have little incentive to cooperate with efforts to streamline medical care or reduce long-term expenses.

In short, Medicaid's inherent flaws guarantee that the program's burgeoning costs will endanger America's fiscal health. Like Medicare and Social Security, Medicaid represents an implicit promise of expensive benefits, the costs of which will far exceed future revenues. But unlike the costs of Medicare and Social Security, future Medicaid expenses won't just show up on the books of a heavily indebted federal Treasury: They also represent one of the largest fiscal obligations of state governments, which, for the most part, are not allowed to issue debt for operating expenses. With the program already accounting for more than one-fifth of total state operating budgets, Medicaid growth will mean painful state tax increases, reductions in basic state services like public safety and education, or some combination of both.

Consider the case of California, one of the nation's hardest-hit states. Already facing a $20 billion budget hole in the current fiscal year, California will see its Medicaid caseload rise by nearly 25% after Obamacare is fully implemented in 2014, costing state taxpayers another $2 to $3 billion a year. "We face enormous challenges just sustaining our existing program," California's Medicaid administrator told Bloomberg News in March. "I just don't see states having the capacity to move forward on these changes in this environment."

It is also important to remember that Medicaid is not just a health-care program. It is the largest single component of America's welfare state, far outweighing the dollar value of cash assistance, food stamps, or housing aid. Like these other programs, Medicaid often provides implicit disincentives to work, since increases in income can mean the loss of eligibility for a very valuable benefit. Unless future policymakers introduce reforms to help break the generational cycle of dependency—fixes based on principles that have worked in other welfare overhauls, like time limits and work requirements—the prospect of losing thousands of dollars a year in essentially free health care will perpetuate strong incentives against moving up the economic ladder. Refusing work, or accepting off-the-books jobs with few long-term prospects, will become rational choices for families facing the steep effective tax rates created by the eligibility rules for Medicaid (and soon to be made worse by Obamacare).

In this sense, as in so many others, the new health-care law makes a longstanding problem all the more difficult to solve. But simply rolling back Obamacare's expansion of Medicaid will not be enough: Any genuine reform of our health-care system will need to address the structural flaws that have long been the basis of Medicaid's woes. Doing so will be enormously difficult—as the problem encompasses more than just issues of design, administration, or health economics.

## THE MANY MEDICAIDS

While Medicaid does formally exist as a single health-care program administered and financed jointly by states and the federal government, it can also be thought of as an amalgam of four different programs—each with its own caseload, rules, and dynamics.

First, Medicaid is a program for healthy low-income children and some working-age adults. Prior to Obamacare, simply having an income near (or even below) the poverty line would not in itself make someone eligible for Medicaid. Generally speaking, children had to be involved—a rule left over from the era in which welfare was aimed at families lacking a breadwinner. Pregnant women, babies, grade-schoolers, and their mothers have thus made up the majority of enrollees in this category, with some states more willing than others to go beyond these mandatory populations. If Obamacare is fully implemented, this category will grow substantially in the coming years; even now, it represents the largest bloc of Medicaid recipients, accounting for nearly three-quarters of the program's caseload. But it is also the least costly per person: Children and young adults have low average medical claims. About a third of the Medicaid budget is spent on these enrollees.

Second, Medicaid covers individuals with severe physical disabilities. Usually qualifying as a result of their eligibility for the Supplemental Security Income program under Social Security, individuals with significant work-impairing disabilities have traditionally made up a small share of Medicaid recipients. They have, however, consumed by far the most expensive services—which include not just medical care, but often a variety of other benefits, including caregiver assistance with daily tasks as well as room and board.

Third, Medicaid covers individuals with severe mental illnesses or addictions. While technically the two groups of disabled recipients are in the same boat when it comes to eligibility rules—together making up about one-fifth of the Medicaid population, but consuming well over 40% of its budget—it is important to recognize that those suffering from mental illness or substance abuse pose special problems for eligibility determination, case management, and even public willingness to support long-term assistance.

Finally, as discussed above, Medicaid also covers seniors requiring long-term care, and therefore plays a significant role in the lives of many seniors when accidents, diseases, or the inevitable infirmities of age render them unable to perform basic tasks. Those who meet the income test, or can show that their resources will swiftly be spent down to the income threshold, can qualify for Medicaid assistance for institutional or home-based care.

This coverage is intended to ensure that truly poor and ill seniors will not be forced to suffer without the long-term care they need to survive, simply because they cannot pay. The unfortunate reality, however, is that there is now a large industry of lawyers, accountants, and financial planners skilled at arranging the assets of middle-class families so that, when the time comes, their parents or grandparents will qualify for Medicaid. By moving assets around, transferring money or property to children, and otherwise gaming the system, middle-class seniors can save their families the immense cost of long-term care (at the public's expense, of course). In total, seniors account for 10% of Medicaid enrollees—and one-quarter of Medicaid spending.

A great deal of the problem with Medicaid, then, is that unlike with Medicare—which, for all its manifest woes, is a relatively straightforward program—just reaching an agreement about *what* needs to be fixed (let alone how) is a serious challenge.

For example, recognizing that Medicaid services are the most valuable of the welfare benefits available to low-income Americans, a reform-minded policymaker might want to apply to Medicaid some of the time limits and work requirements that have proven successful in reducing cash-welfare rolls. Such an approach, however, would make little sense in the case of an institutionalized person with a permanent disability. Similarly, measures to encourage families to save, buy insurance, or otherwise prepare for the possibility that aging relatives will need long-term care may help moderate Medicaid's costs in the future. But they won't do much to reduce Medicaid rolls in the short run, given, for instance, the number of seniors already receiving long-term care on the public's dime.

So before we outline a coherent, realistic strategy for reforming Medicaid, we must think through how the various Medicaids we currently have match up with America's financial realities, constitutional principles, and public expectations. After all, what we choose to do about Medicaid depends on how we choose to define federalism, and how we conceive of the proper role of government in providing a medical safety net for a diverse group of citizens — including poor children, the mentally ill, addicts, the disabled, and chronically ill elderly people who have little support from their families or communities.

It is also crucial to think through the difficult political obstacles standing in the way of serious reform — obstacles that have been made all the more daunting by the passage of Obamacare this spring. If Republicans win control of one or even both chambers of Congress in November, they may well be able to revise or, through the appropriations process, slow the implementation of parts of the legislation over the following two years. But an outright repeal of the bill — including the forthcoming Medicaid expansion — would be unlikely to overcome a presidential veto; a complete rollback, therefore, would need to wait until after 2012.

A detailed and forceful case for a different approach, however, cannot wait that long. A clear explanation of Medicaid's problems, of the reasons why expanding the program and putting it at the center of our health-care system would be a disaster, and of the ways in which the program can be improved must be part of the larger case for undoing Obamacare (and for replacing it with genuine health-care reform).

Starting now, reformers need to outline a strategy for fixing Medicaid that conforms with political realities; offers a clear vision of what government should and should not do to subsidize medical assistance; and restores the important roles of individual thrift, family care, private charity, community action, and state policymaking—values that an increasingly federalized Medicaid system has weakened or supplanted.

## FIXING MEDICAID

A meaningful reform of the Medicaid system will need to reduce the program's size, scope, and cost to taxpayers; increase self-reliance among the middle class; eliminate disincentives for poor Americans to become middle-class Americans; return power and responsibility to states, localities, charities, and families; and ensure that our scarce public resources actually end up serving those most in need of public help. Policymakers can begin by dividing the work into four key reform elements.

First, they should work to convert Medicaid itself into a more specialized program of medical assistance to those with chronic physical or mental infirmities who are, for all practical purposes, wards of the state. This was, after all, the original idea behind the state-based relief programs that Medicaid was created to bail out nearly half a century ago. Both conceptually and practically, it makes sense to distinguish individuals with chronic medical conditions—those likely to produce long-term dependency on the state—from healthy individuals who, due to job loss or other short-term emergencies, find themselves without health insurance or savings. Medicaid ought to be focused on the needs of the former, not the latter; efforts to provide a temporary safety net to people who are, by and large, working and contributing members of society should take a different form. Congress should rewrite eligibility standards accordingly, creating a separate program to subsidize private health-insurance premiums for the able-bodied poor (as described below).

As for the management of the remaining long-term Medicaid caseload, states should receive more latitude to experiment with initiatives to coordinate care, both within the practice of medicine and between Medicaid and other state agencies. For example, state agencies need to work together to avoid creating massive costs for one another—such as when a Medicaid-eligible patient with severe mental illness or addiction goes off his medications, commits crimes or public disturbances, ends up in jail, and then gets transported to a psychiatric hospital or detox center. Tracking patients through the system can help limit these destructive cycles.

In experimenting with such initiatives, states should be careful to avoid the myth of prevention savings: the notion that spending more money on the front end can save much more money on the back end. Preventive medicine is often good medicine, as it helps avoid chronic diseases like diabetes or heart disease; but, as decades of data have shown, it does not save money. Preventive medicine is itself quite expensive, and in most cases people who consume a preventive service would not have needed a more expensive intervention later on anyway (that is, they would not have developed diabetes or heart disease even without the preventive care). As a result, the costs to the system as a whole outweigh the financial benefits. Preventive care must therefore be counted as an expense — even if often a worthwhile one — not a savings.

There are, of course, other proven and effective ways to save — by using vouchers to encourage careful spending or by assigning case managers to help recipients use their benefits efficiently, for instance. And while there is no silver bullet, state policymakers should be encouraged to try those streamlining efforts that they think stand the best chance of reducing Medicaid waste in their states. Above all, states must have the right incentives to lower costs — for example, the ability to keep all of the potential savings from a politically difficult yet effective reform — as well as good reasons to strictly enforce eligibility rules, so that new costs do not overwhelm any savings their reforms might produce.

Second, policymakers should convert Medicaid coverage for low-income but healthy children and working-age adults into a system that subsidizes the payment of premiums for private health-insurance plans. For instance, a future Congress could convert Obamacare's bewildering array of cash payments and tax credits into a universal tax credit, conferring what amounts to an exemption from income and payroll taxes for a fixed amount of household spending on (or saving for) health care.

The tax credit could take the place of the existing unlimited exemption for employer-based plans (as proposed by John McCain in his 2008 presidential campaign, and by several Republican members of Congress since). Such a fixed-dollar credit would be worth most to individuals with children and low incomes, reversing the current dynamic in which unlimited tax deductibility confers the greatest benefit on upper-income Americans and those who work for large employers. Families would be free to apply their tax credits to the purchase of health plans and toward health savings accounts (into which states should be allowed to contribute additional funds now earmarked for Medicaid to help lower-income people).

The key to a successful system of direct premium supports for jobless or low-income Americans and their families, however, is ensuring that it is thought of more as a welfare program than as a health-care program. Recipients should be required to meet the same work or job-search rules currently required for cash welfare benefits. The intention should be to provide temporary, transitional assistance for those down on their luck, not a means of perpetuating dependency.

Third, policymakers should convert the current complex system of federal Medicaid funding into annual block grants to the states, adjusted annually to accommodate medical inflation. Today, Medicaid is an open-ended entitlement: The states set eligibility standards, spend money to cover services for people who meet those standards, and essentially bill the federal government for its share of the costs on a rolling basis. The levels of spending are therefore never fixed, and states do their best to extract more money from Washington by gaming the system's arcane rules.

A single annual block grant would instead allow state policymakers to know exactly how much federal money they will receive for the year and to budget accordingly; it would also allow federal policymakers to have more predictable levels of spending. An added benefit of a block-grant system is that it would give state governments more responsibility for their Medicaid funding: If states choose to expand eligibility or benefits in their programs, they should be required to raise the additional funds beyond their block grants (either by cutting spending elsewhere, or raising taxes). Because most states must balance their budgets every year, they won't be able to paper over Medicaid expansions with additional debt, as Washington can do. Forcing states to responsibly manage one lump sum of money will thus make it harder for government to deceive taxpayers about the real costs of the program. And on the other side of the ledger, states should be able to recoup most of the savings from any disease-management initiatives, asset-recovery programs, or benefit reductions they implement, rather than being forced to send most of the savings they may obtain (often at great effort and political risk) back to Washington to be redistributed to other, more profligate states.

As for Medicaid's current array of mandatory and optional services, federal policymakers should simplify the rules by setting the initial federal grant at the amount required to fund only mandatory services (like doctor visits and hospital stays). States would be allowed to provide additional coverage (for medical needs like dentures and eyeglasses), but only using their own dollars.

This would be a marked departure from the current system, under which state politicians have generally been able to expand Medicaid services and eligibility only to the extent that they could convince voters that the increases would be funded largely by the federal government. Some politicians have been more successful at selling this argument than others, which is why there are such enormous differences in Medicaid spending across the states. Moreover, while liberal states typically offer more generous programs and politically conservative states offer less generous ones, there does not seem to be much evidence that the states with more generous Medicaid programs have better health outcomes. So by getting the federal government out of the matching-grants business — and by letting states make and fund their own decisions about program expansions — policymakers will increase the likelihood that any additional tax dollars committed to Medicaid will make a real difference in the quality and availability of medical care.

Of course, one big political obstacle to block granting will be the debate over setting the initial grant baseline. Higher-spending states will want to freeze their current funding levels in place, which lower-spending states will see as unfair. Although a block-grant conversion would confer fiscal benefits on the country regardless of the starting point (by encouraging wiser spending decisions in the states), it would be preferable for Washington to set a baseline that, as much as possible, allocates a similar amount of federal funding per mandatory enrollee, adjusted for regional differences in medical prices. Under such a computation, New York would still receive substantially more federal dollars per low-income person than Mississippi; the difference in actual purchasing power, however, would be minimal.

Fourth, policymakers should encourage American families to save for long-term care. Beyond reversing Obamacare's attack on tax-free health savings accounts, this can be achieved by establishing generous tax relief for private long-term-care insurance, by dramatically tightening Medicaid eligibility rules, and by seriously stepping up eligibility enforcement.

While statistics show that most Americans entering retirement will not require lengthy and expensive nursing-home stays, some certainly will. Even more seniors face the prospect of other long-term expenses, such as home-based health care. Furthermore, the share of the population over the age of 85 is expected to increase by more than 50% in the next 15 years (as older people are in better health than ever before), so we can expect a significant increase in the number of seniors needing long-term care.

As with other major life expenses—like sending a child to college, or losing a job—public policy should encourage families to plan for the possibility of long-term care through prudent saving and insurance coverage (rather than encouraging reliance on the government to pay the bills, using taxes collected from thriftier families). And one obvious way federal and state policymakers can encourage thrift is by changing tax policy—restoring, and expanding, the health savings accounts that Obamacare strictly limits, and creating the aforementioned universal tax credit for health care (including the purchase of long-term-care insurance).

Still, those who study and sell such insurance insist that tax incentives alone won't be enough to induce American families to take the necessary steps to protect their assets against future long-term health-care expenses. The Medicaid-fraud industry of lawyers, accountants, and benefits consultants has been too successful in marketing the message that, with creative planning, middle-income families can ensure that their elderly relatives will qualify for Medicaid.

The only realistic way to change this public perception is to change the law so that it becomes both difficult and unappealing for middle-class seniors to qualify for Medicaid. To begin with, it should be made more difficult for people with expensive homes to receive coverage. Today, an individual's home equity up to $500,000 (and in some states up to $750,000) is excluded from the calculation of assets when determining Medicaid eligibility. Congress should set a date—far enough into the future to reduce political blowback and to allow families to adjust their plans—for phasing out all exemptions of home equity from these calculations. In addition, the existing rules against seniors' transferring assets to family members in order to meet Medicaid eligibility requirements—which take into account transfers of wealth reaching back five years before a person applies for Medicaid, and then limit that person's eligibility based on the amount transferred—should be extended to reach back at least 10 years.

At the same time, states should be far more aggressive in enforcing these rules, keeping in mind that every dollar not spent subsidizing the inheritance of a middle-class family is a dollar that can be spent on a truly needy senior with no family to rely on. Americans should be made to understand that if they want to place a relative in long-term care through Medicaid, they will have to either spend down *all* of the relative's assets — including the value of a home — or transfer those assets to the state after the relative's death (as current law already requires when a senior turns out to have had more assets at the time of his death than when he applied for Medicaid coverage). Families must be made to recognize that if they want to avoid these unpleasant eventualities, they will need to buy private insurance — not try to game the state.

### STEPPING BACK FROM THE ABYSS

Reforming Medicaid has never been an easy prospect — and the passage of Obamacare has only made it more difficult. Many of the most powerful lobbies in Washington and in state capitals will work against any effort to fix what ails this deeply flawed entitlement. Liberal politicians, too, will obstruct the reform process at every step, recognizing (correctly) that such a restructuring of Medicaid would move America as far away from their ultimate goal — single-payer, government-run health care — as Obamacare moved America toward it.

But the simple truth is that American taxpayers cannot afford the status quo. Even before Obamacare, the combined cost of Medicaid, Medicare, and Social Security was projected to consume nearly 15% of gross domestic product by 2030 — up from less than 10% today. These entitlements are already falling into the red, and have an unfunded liability of nearly $100 trillion through the end of the century.

Obviously, all three programs are in need of serious change. But from the perspective of America's long-term fiscal health, Medicaid presents the most urgent challenge — because the program involves state governments that have far fewer options for contending with debt than Washington.

As much as Obamacare has complicated matters, it has also stirred up a great deal of public furor. This presents policymakers with an opportunity to roll back the law, and to implement meaningful reform of Medicaid in its place. Given what is at stake for the nation, it is an opportunity Americans cannot afford to let pass by.

*Originally published as "How to Fix Medicaid" in the Summer 2010 issue of* National Affairs.

# How to Fix Social Security

## Charles Blahous

*WINTER 2010*

IN THE WAKE OF A CRUSHING RECESSION, with sharp declines in employment and government revenues, Social Security is much closer to going into the red than earlier projections had estimated. Last spring, the Social Security trustees reported that more than 75% of the program's previously projected near-term surplus had vanished. In September, the Congressional Budget Office offered an even more sobering prediction: Social Security will begin running deficits in 2010, and by 2019 will face annual shortfalls in the neighborhood of $60 billion, which will have to be made up out of general revenue.

These reports highlight the growing urgency of Social Security's troubles and the pressing need for change. But merely ringing the alarm bells will do little to improve the political prospects for fundamental reforms. Interest groups purporting to represent seniors are still dogmatically opposed to changing the system; the country as a whole is disinclined to do anything seen as jeopardizing benefits for the elderly; and the downsides of many of the most commonly proposed reforms are often far easier to see and explain than the long-term fiscal benefits they would bring.

Indeed, the nature of the Social Security system complicates any purely fiscal case for reform. Normally, advocates of government spending must choose between adding to the tax burden and adding to the deficit. But when future Social Security benefits are promised well in excess of projected revenues, the cost does not show up in measures of today's deficit. Instead of adding immediately to the tax burden, policymakers add to the burden of the *next* generation, a practice that permits them to duck near-term responsibility for raising taxes while

CHARLES BLAHOUS *is a senior fellow at the Hudson Institute. He is the author of* Social Security: The Unfinished Work *and a member of the Board of Trustees of the Social Security Trust Funds.*

blurring the long-term budget realities by quibbling over projections. And as with other entitlement programs, cost increases in Social Security occur on autopilot, so that by default the program stays on a course of ever-rising costs—however unsustainable it may be in the long run. Reforms cannot be made without new legislation that could easily be painted as either raising taxes or cutting benefits. The status quo is well entrenched.

Reformers are badly in need of a different way of thinking about fixing Social Security. Rather than treat the program purely as a fiscal problem for government, and so leave themselves open to the charge of opposing its objectives, they should advance their own values-based vision. They should put themselves squarely on the side of the broadly shared American principles of respecting and rewarding work.

In a number of serious and largely unintentional ways, Social Security now discourages seniors from continuing to work. A set of reforms aimed at correcting these distortions would significantly improve the system's finances while also conveying solidarity with seniors who extend their working careers—either by choice or, because of the financial crisis, out of necessity. At a time when the political landscape makes a more fundamental redesign of the program highly unlikely, correcting the distorted relationship between Social Security and work offers a promising avenue for easing the program's woes.

### AN AGING ENTITLEMENT

When President Franklin Roosevelt and the Congress first established Social Security in 1935 as one of several federal responses to the Great Depression, the age of benefit eligibility (65 years) was set to be higher than the life expectancy of the typical American male at birth (61 years at the time). Today, however, Americans are living longer than ever before, while claiming benefits even earlier—meaning the typical beneficiary now collects Social Security for more than 18 years. Meanwhile, the vast Baby Boomer generation is starting to drift onto the retirement rolls, after having produced too few children to adequately fund the benefits they are told they will receive.

The result has been a dramatic shift in the balance between beneficiaries and taxpaying workers. In 1960, there were five workers for each beneficiary. Today that ratio hovers just above 3-to-1. As the Baby Boomers exit the work force, it will plunge rapidly to 2-to-1 within a generation.

This massive demographic change threatens to unleash unprecedented tax burdens upon younger generations. Put simply, when there are fewer workers to support each beneficiary, each worker must pay more. In 2008, the cost of paying Social Security benefits absorbed roughly 12 cents out of every taxable dollar workers earned. Without fundamental change, this toll will rise nearly 40%—to more than 17 cents of every taxable dollar—in a generation. For perspective, consider that the $700 billion cost of the TARP program (the federal government's huge, unprecedented intervention to stabilize the financial markets) amounts to less than *half* of what our children would pay in taxes to cover just a *single year* of Social Security benefit payments 25 years from now.

Add in the similar aggregate cost growth in Medicare, and our children will be paying fully one-third of their wages to support just two federal programs. This one-third levy would be taken from their earnings before funding all of the other things that federal, state, and local governments tax them to accomplish—whether providing for the national defense, paving the highways, or funding their own children's education. If we do nothing to avert this outcome, we will bequeath to our children a lower after-tax standard of living than our own.

The financial crisis and the ensuing economic downturn have only made matters worse by reducing Social Security's payroll-tax revenue and prompting an uptick in disability-benefit claims just as the program last year paid out its largest cost-of-living adjustment in 27 years.

As a result, the Social Security shortfall—long derided by defenders of the status quo as a "phony crisis"—is now rushing at us faster than either Social Security's trustees or the CBO previously predicted. Even the Obama administration's budget numbers demonstrate that government finances are on an unsustainable course unless Social Security, along with other federal entitlements, is reformed.

And the longer we wait to deal with Social Security, the more we increase the proportion of the eventual solution that will necessarily take the form of higher taxes. This is largely due to the overwhelming consensus that we should not cut benefits for those already in, or even near, retirement. We simply won't pay someone a $2,000 benefit in January, and cut it to $1,600 in February. As a result, we lock in higher tax burdens with each passing year.

The cost of falling into this trap is formidable. According to the 2009 report of the Social Security trustees, current participants in the Social Security system are scheduled to receive $18.7 trillion *more* in future benefits than they will pay in future taxes. Another year's delay, as more and more Baby Boomers retire, further increases the proportion of this figure that becomes untouchable in political negotiation. To make matters worse, the sacrosanct benefits of each new class of retirees raise the bar for the minimum politically acceptable level of benefits for those who follow. It is unlikely that even the most fiscally conservative members of Congress will countenance Social Security benefit declines relative to inflation.

As a result, the window for avoiding substantial tax increases is closing fast. For those committed to a wage-indexed benefit formula, it has indeed already closed. But even for those willing to limit the growth of workers' benefits to inflation, the window for avoiding a tax increase is likely to slam shut within the decade. Every year we creep closer to insolvency, the amount of the shortfall that will have to be made up by taxes creeps up as well, regardless of which party wins the intervening elections. To bring Social Security into the black at the point of insolvency in 2037 would require a benefit cut in that year of 24%. This assumes, moreover, that we are willing to allow those already in retirement to suffer benefit cuts. Assuming instead that previous retirees' benefits will be protected, nearly all benefits for new retirees in 2037 would need to be wiped out to keep the system whole without a tax increase. This obviously will not happen. If we want to fix Social Security without imposing enormous tax increases on our children, time is of the essence.

### MYTHS AND REALITIES OF PERSONAL ACCOUNTS

The most widely debated reform proposal of recent years has been the establishment of personal accounts. In 2005, President George W. Bush proposed progressive indexing of the Social Security benefit formula as a means of addressing the fiscal shortfall, and voluntary personal accounts to improve the program's treatment of younger workers. But the Congress failed to vote on this proposal — or on any other that would have improved the program's long-term outlook.

Many conservatives continue to believe that by failing to enact personal accounts when Republicans held a majority, they missed an opportunity to cure Social Security's fiscal troubles. But while personal accounts would have been a change for the better, they were not a panacea, and would have dealt with only one aspect of the system's woes. They could provide an effective means of funding future benefits, but not a pain-free way to fully close the gap between projected revenues and costs. Even if personal accounts succeeded in saving a portion of future Social Security payroll taxes, there remained a large gap between the amount of those taxes and the cost of promised benefits.

More recently, the combination of stock-market turbulence and federal deficits approaching $2 trillion has strained budgetary resources—as well as the public's appetite—for establishing personal accounts. It is worth noting that this loss of appetite has more to do with perception and spin than with the reality of proposed personal accounts. Personal-account opponents have groundlessly claimed that the stock-market decline would have devastated beneficiaries if the Bush administration had enacted such accounts in 2005. In reality, under President Bush's proposal, not a single person now receiving Social Security benefits would have held a personal account. Last year would have been the first in which accounts would even have accepted contributions from current workers. Young workers starting their investments would now have been buying in a down market. And going forward, the total proportion of a typical worker's Social Security benefit subject to investment risk would have been less than 1.5% for each year of account participation. (The precise percentage would have been higher for higher-wage workers, lower for lower-wage workers.)

Though few yet appreciate it, the market plunge could actually prove a long-term blessing for the cause of personal accounts (albeit, paraphrasing Winston Churchill, a very well-disguised one). If nothing else, the downturn has successfully smashed the idea that the case for accounts should be premised on stock-return projections. There has always been a tradeoff between higher returns and higher risk; the former could never be promised without the latter. To the extent that the case for personal accounts can be liberated from the siren song of ever-rising stock returns, it will be much stronger.

The true advantage of the personal-accounts approach is that it is far fairer to the young than continuing indefinitely with pay-as-you-go financing. As the worker-to-beneficiary ratio drops, each succeeding generation in a pay-as-you-go system is treated worse than the one before it. Personal accounts offer a way around this dilemma, allowing today's workers to save in advance for a future in which fewer workers will be around to fund their retirement. No one in his right mind would say, "The stock market is collapsing. I had better not save for retirement." But that is exactly the sort of myopia we will perpetuate if we continue to finance Social Security solely on a pay-as-you-go basis.

The other major criticism of personal-account proposals — their supposed expense — looks positively quaint now. Consider, for example, the 2005 debate over the allegedly enormous "transition cost" of personal accounts. President Bush's proposal aimed to have roughly $675 billion invested in personal accounts over the program's first ten years (CBO predicted the amount would be closer to $300 billion). This amount has already been exceeded by President Obama's stimulus package ($787 billion) and by the TARP rescue ($700 billion to date). It would also be far surpassed by the Obama administration's proposed health-care overhaul. These dollar-figure comparisons, moreover, obscure an important distinction: Each of these other three initiatives represents a *new* commitment of federal tax dollars, while the personal-account proposal would have funded *existing* commitments of Social Security.

Indeed, the Obama administration's own support for a universal auto-IRA account — which would have employers automatically send a portion of each paycheck into a retirement savings account for workers who so choose — implicitly acknowledges the prudence of long-term saving in accounts under individual ownership and direction.

The case for personal accounts, provided it includes a healthy grasp of their limits, remains strong and well grounded. But being right doesn't make the politics of Social Security reform generally, or of personal accounts specifically, any easier today. In a time of Democratic dominance of Washington, personal accounts funded by Social Security payroll taxes will not see the light of day. Meanwhile, the task of repairing Social Security's finances continues to grow more urgent. Reformers on both sides of the aisle are thus in dire need of new and viable ideas for Social Security reform — ideas that are fiscally responsible, and yet will resonate with a wide swath of the body politic.

KEEPING SCORE

The first idea serious reformers should promote is an essential prerequisite for a more honest debate about the condition of Social Security: transparent, objective accounting. Perhaps the most important thing that reformers need to understand in any future Social Security negotiation is how the policy result — and especially the balance between cost restraints and new taxes — will be driven by the program's unique scorekeeping.

Reformers must avoid a negotiation predicated solely upon the concept of a "75-year actuarial balance" — at least as the balance has been calculated since a 1988 change in actuarial methods. This metric heavily tilts the playing field in the direction of tax increases in a number of ways.

First, it simply ignores any and all tax increases required to pay off the Social Security Trust Fund — as though it were money that has all been saved, rather than a debt that future taxpayers must yet redeem. Recall that it cost 12 cents out of every dollar earned by workers to pay for Social Security benefits in 2008, and that by 2036, this cost will rise to 17 cents of every dollar. As a result of the Trust Fund's legal claim on government funds, this gap between payroll-tax collections and the cost of paying benefits must be made up by raising additional general revenues (read: income taxes). The 75-year actuarial balance method simply assumes at the starting point that taxpayers will provide this substantial additional revenue.

Second, the metric counts the tax revenues raised from many workers' wages but not the benefits they will be paid. To see how this distorts our understanding of the program's finances, suppose that we only looked at the system over ten years. If we did so, we'd see the taxes paid by a 25-year-old worker, but not the benefits he will receive when he retires 40 years from now. Thus, a ten-year actuarial window would credit us with savings if we raised his taxes, but not if we constrained his benefits. The same problem exists regardless of where the time window is cut off. Whether we look at the system over ten years, or 25, or 75, by counting millions of workers' taxes but not their benefits, the metric finds that much more will be readily achieved by concentrating on the tax side.

Third, the metric makes future shortfalls appear to be smaller than they really are. This is because the scorekeeping was changed in 1988 to discount future shortfalls more heavily — employing a discount rate equal to the rate of interest presumed to be "earned" on the Social Security Trust Fund. The interest is assumed even if the money in the Trust Fund is not actually saved. This same assumption of earnings also greatly overstates the fiscal benefits of raising taxes now to address the shortfall.

When negotiating the 1983 reforms, policymakers used a simpler method, which recognized that benefits would be financed by taxing workers at the time that they are paid. It treated a deficit that would absorb 4% of wages in one year as being twice as large as a deficit absorbing 2% of wages in another year. The post-1988 discounting method, however, finds implicitly that future workers face smaller Social Security deficits, even in many instances where the tax rates threatening them are far higher.

These are among the reasons why reliance on the 75-year metric would inevitably drive negotiators to "solve" the problems of Social Security primarily by raising taxes. Raising the tax cap to cover 90% of all taxable wages, for example, would reduce the dollar amount of the outyear Social Security shortfalls by only 15%. Using this flawed metric, however, such a move would appear to solve more than 40% of the problem. If believers in limited government enter into negotiations without understanding these scorekeeping biases, they won't have a chance.

Given all this, what metrics should negotiators use? There are a number of better possibilities. One is very simple, and is a calculation that the Social Security actuary's office has performed consistently for the past decade. This metric would require that Social Security—or at least, any pay-as-you-go element within it—be returned to *annual* cash balance (or surplus) within the 75-year period, and be on a trend to stay there.

Another option would be to return to the actuarial methodology used in 1983. This method was imperfect in that it did not account for imbalances in *annual* program operations, and thus is not a complete substitute for insisting on sustainable annual cash flows. But this method would still be a useful component of improved scorekeeping, because it avoids a number of the problems cited above: It eliminates the problem of how to account for the Trust Fund, and it also values future deficits as they would actually be felt by future workers. This would do much to level the policy playing field between raising taxes and constraining costs.

### VALUING WORK

Leveling this analytical playing field is an important prerequisite for reform. But to take meaningful steps in the right direction, reformers must also bring a coherent and potent policy agenda to the table. They need to make the case for changes that will lessen the pressures now driving Social Security toward insolvency, and that will send the right message about the valued place of older Americans in our society. Reformers should therefore champion ways of honoring and rewarding taxpaying work.

Experts have long understood that Social Security is effectively designed to drive seniors out of the work force. American Enterprise Institute scholar Andrew Biggs has found that the marginal return on contributions made by seniors who choose to extend their working lives is a ridiculous -49.5%. (To be clear: That's *negative* 49.5%.) This may have made sense in 1935, when the nation was trying to move seniors out of the work force to give young male workers a competitive shot at a smaller pool of jobs. But it makes no sense whatsoever given the economy, demography, and culture of our day.

Correcting these flawed incentives in Social Security will require both sticks and carrots. The carrots make for easier politics than the sticks, but reformers need to resist political pressure to simply make the system even more expensive. They should offer cost-saving measures that provide incentives to work, which would reduce the remaining shortfall that must otherwise be offset by more politically difficult fixes in the future. Reformers should trust that the American people, if fully informed, will choose rewarding work today over raising taxes tomorrow.

First, policymakers should re-evaluate the Actuarial Reduction Factor and the Delayed Retirement Credit. Under Social Security's current structure, benefits are reduced if they are claimed early, and increased if claimed late. This is done so that, if one lives an average lifetime, one's total expected Social Security benefit does not change. It also prevents individuals from gimmicking the system by manipulating the date of their benefit claims. The proportional adjustment is 20% downward if claimed three years before normal retirement age (13.33% if claimed two years before, etc.), and 8% per year upward (for up to three years) for claims made after.

This sounds reasonable at first. The problem is that individuals' work and benefit claims are correlated: People often claim benefits when they stop working, and vice versa. If they continue working and paying taxes, therefore, they often make these additional tax payments without receiving any additional benefits.

To correct this, the Actuarial Reduction Factor and Delayed Retirement Credit could both be increased to reflect, at least in part, the value of additional payroll taxes paid. One possibility is to raise the ARF from 20% to 25% for those claiming three years early and the DRC to 10% for each year after the Normal Retirement Age. These adjustments would serve as a proxy for the expected actuarial value of the additional payroll taxes contributed by a typical senior who extends his working career. Implementing these changes would strengthen work incentives over a wide range of ages, increasing both the reward for delayed retirement and the penalty for early benefit claims.

Workers could also be offered an additional choice: the opportunity to receive the DRC as a lump sum. Few workers take the DRC now, as they are not greatly enticed by the prospect of an extra few hundred dollars per month. A lump-sum DRC, however, could well equal tens of thousands of dollars at the time of retirement — and provide a powerful motive to continue taxpaying work.

A second change worth pursuing is an improvement of Social Security's Average Indexed Monthly Earnings calculation. The current system does two things that fit together somewhat awkwardly: On one hand, it keeps track of a worker's career wage history and assigns to it an "average indexed monthly earnings" figure on which benefits will be based. On the other hand, it follows a progressive model, offering worse returns as a worker's AIME rises. As a result, for each additional year that a person works, his AIME figure climbs higher, and so his return on that year's work declines. For seniors contemplating whether to extend their working lives, the returns are especially poor.

Splitting these two functions would preserve Social Security's progressivity while also improving its work incentives. Currently, the system indexes one's past earnings history into today's terms, identifies one's top 35 earning years, and then averages them. It afterward applies the progressive benefit formula to this total. Instead, it could simply apply the current benefit formula to *each* of a worker's past earnings years. Then one's total benefit could be computed by simply adding up each of these annual benefit accruals. Instead of returns growing worse with each year of work, each worker would in effect start "fresh" with each additional work year; every new year would offer just as large a benefit reward as the year before.

This reform would reduce system costs, and would somewhat favor the steady low-wage earner over the intermittent high-wage earner. It would also enable Social Security to reward work in a manner more similar to a private-sector pension plan, in which benefits accrue with each additional year worked.

AIME reform has the added benefit of helping to repair other oddities of Social Security law. For example, the current system inaccurately perceives certain high-income workers to be low-income workers — especially immigrants (whose earnings abroad are invisible to Social Security) and state-government employees (those who spent part of their careers not participating in Social Security). As a result, it pays the generous returns intended for low earners to a subset of high earners. AIME reform would result in an appropriate return paid for each year of covered work.

Third, reformers could encourage work by eliminating Social Security's earnings test. Currently, seniors earning money between early and normal retirement age must pay a penalty of one dollar for every $2 they are paid over the earnings limit of roughly $14,000. This isn't technically a benefit reduction, but rather a benefit deferral, because the money is later returned in the form of higher monthly benefits. Nevertheless, the earnings limit sends exactly the wrong message to seniors, driving them out of the work force during the critical years between 62 and 66, when many might otherwise continue to work.

The principal effect of the earnings limit now on the books is not to prevent early benefit claims — indeed, the earliest possible age of 62 remains the most popular age of claims, despite the existence of the test — but rather to discourage paid work. This is precisely the wrong message for the government to send, and may actually have the paradoxical effect of increasing elderly poverty by inducing a too-hasty departure from the work force. Since the rationale for the current earnings test rests on the unfounded predicate of mitigating poverty among seniors, and since its adverse effects upon work are apparent, it should be an obvious target for elimination.

A fourth attractive reform is payroll-tax relief for working seniors. Many good proposals have been put forward to reduce the tax burden associated with employing seniors; these need to be thought through carefully if the government is to avoid practicing outright age discrimination. Still, two measures in particular seem worthy of consideration.

One is to exempt seniors and their employers from the disability tax. Once seniors hit the normal retirement age, they are no longer eligible for disability benefits. It seems unfair to tax them for benefits that they cannot receive. To offset the revenue lost to the disability program, the current Old Age and Survivors Insurance and Disability Insurance taxes could be adjusted.

Another promising idea is to eliminate the Social Security payroll tax entirely after 45 years of earnings, as recently proposed by Mark Warshawsky. Unlike simply eliminating the payroll tax at a given age, this approach would avoid overt age discrimination and also provide a positive work incentive on the way toward, as well as at, 45 years. It would also better avoid charges of gender discrimination: Men and women resemble each other more closely in work-force attachment than they do in life expectancy.

Another way to improve both system finances and work incentives is by capping the growth of Social Security's non-working spouse benefit.

We should not completely abandon the benefit, which recognizes the value of stay-at-home work—but there are shortcomings in its current design that can certainly stand to be improved.

To begin with, the current non-working spouse benefit produces many unnecessary and regressive transfers of income. A high-income, one-earner couple, for example, receives a higher rate of return from Social Security than a two-income, low-earner couple. The structure of the benefit is also the leading culprit in the low (-32%) incremental return on contributions to the system made by women. Moreover, the non-working spouse benefit is poorly targeted: Though intended partly to recognize the effort of raising the wage-earners of the future, it strangely provides the same entitlement whether the non-working spouse has many children, few children, or none at all.

Under today's system, a single working mother who earns half of the average wage gets a smaller benefit after a lifetime of contributions than someone who simply marries a maximum-wage earner. Capping the growth of the non-working spouse benefit so that it does not exceed benefits earned by a significant portion of the low-income working population would improve both the system's fairness and its work incentives.

Finally, work incentives cannot be fully repaired without examining Social Security's eligibility ages. Admittedly, raising the early eligibility and normal retirement ages is tougher political medicine than the other ideas discussed here. But it may be the most powerful work incentive of all: More people choose to retire at the age of earliest eligibility than at any other age. Indeed, people now tend to claim Social Security at younger ages than when the program was first established, despite the vast increases in life expectancy and personal health we have experienced since then.

The usual objection to raising the ages of eligibility is the burden it would place on laborers in physically demanding jobs. Whatever the merits of this argument (and the empirical evidence suggests they are not great), the fact remains that it was considered just fine for Social Security to provide benefits only at age 65 throughout the 1940s and '50s, when there were many more such physical laborers than today. Furthermore, the current rules allowing *everyone* to retire at 62 are a grossly inefficient way to address this perceived problem.

Moreover, raising the age of earliest eligibility is probably a useful, if somewhat paternalistic, way to address the objections to reforming the Actuarial Reduction Factor for early retirement. If the early retirement penalty is increased — however fairly from a work-reward perspective — and individuals nevertheless continue to retire at 62 despite lower benefits, there would be some increased risk of poverty among seniors who outlive their other retirement savings. By raising the age of earliest eligibility, however, reformers would implement a change that not only makes sense from a demographic standpoint, but also seems likely to help reduce elderly poverty, especially among the very oldest seniors.

### PREPARING THE GROUND

By engaging the public along these lines, Social Security reformers could appeal to broadly shared American values that honor work, basic fair play, and the idea that individual choices — rather than the whims of federal policymakers — should be the principal determinants of one's prosperity. Americans will instinctively respond to the message that if they keep working and keep paying into Social Security, they should be entitled to some of the benefits of that extra work without the government taking it all away (as it now does in too many cases).

Such reforms would also speak to the difficult choices many Americans must make in the current recession. Unfortunately, all across the country, people are being pushed to extend their working lives in order to recover retirement assets lost in the financial-market meltdown. Those who remain in the work force will contribute their productivity to our economic recovery, and the system should support them as they do.

Of course, enacting these reforms will also contribute significantly to addressing Social Security's fiscal problems. The projected long-term gap between the system's annual income and costs could be reduced by as much as 40% simply by enacting the common-sense reforms described here. This would considerably reduce the difficulties faced by reformers negotiating among more politically polarizing options to finish the rest of the job.

It is time, therefore, for a new approach to Social Security: one based on honoring the labor of American workers, one that offers a way around the quicksand of today's Social Security politics, and one that charts a clear and politically plausible path to meaningful reform of the system.

*Originally published as "Social Security and Work" in the Winter 2010 issue of* National Affairs.

# How to Get Means Testing Right

## Andrew G. Biggs

FALL 2011

AMERICA FACES A MASSIVE CRISIS of entitlement spending. The Congressional Budget Office projects that, just a decade from now, government debt will be greater than the nation's entire gross domestic product—and that the main driver of that debt will be entitlement programs. Because of America's aging population and rising health-care costs, Social Security and Medicare have simply been pushed to the brink.

Meanwhile, today's trillion-dollar deficits, depressed federal revenues, and ballooning discretionary spending restrict the range of possible solutions. There is no more cushion of either funding or time. Slow and steady increases in the retirement age and minor tweaks in benefit formulas can no longer stave off disaster: Reformers must now entertain policy solutions once considered unimaginable. And prominent among those solutions is subjecting Social Security and Medicare to some form of means-testing, by which poorer seniors would receive more generous benefits and the wealthy would receive less (or none at all).

The appeal of means-testing is easy to see. It would dramatically reduce entitlement spending, and in a way that could be justified as commonsense: Since we don't have the money to give benefits to everyone, we should give benefits only to people who need them most. Why should a billionaire like Michael Bloomberg have his health care heavily subsidized by overburdened taxpayers? Means-testing entitlements would save huge amounts of money by not paying out benefits to wealthy Americans who can get along just fine without them. At the same time, it would still allow Medicare and Social Security to serve their basic purpose: providing a safety net to the elderly.

But means-testing also has some serious drawbacks, especially when it comes to how the policy might shape Americans' financial decisions.

ANDREW G. BIGGS is a resident scholar at the American Enterprise Institute.

Means-testing entitlement benefits could punish the very people who work the hardest and save the most, depressing economic activity and discouraging good behavior. The cure for our fiscal problems could thus end up being worse than the disease.

If reformers are to reduce the costs of Medicare and Social Security without inviting counterproductive side effects, they must pay careful attention to the design of their policy reforms, and remain open to solutions that go beyond simple means tests. Embracing the idea that the rich should receive less generous entitlement benefits than the poor could help avert America's entitlement crisis — but the devil, as always, will be in the details.

### THE UNIVERSAL ETHOS

Originally, both Social Security and Medicare were designed as "social insurance" programs meant to ensure that, regardless of what might happen with their personal finances and retirement savings over the course of a lifetime, elderly Americans would be protected by a government-backed safety net that would prevent destitution in old age. Since the net extended to nearly every senior, these programs can be best understood as universal benefits.

Social Security provides a monthly retirement-benefit check to some 46 million Americans, as well as disability benefits to another 10 million. The program, which now costs roughly $730 billion per year, is the largest line item on the federal budget. It is funded by a nearly universal flat payroll tax of 12.4%, half of which is paid by the employee and half by the employer.

Each person's retirement benefit is determined by a formula that takes into account the age at which he chose to retire (those who retire early, starting at 62, receive lower benefits than those who wait until the normal retirement age, which is now 66) and a measure of his earnings during his working years — and therefore of the amount he paid in Social Security taxes. That measure is based on an average of the highest 35 years of his covered earnings (that is, of pay that was subject to the payroll tax), adjusted for wage growth and then divided by 12 to yield a monthly amount. That amount is then inserted into a progressive benefit formula designed to ensure that Social Security benefits replace a larger proportion of pre-retirement earnings for people with low average earnings than for those with higher earnings.

For instance, a worker who becomes eligible to retire this year will receive 90% of that monthly amount up to $749, plus 32% of the remaining amount between $749 and $4,517, plus 15% the remaining amount above that level. This means that workers with lower lifetime earnings receive a *proportionately* higher (though generally still *nominally* lower) benefit. The benefit formula provides an added protection to the poorest seniors, but the program is still designed to offer a fundamentally universal benefit: Rich and poor alike receive Social Security checks in retirement, and the rich tend to receive larger ones. As the Social Security Administration says on its web site, Social Security "is not and was never intended to be a program to provide benefits based on need. Rather, it is a system of social insurance under which workers (and their employers) contribute a part of their earnings in order to provide protection for themselves and their families if certain events occur."

Medicare—which provides comprehensive health insurance to essentially every American over the age of 65—carries this universal ethos even further, offering the same health benefits to all retirees regardless of their circumstances. The program now costs roughly $550 billion per year, a figure that is growing much more quickly than the cost of Social Security, thanks to galloping health-care inflation. Medicare, too, is funded in large part by a flat payroll tax (at a rate of 2.9%, shared equally between employers and employees), though some elements of the program are also funded by general revenue and by premiums paid by enrollees. Eligibility for benefits is based upon Social Security eligibility, but unlike Social Security, Medicare benefits do not vary based upon prior earnings or contributions to the program. Therefore, those benefits, too, are not based on need, nor are they based on what retirees paid into the program while they were working.

Indeed, although Social Security and Medicare are both considered earned social-insurance benefits, neither involves a direct relationship between money paid into the program and money drawn out of it. The structure of both programs means that current workers fund the benefits of current retirees; workers do not put money into a fund that will support their own benefits later. In Medicare, the average retiree actually draws far more money in benefits than he put into the program while working: According to Eugene Steuerle and Stephanie Rennane of the Urban Institute, a two-earner couple with average wages turning 65 this year will have contributed $119,000 to Medicare in taxes but will receive $357,000 in benefits during retirement. In Social Security, a similar average couple retiring today at age 67 will actually receive somewhat less in benefits ($560,000) than they put in to the program while working ($611,000).

In both cases, however, the level of benefits bears no relation to economic need. It would thus be a significant departure from the programs' histories and purposes to subject them to means-testing. Under a means test, the government assesses the resources available to an individual — his income and assets, aside from the benefit payment in question. To the degree that those other resources exceed some pre-set level, the government then reduces (or eliminates) the individual's benefit payment.

Means-tested benefits are relatively common in the United States in welfare programs aimed at reducing poverty. Familiar means-tested benefits include the Earned Income Tax Credit, Medicaid, and Supplemental Security Income, while a large number of tax credits or deductions (like the child tax credit, new homebuyers tax credit, and deductions for pension contributions) are phased out as incomes rise. America's reliance on means-tested programs stands in contrast to most European countries, where universal benefits are far more prevalent. Many European countries pay, for instance, a universal child credit to all parents, and provide universal health coverage (not only to the elderly) regardless of income.

Means-tested benefits have the advantage of being more narrowly targeted, and therefore less costly, than universal benefits. One disadvantage, however, is that a means-tested benefit imposes an implicit marginal tax on people with earnings close to the income level at which the benefit phases out. For instance, for an eligible taxpayer (or couple) with two or more children, the benefit received through the Earned Income Tax Credit declines by 21 cents for each dollar earned above the prior year's income, imposing an implicit marginal tax rate of 21% on recipients' increased wages.

When one considers the implicit penalties for earning additional income imposed by all federal welfare programs, and combines them with explicit federal and state taxes, households in poverty can face higher marginal tax rates on taking a new job or working more hours than do households earning significantly more (as much as five times the poverty level, in fact).

The negative effects of these incentives on work are mitigated, however, by the fact that most people cannot easily choose how many hours to work. For the overwhelming majority of Americans, the choice is essentially to work a full-time job (40 hours per week) or not to work at all. Moreover, because of the complicated ways in which federal welfare programs and taxes affect one another, the effective marginal tax rates can be nearly impossible to decipher; their negative incentives thus become difficult to act upon. The result is that most people in the prime of their working years—whether they qualify for government benefits or not—will work as much as they can, regardless of marginal incentives.

But the story is different with older Americans. Often, seniors have far more flexibility—fewer immediate financial obligations, and more accumulated resources to cover the obligations they do have—as well as real choices about whether to work and how much to save. Marginal incentives can therefore make a very real difference for them (as we shall see). This is one reason why means-tested benefits—though common among federal programs targeted at the poor—have, for the most part, not been applied to Social Security and Medicare.

Of course, means tests for these programs have not been *entirely* rejected; there are some very modest instances of the practice in both Social Security and Medicare. For example, since the Social Security reforms of 1983—implemented to improve the program's shaky finances—a rising share of Social Security benefits has become subject to income taxes. Currently, retirees with "combined incomes"—defined as adjusted gross income plus non-taxable interest income, plus one-half of the Social Security benefit—between $25,000 and $34,000 pay the income tax on up to 50% of their benefits. Seniors with combined incomes over $34,000, meanwhile, pay the income tax on up to 85% of their benefits.

This tax structure can be considered a means test, especially as the taxes levied on the first 50% of benefits flow directly back to Social Security (the taxes levied on the increment between 50% and 85% of benefits flow to the Medicare program, a policy instituted under President Clinton's 1993 budget package). Taxing Social Security benefits to fund Social Security in this way constitutes an effective 3.4% "clawback" in the total benefits of high-income seniors. And crucially, because the income thresholds for benefit taxation are not indexed to inflation or wage growth, ever-increasing shares of total benefits will become subject to this means test over time. By 2050, nearly 5% of total Social Security benefits will be taxed back.

But such taxation of Social Security benefits has at least a plausible foundation in the principle of tax neutrality—by which a tax system is designed not to influence investment, the allocation of capital, or other individual economic decisions—and thus is not simply a means test. While the 6.2% employee share of the payroll tax is paid after income taxes, the matching employer contribution is not subject to either personal or corporate income taxes. As a result, imposing income taxes on half of a person's Social Security benefits is similar to the taxation of 401(k) or Individual Retirement Account withdrawals—essentially just deferring taxation from one's working years to one's retirement. Moreover, the effective increase in marginal rates through the taxation of Social Security benefits is modest. Researchers at the Urban Institute have found that eliminating the taxation of Social Security benefits entirely would reduce the implicit tax on continued work in retirement by only three to four percentage points.

Medicare offers a clearer case. The premiums for Medicare Part B (which covers physician services, outpatient care, and medical equipment) and Part D (which covers prescription drugs) are higher for wealthier retirees. For instance, Part B premiums range from $110 per month for retirees with incomes of less than $85,000 to $369 per month for retirees with incomes over $214,000. The result is that, for seniors earning between $85,000 and $214,000 a year, an implicit effective tax rate of around 2.2% of income is imposed by Medicare. Today, roughly 5% of retirees pay higher Part B premiums based on their incomes (though this share will rise to around 14% over the next decade because of Obamacare, which ends the practice of adjusting income thresholds for inflation). Under the Part D prescription-drug program, around 3% of beneficiaries currently pay income-adjusted premiums; this number, too, will rise under Obamacare, to around 9%.

These are both exceedingly modest means tests, however, and bear little resemblance to the sorts of eligibility tests employed in programs intended for the poor. Our old-age entitlements thus retain a fundamentally universal character—for as much as there is disagreement over entitlement reform, one broadly unifying theme has long been a commitment to universality. For example, the bipartisan Advisory Council on Social Security, appointed by President Clinton in 1994, was at odds over several major issues—but one conclusion the group supported unanimously was that "[c]onventional means-testing of Social Security is unwise." The group further declared:

The fact that benefits are paid without regard to a beneficiary's current income and assets is the crucial principle that allows—in fact encourages—people to add savings to their Social Security benefits and makes it feasible for employers and employees to establish supplementary pension plans.

Moreover, means-testing would send the wrong signal to young people and wage earners generally. The message would be: "If you are a saver and build up income to supplement Social Security, you will be penalized by having your Social Security benefits reduced." This message is both unfair to those who work and save and creates the wrong incentives.

These statements represent the conventional wisdom on both sides of the entitlement debate, although different ends of the political spectrum have opposed means-testing for different reasons. Thus, if any form of means-testing is to offer hope of resolving the problems with Social Security and Medicare, it is essential for reformers to understand the nature of this opposition—and then formulate an adequate response.

### LEFT AND RIGHT

People on the left tend to oppose means-testing based on the view—perhaps most notably espoused by Wilbur Cohen, an official of the Social Security Administration right after the program's founding and later Lyndon Johnson's secretary of Health, Education and Welfare—that "a program just for the poor is a poor program." They believe, in other words, that Americans will not adequately support (and fund) policies in which redistribution toward the poor is too overt. For instance, in the late 1990s, traditional liberals like Senator Edward Kennedy opposed increases in Medicare premiums for high earners, while in the 2000s influential liberals argued that adding personal accounts to Social Security would weaken support for the program among middle and high earners, who would see most of their benefits coming from their individual accounts rather than from the traditional program.

But this view is empirically dubious. Programs such as the Earned Income Tax Credit have retained bipartisan support and even been expanded; the Medicaid program, which provides health care to the poor, is among the largest and fastest growing in the federal budget—costing federal and state taxpayers more than $400 billion each year. Moreover, the argument that, because Americans won't support redistribution if they know it is taking place, policymakers should therefore disguise redistribution by mixing it with benefits paid to middle and high earners is insulting to voters. It implicitly holds that most Americans will act only out of selfish motives, and so must be convinced that redistributive programs in fact serve their own interests. It also suggests that government aid to the poor must be rooted in a lie.

Strangely, the concern that voters will not pay for government programs from which they themselves do not benefit hasn't chilled the left's fervor for progressive *funding* of entitlements. After all, high earners already pay more into Social Security and Medicare than they are likely to receive back in benefits. And most proposed liberal reforms to entitlement programs would simply extend this trend, requiring the wealthy to pay more while they are working. For instance, the most popular Social Security reform proposal on the left these days is to raise (or eliminate altogether) the annual cap on earnings subject to the Social Security payroll tax, currently $106,800. Eliminating the cap would constitute an enormous tax hike on individuals earning more than the current maximum, effectively raising the top marginal tax rate by 12 percentage points.

It is not clear why large benefit cuts for high earners would reduce their support for entitlement programs, as the left believes, but even larger tax increases would not—unless we assume that the best-educated and hardest-working Americans are extremely bad at math. One potential answer is that tax increases on high earners are more acceptable simply because they can raise more money for the program than can benefit cuts applied to the same people. Clearly, there is a limit to how much government can cut a person's benefits: The top Social Security benefit for a person retiring in 2011 is around $29,000 a year; no more than that amount can flow back into the program's coffers from cuts to his benefits. Eliminating the payroll-tax ceiling, however, could raise vastly more for the Social Security program: Under current rates, lifting the cap would mean garnering an additional $29,000 a year from every person earning $350,000—and much more from people earning still higher incomes. Moreover, the savings from cutting or reducing a senior's benefits would accrue only in the years between his eligibility and death. By contrast, the added revenues from lifting the tax cap would stream onto the program's balance sheets over Americans' entire working lifetimes.

The right, meanwhile, has tended to oppose means tests for economic reasons. Chief among them is that reducing a person's government benefits as his outside income increases creates a disincentive to work and save. In other words, means tests can produce implicit taxes every bit as harmful as explicit taxes. And since we want individuals to work and save more to provide for themselves in retirement (let alone to sustain the American economy), it would be both counterproductive and unfair to penalize them for doing exactly that.

There is some evidence to support these arguments. For instance, seniors who retire early and earn money between today's Social Security early-retirement and full-retirement ages (that is, between the ages of 62 and 66) have their benefits reduced during those years by one dollar for every $2 they are paid over the annual earnings limit of roughly $14,000. In effect, retirees perceive this earnings test as a 50% marginal tax on income over the $14,000 threshold, and research indicates that many retirees earn up to the threshold and then cease working in order to avoid the earnings test. As it happens, an unadvertised aspect of the Social Security earnings test is that, as soon as an "early" retiree turns 66 and reaches the full retirement age, his benefits are increased to account for any past reductions he experienced because of the test. The "earnings test" is therefore not a true tax: Lifetime benefits remain roughly the same with or without the test. Nevertheless, it is widely *perceived* as a tax, and the effects on seniors' earnings behavior are significant and troubling.

Many conservatives are also concerned about the administration and enforcement of means tests. To run a means test, the government quite obviously needs to know the scope of a person's means, entailing a more intrusive IRS than many would prefer. For instance, individuals do not currently file information regarding the value of their assets or bank-account balances along with their tax returns, but this information would be necessary to administer an effective means test. Moreover, as is painfully evident in Medicaid's provision of long-term care for the elderly (which is available only to seniors below a certain income and asset threshold), potential beneficiaries will seek to avoid a means test if possible by, for example, shifting assets to family members. This makes the administration of means-tested programs a race between individuals seeking to game the system and administrators devising new rules to prevent them from doing so—a pattern that often results in gross inefficiency and waste, as well as fraud.

Others argue that wealthier Americans have put more into the Social Security and Medicare systems during their working years, so that reducing their benefits to pay for those who have put less into the system is tantamount to a tax increase, and would mean turning a social-insurance program into a more redistributive welfare program.

Still, despite these concerns, support for large-scale means tests has been growing among some conservatives in recent years. They view means-testing as a way to generate quick and significant savings without undermining the safety net for the truly needy. Conservative commentator Charles Krauthammer, for instance, has called for means-testing Social Security "so that Warren Buffett's check gets redirected to a senior in need." Mitch Daniels, Indiana's Republican governor and a prominent fiscal conservative, has also called for a Social Security means test for better-off retirees. And many on the right have suggested that Medicare benefits should be significantly greater for seniors in need, so that people who can afford to pay more can help avert the program's looming fiscal collapse.

But this newfound enthusiasm for means-testing has too often failed to account for the real-world consequences of such tests.

### IMPLICIT TAXATION

To illustrate both the positive potential and the risks involved in means-testing our old-age entitlements, consider the provisions of a budget-reform plan proposed by the conservative Heritage Foundation in May. The plan, which Heritage calls "Saving the American Dream," would include (among other reforms) means tests for both Social Security and Medicare benefits.

It would begin reducing Social Security benefits for retirees with annual incomes of $55,000 (excluding Social Security benefits), and would then gradually reduce benefits for seniors with incomes above that level until completely eliminating benefits for retirees with incomes above $110,000. According to the Census Bureau's Current Population Survey, in 2009, the typical retiree with an income of $55,000 to $59,000 had a Social Security benefit of around $14,000 per year; thus, under Heritage's proposal, as a senior's income rose from $55,000 to $110,000, his Social Security benefits would fall from $14,000 to zero. In effect, the individual would lose around 25 cents in Social Security benefits for each dollar of income above $55,000. This would generate an implicit tax rate of 25%, in addition to other taxes this person might pay.

The plan includes a similar approach to Medicare. It proposes transforming the Medicare program into a premium-support system similar to the one envisioned by House Budget Committee chairman Paul Ryan, in which the government would contribute toward individual purchases of private insurance coverage. The Heritage proposal, however, would adopt a much more significant means test than the Ryan approach. The premium-support benefit would be modified based upon the age, health costs, and income of each senior, gradually phasing out for seniors with incomes between $55,000 and $110,000. Assuming an annual government contribution of $11,000 — roughly the level of per-beneficiary Medicare spending today — the Medicare and Social Security means tests combined would produce an implicit marginal tax rate of around 46%.

While Heritage cites the current taxation of Social Security benefits and progressive Medicare parts B and D premiums in defense of its reforms, the effects of its proposed means tests would be more than an order of magnitude larger. Even under Heritage's accompanying proposals to reform the tax code — replacing the current system with a flat tax of about 25% — total marginal tax rates in retirement could reach 72%.

These results could, of course, vary based upon other policy parameters. For instance, if, at the same time it imposed a means test, the plan adopted a significant, across-the-board tightening of Social Security and Medicare benefits for *all* seniors, the implicit tax rates imposed by the means test would be smaller — simply because fewer benefits would be available to be "lost" through the earning of extra income. Alternatively, if the income thresholds at which the means test was applied were not fully indexed for the growth of incomes over time, the means test could apply to larger and larger numbers of retirees each year, and its effects would be greater.

The precise long-term effects of such a plan are therefore difficult to pin down. But the broad conclusion should be clear: Means tests can impose very high implicit taxes on work and saving upon individuals whom we would otherwise wish to encourage to work and to save more. The growing embrace of means-testing on the right is thus somewhat puzzling, given the opposition of conservatives to far smaller increases in top marginal income-tax rates proposed by the Obama administration.

That puzzle can be at least partially solved by considering what else means tests offer: a vastly improved budget outlook, intensely craved by fiscal conservatives. Heritage's budget plan was produced at the invitation of the Peter G. Peterson Foundation, which asked six prominent think tanks spanning the ideological spectrum to provide their blueprints for addressing the federal government's fiscal problems. Of the six (one of which was produced by scholars at the American Enterprise Institute, including me), Heritage's was the *only* plan that would actually balance the budget within the coming decade; that balance would be reached largely by reducing Social Security and Medicare outlays by more than a full percentage point of GDP over a four-year period. Other proposals settled merely for so-called "primary balance," in which spending (excluding interest payments) would not exceed revenue. But while this approach would stabilize the ratio of government debt to GDP, it would not bring revenues fully into line with outlays.

The means by which the Heritage budget would achieve its impressive feat highlights a crucial point: It would be difficult, and perhaps impossible, to bring the federal budget into balance quickly without touching the Social Security and Medicare benefits of those already on the programs' rolls. The budget deficit is too large, and the non-entitlement elements of the budget too small, to make balancing the budget possible without affecting current retirees. Traditionally, reformers have pledged to protect seniors receiving benefits and people near retirement against any changes, in a (generally unsuccessful) effort to neutralize seniors' opposition to entitlement reforms. This strategy made sense as long as fiscal calamity remained in the distant future and the true budget challenge could be addressed over the long term. But in today's environment of mounting annual trillion-dollar deficits, slow and steady may no longer be a viable approach.

A significant overhaul of entitlements in the near term may therefore be simply unavoidable. And of the various options available, providing less generous benefits to wealthier retirees certainly seems like a prudent and effective way to go about such changes. Yet a stubborn truth remains: Straightforward means-testing will have some enormously counterproductive consequences. So what can reformers do?

A BETTER WAY

There is an alternative approach — one that achieves many of the ends of traditional means-testing, but without inviting many of its drawbacks. The plan's essential and distinguishing feature would involve limiting benefits based not on individuals' incomes in retirement, but rather on their *lifetime* earnings. As noted above, Social Security already effectively does this, by paying proportionally lower benefits to people with higher average lifetime earnings. Today's reformers could do the same, if to a greater degree.

For instance, the Social Security Administration already tabulates individuals' average lifetime earnings as an intermediate step in calculating their retirement benefits. Reductions in Social Security or Medicare benefits, or increases in premiums, could be based upon this measure of average lifetime earnings rather than on income in retirement.

Unlike a strict means test, this approach would avoid creating powerful disincentives to save. Indeed, individuals facing lower Social Security benefits in retirement would have an incentive to save *more* during their working years to make up for the loss. And these increased savings would benefit not only the savers, but the economy as a whole: To the degree that retirement savings generally take the form of investment portfolios, increased saving for retirement would generate more investment capital — in turn boosting economic output and wages over the long term.

Incentives to work would still be undermined somewhat under such an approach. Reducing benefits based upon lifetime earnings would mean that, for each additional dollar an individual earns, the return through Social Security would be smaller. Thus, the "net tax rate" under Social Security — that is, the net value of taxes paid and benefits earned — would increase, and obviously higher tax rates discourage work.

But it is likely that these negative effects would be significantly smaller under a lifetime-earnings approach than under a traditional means test. After all, these net tax increases would be relatively small at any given time, since they would be spread out over a full working lifetime rather than concentrated in retirement. This makes an enormous difference, as public-finance economists hold that the negative effects of taxes — known as the "deadweight loss" — rise with the *square* of the tax rate. The implication is that it is far better to spread a smaller tax increase over a larger number of years than to concentrate a large increase over a shorter period of time. In effect, this approach would take the favorite maxim of tax reformers — broaden the base while lowering the rate — and apply it to reductions in entitlement benefits, yielding, in essence, a lower effective tax over a larger number of years.

Moreover, as noted, there is reason to believe that people are more responsive to marginal tax rates during or near retirement—when the option not to work is clearly available—than during their prime working years, when the need to support a family and save for retirement means that most people will work as much as they can. In a 2008 study of workers over the age of 70, Lucie Schmidt of Williams College and Purvi Sevak of Hunter College found that "a reduction in the marginal tax rate that would increase the payoff to working by 10% would increase labor force participation by 7.5% among men and 11.4% among women." These are far greater responses to tax incentives than have been found among younger workers. For the population as a whole, the Congressional Budget Office assumes a response about one-third this size. The effect on marginal tax rates of the means test proposed in the Heritage budget would be almost four times larger than the increase studied by Schmidt and Sevak—and in the wrong direction—and so would be likely to yield a powerful undesirable response. Similarly, a study by Eric French of the Federal Reserve and John Jones of the State University of New York found that labor-force "participation decisions are most sensitive to financial incentives when workers are old." Means tests would thus impose powerful negative incentives precisely when people are most responsive to them.

Of course, the major problem with cutting benefits for well-off retirees based upon their lifetime earnings is that such a reform would require a lifetime to take full effect. And the federal budget doesn't have a lifetime to wait. This dilemma highlights the cost of delay on entitlement reform: We have known since the late 1980s that Social Security would require reforms beyond those passed in 1983; had these more significant fixes been passed at the time, they would now be fully effective. They would have put the program on a sustainable path while giving individuals enough time to adjust their saving and retirement plans.

The same is true of Medicare. The scope of the coming problem, and the shape of a plausible solution, have been clear since at least the mid-1990s, when a bipartisan Medicare reform commission appointed by President Clinton and congressional leaders endorsed a premium-support structure that closely resembles the one House Republicans are pushing today. Time, then, really is the resource that budget reformers need the most—yet it has become the most elusive.

If we wish to balance the budget in the near term, the key is to devise approaches that generate targeted, immediate savings without imposing significant disincentives to work and save. In economic terms, we wish to impose a negative "income effect"—that is, a loss of income that individuals will seek to make up through additional work—without imposing a negative "substitution effect" that reduces the rewards to additional work.

Striking this balance will not be easy. If immediate reductions in Social Security and Medicare benefits are required, then the best option might be a combined approach: changing the benefit formula based on lifetime earnings so that the reform takes effect over the long term, but also implementing shorter-term changes that, while rooted in the same principle, are more incremental. For instance, we might pay wealthier individuals with higher Social Security benefits lower annual cost-of-living adjustments than those receiving lower benefits. A progressive COLA could reduce high-end benefits by reasonable amounts in the near term while generating incentives—not disincentives—to work or save. A policy in which the highest third of beneficiaries received no COLA, the lowest third received a full COLA, and the middle third received half the current COLA would reduce Social Security outlays by around 12% over the first ten years. In fact, the savings from this measure alone would be enough to balance the program's finances over the long term.

There could be many variations on such an approach, of course, and they need not necessarily involve the COLA. But all must seek to reduce outlays while hurting neither the most vulnerable retirees nor Americans' incentives to work and save.

In Medicare, the fiscal challenges are even greater, but the basic logic of reform would be much the same. For instance, Medicare beneficiaries might be subject to an annual deductible based on their average lifetime earnings.

FAIR AND SUSTAINABLE

It is inevitable that Social Security, Medicare, and other government programs will become less generous toward the rich than they are today. The only alternative is ever-increasing taxes and their toll on personal welfare, individual freedom, and economic growth.

It is impossible to support a European-style universal welfare state without European levels of taxation, so the provision of relatively generous entitlement benefits to rich and poor alike must shift over time to a more targeted approach. But that targeting must bear in mind the crucial insights of market economists in recent decades—that individuals and the economy as a whole are complex and dynamic, and respond to incentives in ways that can stymie the seemingly simple answers suggested by static economic analysis.

Means tests are a good example of this very principle. On paper, they can provide significant budgetary savings while sparing the poor from benefit reductions. In practice, however, they can generate disincentives to work and to save, and do more harm than good. The challenge for today's policymakers is to craft policies that make the most of the benefits of means-testing while avoiding its worst consequences.

*Originally published as "Means Testing and Its Limits" in the Fall 2011 issue of* National Affairs.

# III. Tax Reform

# How to Think about the Tax Code

## Donald B. Marron

SUMMER 2011

WITH THE UNITED STATES on track for a third year of trillion-dollar deficits, public debate is now focused on getting America's fiscal house in order. The challenge is straightforward: The federal government spends much more than it collects in tax revenue each year and will continue to do so even after the economy recovers.

The argument over how to close that gap is often dominated—sometimes debilitated—by sharp disagreements about how much should come from spending cuts and how much from tax increases. But that division can be misleading. A great deal of government spending is hidden in the federal tax code in the form of deductions, credits, and other preferences—preferences that seem like they let taxpayers keep their own money, but are actually spending in disguise. Those preferences complicate the code and often needlessly distort the decisions of businesses and families. The magnitude of these preferences raises the possibility of a dramatic reform of the tax code—making it simpler, fairer, and more pro-growth—that would amount to simultaneously cutting spending and increasing government revenue, without raising tax rates.

Such a reform would not eliminate the need for serious spending cuts, of course, nor would it take tax increases off the table. But it could dramatically improve the government's fiscal outlook and make the task of budget negotiators far easier. It will only be possible, however, if we clearly understand how spending is hidden in the tax code and what reformers might do about it—if we see that tax policy and spending policy are not always as distinct as we might think.

DONALD B. MARRON *is director of the Urban-Brookings Tax Policy Center. He has served as a member of the President's Council of Economic Advisers and as acting director of the Congressional Budget Office.*

To illustrate, consider a dilemma that President Obama faced in constructing his 2012 budget. Because of inflation's ups and downs, Social Security beneficiaries did not receive a cost-of-living increase in 2011, just as they did not receive one in 2010. Nor did many benefit from the payroll-tax holiday enacted as a form of stimulus at the end of last year (since few retirees are still working and paying payroll taxes). For these reasons, President Obama wanted to make a special, one-time payment of $250 to each American receiving Social Security.

But that idea raised a question of basic fairness. Some retired government workers do not participate in Social Security. But they are just as retired—and arguably just as deserving of an additional benefit—as Social Security recipients. So the president wanted to give them $250, too. But how could he get the money to the retired government workers? The government doesn't have a master list of retirees outside of Social Security. Even if it did, it would make no sense to have Social Security send checks to retirees who had never participated in the program to begin with. Another agency had to deliver the benefit—one that was already in contact with most retirees, could enforce eligibility requirements, and, most important, could deliver the money. Only one agency fit the bill: the Internal Revenue Service. The president thus structured his special, one-time payment as a $250 refundable tax credit for any retiree who did not qualify for Social Security. In Beltway parlance, he offered these men and women a tax cut.

But was it really a tax cut? The president's $250 credit would have the same budgetary, economic, and distributional effects as his $250 boost in Social Security benefits. Both would deliver extra money to retirees, and both would finance those payments by adding to America's growing debt. One benefit would arrive as a Social Security check, the other as a reduced tax payment or a refund. These superficial differences aside, however, the proposed tax credit would be, in effect, a spending increase.

This is just a small example of a widespread practice that involves hundreds of billions of dollars each year. Because tax cuts often sound more appealing to policymakers and voters than spending increases—especially in today's political climate—the temptation to spend through the tax code is enormous. And the confusion surrounding such spending allows politicians to claim they are saving taxpayers' money when, in fact, they are really spending it.

With America deep in the red, this point is particularly important to keep in mind when considering proposals to reduce the federal deficit. It is neither feasible nor desirable to reduce deficits with tax increases alone. But revenues must be part of the conversation — even among lawmakers who loathe the very idea of "tax hikes." With our aging population and rising health-care costs, America will not be able to restrain spending enough to avoid increasing federal revenue above historical levels.

But these combined pressures do not mean that income tax *rates* have to go up. By properly taking account of spending disguised as tax breaks, policymakers can raise new revenue — and potentially even pay for some tax-rate *reductions* — by cutting back on the many spending-like provisions in our tax code. After all, that hidden spending should get the same scrutiny — and inspire the same enthusiasm for cuts — as the spending on entitlements, domestic programs, and defense that is targeted by today's fiscal hawks.

A SEA OF TAX PREFERENCES

Identifying all of the spending programs hidden in the tax code is no easy matter. The code is notoriously complex, and distinguishing between tax provisions and spending-like provisions can involve as much art and philosophy as it does science and accounting.

The best place to begin is the list of tax preferences that the Treasury Department compiles each year for the president's budget. This year, that list identifies more than 170 distinct preferences in the individual and corporate income taxes. These preferences fall into five categories.

First, *credits* reduce a taxpayer's liability dollar for dollar. If a taxpayer's total liability is low enough, and a credit is refundable, it can even result in a direct payment from the government to the taxpayer. The two largest credits are the Earned Income Tax Credit for low-income, working Americans (which provided its recipients with about $60 billion in 2010) and the child tax credit (which gave $48 billion to low- and moderate-income families). The most significant business credits include those for research and experimentation and for developing low-income housing, each of which amounted to almost $6 billion last year.

Second, *deductions* reduce the amount of income subject to tax. In the personal income tax, the most important deductions include those for mortgage interest ($79 billion in tax savings in 2010), charitable giving ($42 billion), and state and local income taxes ($27 billion). On the business side, the largest deductions are for accelerated depreciation (the ability to write off investment costs faster than capital actually depreciates), which amounted to a savings of $40 billion, and the deduction for manufacturing activities that take place in the United States ($13 billion).

Third, *deferrals* allow taxpayers to postpone the date at which income gets taxed. Individual taxpayers get deferrals through various tax-advantaged saving programs; 401(k)s, for example, allowed taxpayers to keep about $52 billion they otherwise would have paid to the IRS in 2010. Corporate taxpayers can defer taxes on most income earned by their foreign affiliates until the income is formally paid to the U.S. parent company, a delay that saved them about $38 billion last year.

Fourth, *exclusions and exemptions* allow certain types of income to avoid taxation entirely. The three largest are the exclusion for employer-provided health insurance ($260 billion in 2010), the exclusion for the imputed rental value of owner-occupied homes ($41 billion), and the exemption for interest earned by holders of state and local bonds ($30 billion).

Finally, *preferential rates* tax certain types of income at lower levels. The most important are the lower personal rates on long-term capital gains ($36 billion in 2010) and qualified dividends ($31 billion).

The estimated revenue losses from these five kinds of preferences total more than $1 trillion annually, almost as much as we collect from individual and corporate income taxes combined, and almost as much as we spend on discretionary programs. In 2010, for example, individual income-tax preferences totaled more than $900 billion in foregone revenue and corporate income-tax preferences more than $100 billion. When one factors in the money disbursed to individuals and corporations through refundable credits, these provisions boost spending by another $100 billion.

That's big money, but these figures come with two important caveats. First, eliminating all these tax preferences would not boost revenues as much as the numbers suggest. For instance, these calculations do not reflect how taxpayers might change their behavior if these preferences were eliminated. Treasury's estimates thus overstate how much money we could raise by eliminating preferences in the tax code. Still, even allowing for these adjustments, the sum of money at stake amounts to many hundreds of billions of dollars each year — and comes to trillions over the next decade.

The second caveat relates to how exactly the Treasury decides which provisions count as tax preferences. Identifying preferences inevitably invites controversy, because it requires a benchmark notion of an idealized tax system against which any deviations are deemed preferences. Perhaps not surprisingly, tax experts differ on what kind of system represents the ideal benchmark. The Treasury, for instance, uses a comprehensive, progressive income tax as its benchmark, with a few adjustments to reflect the practical realities of administering the tax system. Other analysts believe a broad-based consumption tax would be a better benchmark. In that case, several important preferences—including accelerated depreciation, lower rates on capital gains and dividends, and some retirement provisions—would be much smaller, or would not be identified as tax preferences at all. Meanwhile, other provisions, most notably companies' ability to deduct interest expenses, *would* be identified as preferences.

Although this disagreement reflects a fundamental debate about tax policy, it does not undermine the basic fact that tax preferences are enormous. Indeed, most provisions that are preferences relative to an income-tax-based system are also preferences relative to a system built around a consumption tax. My colleague Eric Toder and I have estimated, for example, that about two-thirds of the dollar value of tax preferences identified by Treasury for 2007 would also be foregone revenue under a consumption tax.

With budget pressures continuing to build, it is no surprise that this large pot of potential revenue has caught the eyes of policymakers. Some tax reformers, like senators Ron Wyden of Oregon and Dan Coats of Indiana, have recommended substantial cuts in tax preferences in order to finance broader reform of the tax code, including reductions in tax rates. President Obama's fiscal commission—as well as the debt-reduction task force chaired by former New Mexico senator Pete Domenici and former White House budget director Alice Rivlin (a committee on which I served)—proposed even deeper cuts, with the aim of financing significant deficit reduction and across-the-board reductions in individual and corporate tax rates.

This focus on tax preferences is a healthy development. Unfortunately, it has been accompanied by rhetorical flourishes that sometimes obfuscate America's real policy challenges. Tax reformers and deficit hawks often refer to tax preferences as loopholes or special-interest provisions. The president's fiscal commission even called them "tax earmarks." Those epithets make for good, quotable copy, and occasionally they even ring true. There is one tax provision, for example, that has as its sole purpose lowering taxes on NASCAR venues. That's certainly heading into earmark territory.

But the real money is not in earmarks, loopholes, or special-interest provisions. It's in the tax preferences that benefit large numbers of Americans throughout the income distribution and that play an important role in the lives of many voters. The exclusion for employer-provided health insurance and the deduction for mortgage interest, for instance, benefit tens of millions of households each year. The Earned Income Tax Credit and the various child-related credits are the two largest federal programs providing financial support to low-income families. Preferential rates on long-term capital gains and dividends reduce the tax burden on millions of individual investors. Tax preferences for research and experimentation reward firms for innovation.

It is therefore important for policymakers to recognize that tax preferences are not merely "loopholes" exploited by narrow interest groups or "earmarks" that favor some congressmen's pet constituencies. Tax preferences are social safety-net programs. They are middle- and upper-income entitlements. They are preferences for capital income. And they are incentives for activities — such as owning a home, saving for college, or investing in new research — that many believe enhance our society. Given these realities, we should not be lulled into believing that cutting tax preferences will be as painless as closing a few loopholes. Such cuts will be as politically painful as cutting popular spending programs.

### ARE PREFERENCES REALLY SPENDING?

How did our tax code become so stubbornly riddled with preferences? Though tax preferences are widespread and have grown rapidly in recent years, they are not a new phenomenon. Indeed, Treasury officials began tracking them in the late 1960s. But rather than brand them as "tax preferences" or "tax breaks," they called them "tax expenditures" — a label intended to emphasize the similarity to spending programs. Congress then wrote that term into law in the landmark Congressional Budget Act of 1974 — legislation that established the rules still governing the federal budget process today.

The rationale for viewing the preferences as expenditures, rather than mere tax breaks, was (and is) that their budgetary, economic, and distributional effects are often indistinguishable from those of spending programs. Consider, for example, the tax-exempt bonds issued by state and local governments. Typically, these bonds pay much lower interest rates than taxable bonds of comparable risk. Because investors focus on after-tax returns, they are willing to accept the lower interest payments in return for the exemption from federal taxes. In the end, many investors come out ahead.

At first glance, this system might appear to offer a major tax break to investors. In reality, however, most of the benefit flows to state and local governments, which pay less in interest on their debts than they would otherwise have to in order to compete with higher-yield taxable bonds. Investors in municipal bonds pay an implicit tax by accepting lower returns, and the state and local governments receive an implicit subsidy. The fiscal effects would be the same if the tax exemption were eliminated, investors paid taxes on their interest, and the revenues were then disbursed to fund state and local projects. But because the money would pass through federal hands, we would call that taxing and spending, not a tax break.

The same is true of the exclusion for employer-provided health insurance, the deduction for charitable contributions, the corporate credit for U.S. manufacturing activities, and many other preferences. In each case, the government could accomplish the same goal — perhaps more cheaply — through an explicit cash subsidy, but has chosen instead to structure the spending as a tax break.

Princeton economist David Bradford once offered a simple thought experiment to illustrate how far such games could go. Suppose that policymakers wanted to slash defense procurement and reduce taxes, but did not want to undermine America's national security. They could square that circle by offering defense firms a refundable "weapons-supply tax credit" for producing desired weapons systems. The military would still get the weapons deemed essential to national security, defense contractors would get a tax cut, and politicians would get to boast about cutting both taxes and spending. But nothing would have changed meaningfully.

The government's ability to use such maneuvers has convinced many observers that tax preferences can be the equivalent of spending. But others continue to argue that the only tax preferences that should count as spending are the refundable credits that result in direct cash payments by the government. All other preferences are tax cuts, they insist.

The conflict between these two perspectives grabbed headlines this spring when Senator Tom Coburn, a Republican of Oklahoma, proposed ending the ethanol tax credit. The credit provides 45 cents to blenders of gasoline for each gallon of ethanol used in blending fuel. The Department of Energy could pay a direct 45-cent subsidy to blenders for each gallon of ethanol they use, but policymakers have instead chosen to run the incentive through the tax code. Senator Coburn introduced an amendment to eliminate the tax credit, arguing that doing so would cut corporate welfare and, in effect, cut spending. In his words, "[e]thanol subsidies are a spending program wrongly placed in the tax code that increases the burden of government [and] keeps tax rates artificially high."

Coburn's amendment was opposed by Americans for Tax Reform—an influential conservative group devoted to keeping taxes low. Since 1986, ATR has asked political candidates and officeholders to sign a pledge committing, among other things, to "oppose any net reduction or elimination of deductions and credits, unless matched dollar for dollar by further reducing tax rates." In the 112th Congress, 235 House members and 41 senators—mostly Republicans, but including a few Democrats—are pledge-signers; one is Coburn.

ATR contended that Coburn's amendment, which the Senate passed in June, would violate his pledge not to raise taxes. It also objected to Coburn's contention that the credit amounted to government spending. "Spending programs and tax relief are not the same thing," said ATR's tax-policy director, Ryan Ellis. He added: "If the government lets Tom Coburn keep a dollar of his own money, that is not the same thing as the government stealing a dollar from Ryan Ellis and giving it to Tom Coburn. The differences between tax relief and spending are unambiguous."

In April, similar views emerged from an unexpected source: the United States Supreme Court. In *Arizona Christian School Tuition Organization v. Winn*, several Arizona residents filed suit to overturn a state tax credit for charitable donations used to pay private-school tuition. Their concern was that Arizona's credit subsidized parochial schools, and thus violated the First Amendment's prohibition against any law respecting the establishment of religion. In a 5-4 decision, the Court ruled that the plaintiffs did not have standing to seek relief against the tax credit. The majority argued that, although taxpayers have long been understood to have standing to raise establishment-clause concerns about government spending, they do not have the same standing when it comes to tax incentives. Writing for the majority, Justice Anthony Kennedy concluded that the tax credit in question could not injure the plaintiff taxpayers because it did "not extract and spend [their] funds in service of an establishment." To argue otherwise, he went on, would be to assume "that income should be treated as if it were government's property even if it has not come into the tax collector's hands."

The key weakness in the arguments put forward by ATR and Justice Kennedy is that they emphasize the technicalities of budget accounting but overlook the practical effects of the tax preferences in question. As Justice Elena Kagan wrote in a dissent in the Arizona case, "Cash grants and targeted tax breaks are a means of accomplishing the same government objective — to provide financial support to select individuals or organizations"; they should therefore be judged by the same standards. Tax breaks can be viewed as a form of government spending, Kagan explained, "even assuming the diverted tax funds do not pass through the public treasury.... Both deplete funds in the government's coffers by transferring money to select recipients."

Americans for Tax Reform and Justice Kennedy also misunderstand how money actually flows between taxpayers and the government. The ethanol credit, for example, may appear to allow blenders to "keep their own money," but that appearance is misleading. By levying an excise tax on the fuel that blenders produce, the government has already asserted a legal claim to a sum of money. In Ellis's language, the government has already asserted its authority to "steal" the money, but has not yet collected it. Before taking collection, the government offers to pay blenders to do something that the government wants them to do: use ethanol. If the blenders go along, they can subtract that payment when they send in their taxes. That payment does not let blenders keep their own money; rather, it is a reward for doing the government's bidding. If it were the blenders' own money, it would not come with strings.

Still, not *all* tax preferences are functionally equivalent to spending. One example is the lower tax rate on qualified dividends. Today, the top marginal tax rate on ordinary income is 35%, but the top rate on dividend income is only 15%. The Treasury identifies the lower dividend rate as a "tax expenditure," but it would be a mistake to confuse it with other tax expenditures that function as spending. The true purpose of the lower rate is to correct a design flaw in our current income tax, not to covertly distribute government spending.

The flaw in this instance is double taxation. If an investor buys stock in a corporation, he faces two layers of tax. The company (of which he is part owner) pays corporate income taxes on its profits, and then the investor pays personal income taxes on any of the remaining profits he receives as dividends. The two layers of tax can boost the effective tax rate on corporate income well above the rate for other sources of income. If both corporate profits and dividends were taxed at 35%, for example, the combined tax rate could reach 58%. Applying a lower personal rate to dividends is one way to soften that double taxation. With dividends taxed at 15%, the combined tax rate on corporate income paid out as dividends would be no more than 45%, much closer to the rate applied to other forms of income.

Accelerated depreciation is another example. The Treasury identifies accelerated depreciation as a tax expenditure because it allows businesses to write off their equipment investments faster than would be appropriate under a pure income tax. Under a consumption tax, however, businesses would be allowed to write off their investments immediately. Accelerated depreciation is thus a compromise between two visions of taxation, not spending hidden in the tax code.

Analysts and policymakers should thus take care to distinguish among the various preferences. Many tax expenditures are indeed spending in disguise, but not all.

BIGGER GOVERNMENT

Spending-like tax preferences not only complicate our understanding of fiscal policy, but also pose a challenge to the way we think about the size of government. This is because, in examining the scope of government, analysts usually focus on official budget measures. For example, we often hear that federal outlays averaged about 20.7% of gross domestic product over the past four decades, while revenues averaged about 18.1%. But those official budget measures do not fully account for tax breaks that effectively function as spending programs.

To get a sense of how large the federal government really is, Eric Toder and I recently added up all the spending-like tax preferences in effect in 2007, the last year before the Great Recession. Using the Treasury Department's estimates, we found that those preferences amounted to

$600 billion (this is about two-thirds of the total tax expenditures that Treasury identified; the other third were preferences that are not spending in disguise). Spending-like tax preferences thus amounted to 4.1% of GDP. This means that government spending in 2007 was 23.7% of GDP when the spending-like tax preferences are included, but only 19.6% using the official budget measure. Our more inclusive measure of government spending was thus more than one-fifth larger than the usual measure.

A similar pattern holds with revenues. The official statistics indicate that federal revenues amounted to 18.5% of GDP in 2007, near their 40-year average. When we add back the 4.1% of GDP in potential revenues that were used to finance spending-like tax preferences, however, our broad measure of federal revenues increases to 22.6% of GDP.

The federal government is therefore bigger than we typically think it is. Conventional budget measures miss hundreds of billions of dollars that are implicitly collected and spent each year through spending-like tax preferences. That measurement error affects spending and revenues equally, so our measures of deficits and debts remain accurate. But the conventional measures do understate the extent to which fiscal policy redistributes income and influences economic activity.

For the same reason, conventional budget measures can misrepresent how changes in tax policy affect the real size of government. When we understand the size of government based on its spending alone, we assume that increases or reductions in revenue have no direct effect on the real size of government—all that matters is government outlays. And when we consider how much of our economy the government takes up based on the taxes it collects, we tend to assume that tax cuts make the government smaller and that tax increases make it larger.

But both approaches to assessing the size of government run into trouble when they encounter spending-like tax preferences. For example, using official budget measures, President Obama's proposed retiree tax credit (discussed earlier) would reduce tax revenues. So if we were to assess the size of government based on how much it spends, the president's proposal would have no effect on government's size; if we measured it based on how much it taxes, the proposal would actually shrink the government. But if we (correctly) recognized the retiree tax credit as a spending increase, we would conclude that the credit would actually *increase* government spending (making the government larger), while leaving the real scope of its tax collection unchanged.

The logic also works in reverse. Suppose policymakers decided that employer-provided health insurance should be subject to the same income and payroll taxes that apply to wages and salaries. Such a measure would increase government revenues by several trillion dollars over the next decade. But it would do so by eliminating the largest example of spending through the tax code. Under conventional measures, federal revenues would increase, but government's role in private insurance markets would actually narrow.

Advocates of smaller government are often skeptical of proposals that would increase federal revenues. But when it comes to paring back spending-like tax preferences, an increase in revenues would mean that government's role would get smaller. This, in essence, is the point Senator Coburn was trying to make with the ethanol tax credit. And it is a point that even the most ardent anti-tax, limited-government purists should keep in mind.

### GIVING CREDIT

The fact that some tax preferences are actually hidden spending programs does not necessarily make them bad policy. Some tax preferences support important policy goals, just as many spending programs do. And sometimes the tax system is the most efficient way to administer specific policies. The personal income tax, for example, provides a natural mechanism for providing benefits that should vary with income, like the Earned Income Tax Credit. The corporate income tax provides a convenient administrative structure for incentives like the tax credit for research and experimentation.

The importance of labeling many tax preferences as spending is not to disparage them, but to account for them honestly. The goal is to highlight the resources that the government directs through these provisions and to encourage analysts, commentators, and policymakers to subject them to the same scrutiny they give traditional spending programs. Some tax preferences provide substantial benefits and can withstand that scrutiny even in times of fiscal tightening. Others should be left on the cutting-room floor.

In addition, many of the tax preferences that *do* stand up to scrutiny—or persist because of their political popularity—would benefit from serious restructuring. Today's preferences for low-income workers and families with children, for example, are painfully complex.

Their byzantine rules impose unnecessary costs on beneficiaries and open the door to errors and fraud. Much better would be a system that consolidated these provisions into simple, streamlined preferences for holding a job and having children. The Domenici-Rivlin task force offered one such approach, in which all existing preferences for low-income families and children would be replaced with an earnings credit and a child credit available to all households, regardless of income.

Other major preferences could accomplish their intended goals at lower cost and with less economic distortion if they were redesigned as credits. The exclusion for employer-provided health insurance, for example, is an exceedingly inefficient way to encourage people to maintain health-care coverage. One flaw is that it offers bigger subsidies to high-income households. Because the exclusion matches the tax rate for each income bracket, the government picks up 35% of the insurance tab for an attorney earning $500,000, but only 15% of the cost for a truck driver earning $50,000. Not only is that "upside down" structure unfair, it also reduces the exclusion's efficiency in promoting health coverage — since high-income families are more likely to get health insurance without a subsidy than are lower-income families. If policymakers want to get as much health-insurance "bang" as possible for the many bucks devoted to health-insurance subsidies, it makes no sense to offer additional government assistance to people who are likely to carry insurance anyway.

Another flaw is that the tax exclusion raises the cost of health insurance for everyone. Because the exclusion is essentially open-ended (i.e., whatever amount an employer spends on a worker's health insurance is excluded from that worker's taxable income), workers have an incentive to choose expensive, high-end insurance plans that cover as much health care as possible. Such plans will usually minimize cost-sharing provisions like co-payments (which consumers usually pay for with *after*-tax dollars) while offsetting the costs through high premiums (which are paid for with *pre*-tax dollars). This system, in turn, drives up health-care costs overall — since the generous employer-provided coverage removes individual consumers' financial incentives to limit their use of health services. Absent this tax distortion, insurers would offer less expensive plans that relied more heavily on co-pays, co-insurance, and deductibles in order to both manage demand for health services and keep insurance costs low.

If policymakers wanted to retain a tax incentive for health insurance, they could correct both of these flaws by converting the current exclusion into a fixed, refundable credit. Individuals and families would qualify for the credit if they purchased health insurance that met some basic standard of coverage. Every taxpayer would have the same financial incentive, and would receive the same financial assistance, regardless of income. Every taxpayer would also be free to get more expensive insurance that exceeded the minimum standard, but the additional cost would not be offset by any extra tax subsidy. The credit would thus encourage the acquisition of basic health insurance across the income distribution, without undermining plans' ability to use co-insurance and other tools to influence the use of health services.

The same is true of the mortgage-interest deduction, another "upside down" preference that is more valuable for people in higher tax brackets. Researchers find that the mortgage deduction does little to encourage home ownership. Instead, it encourages middle- and upper-income taxpayers to buy bigger homes and take on more mortgage debt — neither of which is an important social goal. There is a good case, therefore, for simply eliminating the deduction. If policymakers want tax incentives for home ownership, they would be better off redesigning the deduction as a credit — one that would be both fairer and more effective. One option would be a fixed credit linked to home ownership, rather than to carrying a mortgage. For example, taxpayers might receive a fixed credit for each year they own a qualifying residence. Every taxpayer would face the same incentive and would receive the same assistance for purchasing a home. But no one would be encouraged to buy a larger house or to take on extra debt.

If policymakers want to use the tax code to encourage certain types of behavior, credits can often achieve the same results as exclusions and deductions, but more efficiently and at lower cost. Some observers may worry that greater reliance on credits would increase the amount of redistribution in the tax code, but changing the structure of tax rates could offset that effect in a broader tax reform. As both the president's fiscal commission and the Domenici-Rivlin task force demonstrated, eliminating spending-like preferences can allow for significant rate cuts even with significant deficit reduction.

### AN ESSENTIAL REFORM

Washington's love affair with tax preferences has spawned a system that is needlessly complex, economically harmful, and often unfair. Tax breaks reach into many aspects of daily life and influence many personal choices—on matters including health care, education, charitable donations, investment, saving for retirement, owning a home, and even raising children. They represent a major exercise of government power, but face less oversight than many activities on the spending side of the budget. They conceal the true size of government, and they confer enormous power upon the tax-writing committees in Congress—which have the ability to simultaneously raise revenue and spend it inside the tax code.

The time has come for serious reform. America needs to fix its broken tax system *and* find additional revenue to help reduce our persistent budget deficits. The best way to achieve both aims is to take a hatchet to the thicket of spending-like tax preferences. Many preferences should simply be eliminated; those deemed to serve important policy goals should be restructured to be simpler, fairer, and more effective. Lawmakers can then use the resulting revenue to cut tax rates across the board and reduce the deficit.

Such reform is long overdue. It won't be easy, but the enormity of our budget problems may finally be enough to get liberals, moderates, and conservatives to join together to get it done.

*Originally published as "Spending in Disguise" in the Summer 2011 issue of* National Affairs.

# How to Fix the Tax Code

## Robert Stein

For more than two decades, free-market economists and poli-cymakers have championed an agenda of comprehensive tax reform. Modeled on President Ronald Reagan's 1981 tax cuts, their plans have sought to combine further cuts in marginal income-tax rates with relief for cor-porations and investors, along with a profound simplification of the entire federal tax code. But unlike Reagan's immensely popular initiative, the reformers' campaign has gained little traction with the public—and has not been enacted even in times of Republican dominance in Washington.

At the core of this failure has been a misreading of Reagan's success. Too often, advocates of comprehensive tax reform have focused on the particular means of Reagan's plan—the lowering of marginal income-tax rates—rather than on its more general ends: correcting economic distortions caused by government policy, lightening the tax burden on American families, and encouraging more work and investment.

Lowering tax rates today could still enhance the incentives to invest, particularly in the corporate sector. But the distortions caused by mar-ginal tax rates are not nearly as great as they were in 1980. And attempts to solve other problems caused by the tax code itself—like the biases in favor of consumption over saving, or home building over business investment—could never in themselves garner the public support nec-essary for a major overhaul.

Instead, tax reformers should understand that the workplace is not the only venue in which incentives matter—and that taxpayers are not simply workers, employers, and investors. Economic man is also a family man, and the next generation of tax reform should address the distortions and burdens our fiscal policy imposes on American families.

*Robert Stein is a former deputy assistant secretary for macroeconomic analysis at the U.S. Treasury Department.*

In particular, it is time to rethink how the tax code treats parents. Too many free-market economists still see families as an afterthought—arguing that the tax code should be "neutral" about raising children, as if parenting were merely one hobby among many. But raising children is hardly just another pastime: It is one of the most important services any American can perform for our country.

Even if we ignore the societal and cultural implications of parenting and consider economic factors alone, no government—especially not a government committed to an entitlement system like ours—can be neutral toward the very existence of future generations of taxpayers. Our nation's long-term economic prospects are threatened by a declining fertility rate that, if it remains constant, will only barely manage to replace our current population. And even as Social Security and Medicare depend on large numbers of future workers, they have created an enormous fiscal bias against procreation, undermining an important motive for raising children: to safeguard against poverty in old age.

By targeting tax reforms to address these problems, policymakers would both offer meaningful relief to American families and create political opportunities to enact other pro-growth policies. Such reforms could eventually yield a much simpler tax code with lower top marginal rates on work and investment, as well as more favorable treatment for families with children. The result would be a tax-reform agenda with the right attitude toward families—and one with a chance to break the political logjam that has prevented serious change for a generation.

## THE REAGAN TAX REVOLUTION

Ever since the imposition of the federal income tax in 1913, the United States has had a system of marginal tax rates. Taxpayers are grouped into brackets based on income; those who earn more are taxed at higher rates. But the bracket into which each person falls describes only the rate at which the *last* dollar he earns is taxed. A person in the 28% tax bracket does not pay 28% of his entire income; rather, he pays 28% only on the money he earns above the income cutoff that separates him from the previous tax bracket.

For example, let's suppose that there are three tax brackets: Income up to $100 is taxed at 10%, income between $100 and $1,000 is taxed at 20%, and income above $1,000 is taxed at 50%. If a worker earns $100, he pays an income tax of $10. If a worker makes $1,000, his first $100 is taxed at 10%, while his next $900 in income is taxed at 20%. He pays a $10 tax on the first $100 of income, and $180 in taxes on the next $900 of income, for a total income-tax bill of $190. But if a worker earns $2,000, he would pay $190 on the first thousand and then a 50% tax (or $500) on the second thousand, yielding a total tax bill of $690. The nature of the marginal tax-rate system means that although his income is double that of the worker earning $1,000, his tax bill is actually more than *three times* larger—and the disproportion would grow with every dollar earned in the highest bracket.

At a certain point, rates can rise so high that workers already living comfortably with substantial income may decide that it is simply not worth working for more. The key insight of conservative economic thinking in the 1970s was that marginal tax rates were so high that they significantly undermined the incentives to work, save, and invest. Conservatives therefore argued that significant tax-rate cuts would not only put more money in taxpayers' pockets, but also encourage more economic activity, and thus greater prosperity, growth, and even government revenue.

Consider that in 1979, there were more than a dozen tax brackets—and in the top one, workers paid an income tax of 70%. Of every dollar earned beyond $108,300, a worker would keep only 30 cents. Moreover, the tax code was not indexed for inflation. So during the high-inflation 1970s, workers had additional reasons to resent the federal tax structure. First, inflation compounded the existing problems of a marginal-rate system; as salaries grew to keep pace, workers—especially those in the highest bracket—saw a greater share of their income taxed at the highest rate. And many other workers found themselves dragged into higher and higher tax brackets while the actual purchasing power of their income rose much more slowly—a process that came to be known as "bracket creep." The tax code thus further depressed the incentive for high earners to increase their productivity, and therefore depressed economic activity, investment, and growth.

In 1980, Ronald Reagan made the Kemp-Roth tax plan—including a 30% cut in all federal income-tax rates—the centerpiece of his economic agenda. Reagan's political success that year, and the strength and length of the economic expansions of the 1980s and '90s, were due largely to this one decision. Once in office, President Reagan cut tax rates across the board and indexed the tax code for inflation. Marginal income-tax rates that had ranged from 14 to 70% were cut to a range of 11 to 50%. The positive impact on work incentives for high-income households was enormous, as the workers with the most control over their work hours, output, and pay structures had a strong reason to be more productive.

In addition, the Reagan program increased the after-tax return on investment by cutting tax rates on dividends and capital gains. By encouraging greater participation in the stock market, and therefore increasing sources of capital for businesses, these improvements helped generate the great economic expansions of the 1980s and '90s. The reduction in tax rates on the highest-income households also paid for itself: As the economic boom increased individuals' wealth, the total income taxes paid by top earners *increased* as a share of gross domestic product following the Reagan tax cuts.

It is worth noting, however, that the Reagan tax cuts improved work incentives much more for higher-income households than for the middle class and the poor. While the highest-income households experienced a 67% increase in the after-tax return on additional work, a more typical middle-class household saw only an 8% increase.

This was neither class warfare nor a peculiar artifact of the Reagan tax cuts. It was the straightforward result of having a highly progressive structure of tax rates with a very high top rate. A strategy of reducing tax rates simply cannot enhance work incentives as much for those workers who already keep most of what they earn. (And in any case, those workers generally have less control over how much they can work than the rich do.)

But regardless of how they stacked up against wealthier families, there is little doubt that middle-class households liked paying less in taxes as a result of the 1981 cut. They also appreciated, and made popular, the president who put an end to inflation-related bracket creep. But it is difficult to make the case that the middle class cared very much how the tax cut was delivered; it wasn't all that meaningful to middle-income workers that they kept more money in their pockets because their *marginal* rate was lower, rather than through other mechanisms such as tax credits or adjustments to corporate taxes. The incentives guiding their economic decisions would not have been all that different had their tax bills been reduced in other ways.

It is also important to recognize that repeating Reagan's feat—using the tax code to boost incentives for the highest-earning workers to the same degree—would be simply impossible today. Even starting from a top income-tax rate of nearly 40% (which we can expect once President Bush's tax cuts expire in 2011), income taxes would have to go to zero—and not be replaced by any other tax system, like a sales tax—to generate the kind of positive work incentives the original Reagan cuts produced.

There is, of course, far more room to improve the incentives for corporate investment, the profits from which currently face two layers of taxation. And policymakers should look to cut tax rates on inherited income, which—because it has been taxed once already at the time it was earned—is also subject to double taxation. But such reforms by themselves could hardly gain the political backing or produce the economic effects of a broad-based income-tax cut.

Repeating something like Reagan's feat today would therefore require not simply imitating the particulars of his tax reform, but rather advancing its underlying aim: eliminating gross distortions that stifle economic growth and punish workers across the income scale. One such distortion does exist today, though not in the arena of marginal tax rates. A move to correct it could build the kind of political momentum ultimately needed for a broad and productive reform of the tax code.

### PARENTS AND THE TAX CODE

Today, most of the middle class finds itself in a 15% income-tax bracket that adjusts annually for inflation—and so proposals that focus on cutting marginal rates simply will not resonate as they did in 1981, when most middle-class families had been watching their marginal tax rates steadily increase for years. But federal fiscal policy still imposes a significant burden on the middle class, and especially on middle-class families. Indeed, our system of taxes and entitlements not only fails to reward parents—it actively discourages Americans from having children.

In more primitive economies, children are the primary vehicle for saving for old age. Parents provide their children with food, clothing, and shelter; eventually, the grown children take care of their elderly parents—often in the context of cultural or religious practices that serve as cross-generational enforcement devices. It all adds up to a natural incentive for fertility. Of course, parents may not explicitly have their advanced years in mind when deciding to have more children. But it is well demonstrated that this consideration—channeled through a wide variety of social and cultural institutions and signals — in fact plays an important role in such decisions.

Advanced economies, meanwhile, tend to have lower fertility rates — in part because adults can save for retirement using financial instruments, which are a partial substitute for raising children. The prevalence of public retirement systems suppresses fertility even further. Across advanced countries, those with larger public retirement systems tend to have lower fertility rates, even when controlling for a wide range of other social and economic variables (such as income levels or the education and labor-force participation of women).

In fact, a growing body of economic literature shows that in the United States, Social Security and Medicare have "crowded out" the traditional incentive to raise children as a protection against poverty in old age. Most workers foresee getting enough support from the public retirement system to stay out of poverty when they get older, making it less likely that they will have to call on direct aid — either in cash or in kind — from their own children. Recent studies (especially work by Michele Boldrin, Mariacristina De Nardi, and Larry Jones and by Isaac Ehrlich and Jinyoung Kim) show that Social Security and Medicare actually reduce the fertility rate by about 0.5 children per woman. In European countries, where retirement systems are larger, the effect is closer to one child per woman. In other words, without government-run retirement systems, both the U.S. and Western Europe would have fertility rates of about 2.5 children per woman — safely above the population-replacement rate — rather than their actual rates of about 2.1 and 1.5, respectively.

Compounding the problem is the fact that even as these systems depend upon a population of productive young workers at the national level, they diminish the economic need for children at the individual level — and so undermine their own sustainability. By having the economic benefits of children accrue only to society in the aggregate — and thereby distancing those benefits from the individual mothers and fathers who make the decisions about how many (if any) children to have — federal policy distorts incentives in ways harmful to the country's future.

Unfortunately, these negative effects on fertility cannot be cured simply by converting old-age entitlement programs into mandatory savings programs, as the Bush administration proposed for Social Security in 2005. After all, requiring workers to save for retirement through private financial instruments would also crowd out the traditional motive to raise kids.

Instead, those seeking to restore the incentives for producing new generations of Americans should push to reduce taxes on families with children. Such a reform would offset the negative bias imposed by the public retirement system. It would also communicate to Americans that people living in societies with public retirement systems must meet two obligations in order to sustain those systems: first, work and pay taxes to support the previous generation; second, raise children to support themselves when they retire. Those who do not raise children are, in effect, enjoying a partial free ride at the expense of those who do. The next great tax reform should thus begin by cutting taxes for parents.

## A NEW CHILD CREDIT

There are, of course, already some modest tax benefits attached to having children. Combining the impact of the $1,000 per-child tax credit with 15% of this year's dependent exemption of $3,650 (15% being the income-tax rate paid by most middle-class parents), it turns out that having a child today reduces the typical household's annual tax burden by a total of about $1,550. But considering both the cost and the value of raising children, $1,550 is much too low.

The exact cost of raising a child is notoriously difficult to estimate, given disparities in spending at different income levels — not to mention the countless unquantifiable factors involved. But if we take the commonly cited Department of Agriculture figure of $13,000 per child per year through age 17 (a figure that does not even account for college-education costs) — and the fact that Social Security and Medicare will absorb about 25% of the labor income of a child born today — we would find that sharing the direct financial costs of raising children to the same extent that the benefits of their future labor income will be shared would require reducing the annual tax bill of parents by $3,250 per child (25% of $13,000).

Another way of looking at the issue is to consider that the present value of future Social Security and Medicare contributions for a typical worker born today is about $150,000. Rewarding parents for creating these future contributions suggests annual tax relief of about $8,500 per child.

To correct for this inadequate treatment of households with children, the existing dependent exemption for children, the child credit, the child-care credit, and the adoption credit should be replaced with one new $4,000 credit per child that can be used to offset both income and payroll taxes. (This amount is set much closer to the $3,250 figure than the $8,500 one mostly to reduce the plan's negative impact on federal revenue.)

The new child credit would accomplish several significant policy goals. First, it would offset the anti-parenting bias created by Social Security and Medicare. Second, the credit would help simplify the tax code by getting rid of other exemptions and credits that apply to children. Third, and very important for many families, it would end the bias against families with a stay-at-home parent now caused by the child-care credit (which applies only if both parents are working for pay). And finally, it would reduce effective marginal tax rates for many middle-class families.

Such an approach would also be very popular with a vital political constituency—middle-class parents—thereby opening the way to further tax reforms that would both help to pay for the new credit and correct other important deficiencies in the tax code. It could stand as the centerpiece of a new tax-cutting agenda.

### THE NEXT TAX REFORM

Reducing the fiscal burden on parents is very important, but it should not be the only prominent goal of the next wave of tax reform. Reformers should also reduce the worst distortions in the income-tax code itself, including the multiple layers of tax on corporate profits and the highest regular income-tax rate. As they do so, their other key aim should be simplification—to help clean up the mess the tax code has become since the last major overhaul in 1986.

All of these goals can be accomplished by making limited changes to the existing tax code, rather than pushing for a utopian "big bang" tax-reform plan (like a flat tax or retail sales tax).

First, to remove impediments to capital investment, we should adopt Columbia Business School dean Glenn Hubbard's proposal to let companies take the profits on which they pay taxes—plus interest earned from tax-free municipal bonds—and distribute them to shareholders tax-free. Corporate profits would therefore no longer face two layers of taxation, just one. Additionally, capital investment should be promoted by letting companies count 25% of plant and equipment spending as business expenses in the year the purchases are made, rather than using the current slower depreciation schedules. Cutting the effective tax rate on capital investment would encourage equity financing of new investment, raise workers' wages, create new jobs, and improve the competitiveness of American firms.

Second, to simplify the tax code, we should scrap the individual Alternative Minimum Tax and all itemized deductions except for two that are very popular with the voting public: those for mortgage interest and charitable donations. These two deductions would then be made available to all taxpayers, not only itemizers. The goal, however, would be to make the revenue losses associated with the two deductions the same as they are under current law — which means the principal amount on which mortgage interest could be deducted would have to be reduced, and the maximum size of the charitable deduction would have to be decreased.

After taking these deductions, but before receiving any tax credits, individuals should face only two income-tax rates (compared to the current six). The rates should be set at 15% and 35%, and the width of the 15% bracket should be twice the size for married couples as for singles. In addition, these tax rates should be halved to 7.5% and 17.5% for inherited income (above generous exemptions) and capital gains (other than on corporate shares, which would get the more favorable treatment of the Hubbard proposal). For reference, the top official income-tax rate is likely to be at least 39.6% once the Bush tax cuts expire in 2011 — and high-earning Americans could see even more of their money go to the IRS, given the way that some exemptions and deductions phase out at higher incomes. Depending on the outcome of legislative efforts to further socialize the health-care system, these rates — and Americans' tax bills — could go far higher still.

Next, whatever taxes filers owe would be reduced by two new tax credits. The standard deduction and personal exemption for each filer would be replaced by a tax credit of $2,000 that could be used to reduce income taxes only. Each year, the $2,000 figure would be adjusted for inflation. This credit would take the benefits of the standard deduction, the personal exemption for filers, and the tax relief associated with today's 10% bracket and compress them into one simple calculation. A married couple with no children, for example, would reduce their income-tax payment by up to $4,000. (Though if they owed, for instance, $3,000 in income taxes before applying the filer credit, their income-tax bill would only go down to zero; they would not get a rebate in excess of income taxes paid.)

After the filer credit, the new $4,000 per-child credit comes into play, offsetting both income *and* payroll taxes. Moreover, with each passing year, the size of the credit would grow at the same rate as the taxable wage base for Social Security, which means it would generally grow faster than inflation.

Why adjust the filer credit by inflation but the child credit by wage growth? The purpose of the filer credit is to ensure that all taxpayers can earn the basic costs of living—food, clothing, and shelter—without having to pay any income taxes. Over time, the basic cost of living should rise with inflation. The purpose of the child credit, however, is not only to let parents deduct the costs of creating the next generation of taxpayers, but also to reward parents for raising the future workers who will support the public retirement system. The amount of that future support will, naturally, be tied to overall wage growth. And if the child credit grew only with inflation, each year would gradually erode the incentive parents have to raise children relative to those children's future payroll contributions—thereby undermining a key rationale for offering the credit in the first place.

Under this new tax system, most singles would get a tax cut of $175 while most married couples without children would get a tax cut of $350. But the biggest impact would be felt by parents. Take a married couple with two children, earning $70,000 a year: Under current law, this family generates income taxes of about $5,800 and payroll taxes of $10,710 (combining the employee and employer sides of Social Security and Medicare). But under the tax structure outlined above, their income taxes would be completely eliminated and they would also receive a $1,500 credit against their payroll taxes. They would thus enjoy a tax cut of more than $7,000 per year compared to what they currently pay.

Notice how the child credit enhances this family's work incentives at the same time that it acknowledges the immense benefits their decision to raise children will confer on the country. If the family generates an additional $5,000 in income, their income taxes do not go up at all. In effect, they face a marginal income-tax rate of zero.

From the standpoint of federal revenue, the child credit and the filer credit are the most "expensive" items, with the child-credit expansion likely reducing revenue by about $200 billion per year and the filer credit costing another $100 billion per year (after accounting for the elimination of the standard deduction and personal exemptions). Some of these costs would be offset by eliminating itemized deductions (other than mortgage interest and charitable contributions). The rest would have to be offset by allowing the top rate of 35% to touch more taxpayers than it currently affects.

Overall, the plan is designed to be revenue neutral—and yet most taxpayers without children will pay a little bit less in taxes, while middle-class families with children under 18 years of age will pay substantially less. So who pays more? Primarily high-income workers, but also upper-middle-class taxpayers who do not have children in the home (either because they have decided not to raise children at all, or because their children have already turned 18).

To be blunt, the plan is a tax hike on the rich and makes the tax code even more progressive than it is today. Given the loss of the state and local tax deduction, the tax hike will be particularly acute for high earners from high-tax states. And although the top income-tax rate would be capped at 35%, that rate would kick in at lower income levels than it does today. The result would be a marginal tax-rate hike—and a corresponding weakening of work incentives—for many workers who today find themselves in the 25%, 28%, and 33% brackets.

But the effect of this change on the overall economy is likely to be small. Most of the income taxed at those rates actually comes from wealthier people, passing through the upper-middle brackets on their way to earning their last dollars in the top bracket. Applying a higher rate of 35% to more of their income will not make them happy, but it should not dramatically change their incentive to work. Meanwhile, with the top rate set at 35%, rather than the 39.6% or more now scheduled for 2011, the very highest earners will have greater incentive to work harder and more productively.

### ANSWERING CRITICS

This agenda would no doubt face resistance from some anti-tax purists. For instance, many conservatives over the years have developed an allergy to any mention of tax credits, and for good reason. Often tax credits phase out over the upper income brackets, which means that earning more money can end up costing a worker his credit—effectively resulting in higher marginal tax rates. Another problem is that checks for tax credits are often mailed out regardless of how much a worker has paid in taxes (or whether he has paid taxes at all); this can convert a tax credit into a de facto welfare payment.

Some may argue that the plan outlined here is much the same thing: a large welfare-style transfer payment. But the child credit is not a welfare check sent to unemployed adults just because they have more kids. If one has no labor income, one simply does not receive the credit. And once a household has no more income or payroll tax to offset, having more children gets the family nothing. Nor does the child credit turn raising children into a money machine: Anyone who has children knows that $4,000 per year is only a fraction of the actual cost of raising them. Moreover, given the generosity the tax code already shows low-wage parents, the new credit would not be available to those taking the Earned Income Tax Credit. It's either-or, not both.

Others may object that, over time, there is actually no net government revenue gain to raising more children, because those children will grow up to draw on public retirement benefits. But in a mature public retirement system, the amount of benefits available for each generation of workers depends largely on the aggregate earning power of that generation's children. Whether those children will get anything themselves is not a foregone conclusion; it depends on the aggregate earning power of *their* children. No matter how you slice it, encouraging more children will mean more government revenue to support current entitlement commitments — and, if the incentives stay on the books, will probably help pay for the next generation's as well.

Some may also worry that having fewer workers pay taxes each year will increase the electorate's appetite for more government, since fewer people would directly feel government's cost. These critics point out that as things stand now, in a given year, the top 40% of earners pay about 99% of federal income taxes. Factoring in other federal taxes — like those on payrolls and corporate profits, and excise taxes — the top 40% of earners each year generate about 85% of that year's federal tax revenue. There is no escaping the fact that the tax proposal outlined here would increase the share of annual taxes paid by the highest earners, and decrease the share of the U.S. population that pays income taxes in a given year.

But annual snapshots can be deceiving, because most workers move across different income groups during their lifetimes. And just as tax cuts for the highest brackets are eventually enjoyed by many more people than those who happen to be in the top brackets during the year the cuts are enacted, so too will people who drop off the tax rolls in one year likely find themselves paying taxes again in another.

Moreover, no economic analysis has actually shown a relationship between moving more citizens off the tax rolls and increased support for larger government. Indeed, there is evidence indicating the opposite. Economist Gary Becker has shown that countries with flatter tax systems tend to have larger governments, as the burden of new spending proposals can be spread across a wider tax base — which means fewer taxpayers care enough at the individual level to resist the expansion of government.

Even more important, the tax proposal outlined here does not simply reduce the tax rolls based on income. Instead, it reduces the tax rolls based on *parenting*. This is a crucial difference. Some low-income earners might imagine themselves earning little for the foreseeable future, based simply on their experience to date. As a result, voting for more government might appear to be a bargain for them. But parents know that their children are not going be 17 or younger forever. And given the generous size of the tax credit, they will know that when their children are old enough to leave home their tax bills will spike — giving parents a good reason to restrain the growth of government. Moreover, reducing the high cost of raising children could make many middle-class parents less likely to support government spending, not more — since a lack of cash resources during their parenting years is one reason they might pursue more government favors in the first place.

One final potential criticism of this plan is that it too heavily favors parents over non-parents. But the plan outlined here includes many work and investment incentives that benefit parents and non-parents equally — such as cutting the top marginal income-tax rate, eliminating the double taxation of corporate profits, and providing faster depreciation for purchases of plant and equipment.

And in the end, it is right and proper to show some favor to parents. Our country is not comprised of individuals who simply fall out of the sky as fully grown citizens — and our civilization's continued existence hinges on the willingness and desire of adults to raise children. Our public policy can no longer fail to reward those who do.

## A PRO-FAMILY TAX AGENDA

Tax policy will soon be front and center again in our politics. Ongoing efforts to expand the entitlement system will inevitably generate a discussion about overhauling our tax system. Treasury Secretary Tim

Geithner and White House economic advisor Lawrence Summers have both refused to rule out tax hikes on the middle class. Next year, at the behest of the president, former Federal Reserve chairman Paul Volcker may even deliver a proposal to impose a European-style value-added tax on Americans.

Opponents of these ideas will need to present their own version of tax reform, and it cannot be the same agenda that has failed to gain traction for decades. They will need a plan that makes the tax code simpler and more efficient, corrects unfair distortions, pulls our entitlement programs back from the brink of bankruptcy, and helps American families with tangible tax relief. For reformers serious about achieving these aims, recognizing and rewarding the vital role of parents is the best place to start.

*Originally published as "Taxes and the Family" in the Winter 2010 issue of* National Affairs.

# IV. Financial and Monetary Reform

# How to Regulate Risk on Wall Street

## Oliver Hart and Luigi Zingales

SPRING 2010

THE FINANCIAL CRISIS OF 2008 had many causes. They ranged from a housing bubble to excessive speculation, and from inadequate accounting rules to reckless corporate governance. But at the heart of the meltdown were the financial industry's distorted incentives — created in large part by decades of misguided government policy — which caused bankers and investors to take enormous risks without due regard for their consequences.

The easiest way to make money on Wall Street was (and remains) heavy borrowing and extreme risk-taking. The reason is simple: There has long been a sense — which has only grown stronger over the past year — that the government will step in if the situation gets out of hand. Anyone who runs a large financial institution and makes a huge bet on a loan or investment understands that one of two outcomes is now possible: Either he'll get lucky and make a bundle, or he'll get unlucky and walk away (with Uncle Sam left holding the bag). Why should the titans of finance bother to keep risk in check if the government is going to bail out ruined gamblers? Being judged too important to the economy to fail is a financial institution's one sure bet.

Although much has changed in the wake of the crisis, this basic dynamic has not. If anything, it has grown worse. This was affirmed in October by Neil Barofsky, the special inspector general of the Treasury's Troubled Asset Relief Program. Responding to a question about whether the situation had improved over the previous year, Barofsky said:

> I think, actually, what's changed is in the other direction. These banks that were too big to fail are now bigger. Government has

OLIVER HART *is the Andrew E. Furer Professor of Economics at Harvard University.*

LUIGI ZINGALES *is the Robert C. McCormack Professor of Entrepreneurship and Finance at the University of Chicago Booth School of Business.*

sponsored and supported several mergers that made them larger. And that guarantee—that implicit guarantee of moral hazard, the idea that the government is not going to let these banks fail—which was implicit a year ago, it's now explicit.

The message to Wall Street has clearly been that large financial institutions are now shielded from the consequences of their own decisions.

It is even possible to assign a numerical measurement to this expansion of the "too big to fail" regime. As a recent study by Dean Baker and Travis McArthur showed, the advantages large banks enjoy over small banks have only increased since the crisis. Between 2000 and 2007, large banks (those with assets of more than $100 billion) could borrow money at interest rates that were about 0.29 percentage points lower than those available to smaller banks. In the period since, the spread has grown to 0.49 percentage points. This increased spread is the market's estimate of the benefit of the implicit insurance offered to large banks by the "too big to fail" policy.

For the 18 American banks with more than $100 billion each in assets, this advantage corresponds to a roughly $34 billion total subsidy per year. This subsidy distorts the marketplace by hampering the ability of small banks to compete, which in turn leads to greater bank concentration. This increases the power of banks at the expense of depositors and borrowers, and all but ensures that banks will be even bigger the next time a rescue gets called in. In 1998, the Federal Reserve Bank of New York only had to coordinate a rescue of Long Term Capital Management, costing the major creditors $3.6 billion. In 2008, the government had to spend $700 billion to save the whole financial sector. What will we face in 2018 if we don't change course?

And yet changing course is far from easy. The government's serial-bailout approach can't just be written off as indulgent folly: In many cases, it has been the most practicable response to very real threats to the financial system, and to the lack of options for assessing and constraining the risks taken by large financial players. But what the Obama administration has proposed as an alternative is hardly an improvement: Its regulatory approach would throw the baby out with the bathwater, preventing American banks from competing and thriving in an attempt to keep their risk-taking in check.

What we need now is a better way to judge and restrain that risk, but without placing undue constraints on economic growth and the freedom of the market. Of course, balancing these two crucial yet seemingly divergent aims will be no small feat.

If "too big to fail" is so evidently bad, what other options do we have? One approach would be to remove the implicit guarantee given to large banks by making it clear that the government will not step in to protect them should they fail. But such pledges alone would not get us very far, as policymakers in a crisis would be very unlikely to hold to them — and might even be wrong to. The sudden failure of a large bank could in fact be catastrophic for the nation's financial system. And when politicians are faced with catastrophe, long-term concerns tend to take a back seat to the immediate crisis.

Another option is to make the alternatives to intervention more palatable. This is the logic behind the Obama administration's proposal that financial institutions prepare so-called "living wills" — contingency plans for how to unwind their obligations in the event of failure at minimal cost to the system. All market players would understand in advance what would be involved in the failure of a particular institution, and it would be clear to all that massive intervention would not be required and, more important, should not be expected. In principle, this is a good idea; in practice, however, every institution would have a strong incentive to sabotage its own "living will" — designing it so that it would fail to protect the system from the shock of the firm's collapse, and so requiring the government to step in and keep the firm afloat.

A third option would be to avoid the circumstances that create the need for interventions, by restricting the risks that financial institutions can take. If neither government nor the firms can be relied on to refrain from passing the costs of excessive risk-taking on to the public, then the risk-taking itself should be prevented.

This is clearly the best option for changing the behavior of large financial institutions and correcting the distorted incentives that produced such disastrous consequences in the past few years. But everything depends on just how the particular remedy would be carried out in practice.

Many proponents of this approach suggest severely restricting the activities in which large financial institutions may engage, in essence radically simplifying the nature and range of permissible transactions. This is what the Obama administration has recently proposed — prohibiting banks from owning, investing in, or advising hedge funds or private-equity funds, and prohibiting proprietary trading with bank funds. Such a policy would be very costly and doomed to fail: very costly because it would require prohibiting the involvement of large financial institutions in an enormous range of financial activities that now allow them to profit and compete; doomed to fail because such regulations are extremely easy to bypass. It takes no time for a clever financier to design a contract that gets around most restrictions. Most important, the 2008 financial crisis was not caused by deposit-taking banks that assumed excessive risk through their proprietary trading desks, but rather by investment banks that took excessive risk in their portfolios and by commercial banks underwriting too many bad real-estate loans. President Obama's proposal would not prevent either of these activities.

Instead of restricting particular activities, then, regulators should restrict the total amount of risk that large financial institutions may undertake. In what follows, we propose a means of doing exactly that, while minimizing the burdens of such restrictions on the larger economy.

In general terms, this is not a new idea in banking regulation. It is in the spirit of the Basel I and Basel II accords of 1988 and 2004, in which many of the world's central bankers agreed to establish some minimal capital requirements for banks to help safeguard their solvency. But our proposal differs from the Basel approach in two key respects.

First, it does not put its faith in the abilities of rating agencies to assess the risks taken by financial institutions, as the Basel accords did. Rating agencies are useful up to a point. But when a change in rating can unleash enormous economic consequences, rating agencies cannot be relied on to make the right call, because they are extremely sensitive to the practical outcomes of their decisions. American International Group was still rated AA two days before it received an $85 billion bailout from the government.

Second, our proposal would not place its trust in regulators themselves to act in time, since the incentives they face almost always argue against swift action before a crisis. There is no political payoff for an early intervention, especially given the uncertainty that surrounds all such decisions. After Washington Mutual was taken over in 2008, there were still people complaining that the government acted too early. Preventive banking regulation is something like pre-emptive war: There is no credit for the pain avoided, while there is plenty of blame for the pain inflicted. Experience shows that regulators simply cannot be relied upon to resist these pressures.

Any successful mechanism to contain the risks that large financial institutions take, and so to avoid future bailouts, would therefore have to be driven not by refereeing institutions but by the market itself. It would need to rely on the market's ability to collect relevant information promptly, and to make it known widely.

### REGULATING RISK

How can the market be expected to assess the risks large institutions take if market players know that those institutions will eventually be bailed out in a crunch? The very existence of the "too big to fail" policy makes it extremely difficult for the market to usefully measure and analyze such risks.

Fortunately, the logic behind "too big to fail" itself may actually offer a way around this problem. As many observers have noted, the government's reason for bailing out large financial institutions is not exactly that these firms are so large that their failures would crush the whole system. Rather, the government's concern has been that these firms are so *interconnected* with other financial institutions—through their various transactions, obligations, and contracts—that a default might trigger losses among an enormous number of counterparties, producing further defaults that would cascade out of control.

To function properly, the financial system needs to operate under the assumption that certain assets, such as deposits, are "worry free." Depositors with money in, say, checking and savings accounts should not have to monitor counterparty solvency, or worry about which banks their bank is dealing with. This sense of security saves a great deal of anxiety and cost—which ultimately allows the system to operate more efficiently. But this belief can be sustained only if the prompt and full repayment of so-called "sensitive" or "systemically relevant" obligations is not in question. People need to know that not just bank deposits, but also short-term interbank borrowing and the network of derivative contracts, are secure enough that they won't suffer even if their bank collapses. In a system built on trust and confidence, the fundamentals have to be secure to allow people to take sensible risks at the margins.

Once we understand that the issue addressed by "too big to fail" is the interconnectedness of large financial institutions, and therefore the stability of the larger system, we can make some important distinctions. Not all of the debt held by large financial institutions, and not all of the transactions they engage in, are systemically relevant in this way, and so in need of such total protection. Specifically, long-term debt is not "systemically relevant." There is no reason for a large financial institution to hold bonds or other long-term debt in other financial institutions. This debt mostly resides in the massive portfolios of mutual funds and pension funds, which can absorb losses in the value of such debt in the same way they absorb losses from equity investments. A default on that debt, therefore, would not trigger a cascade of bank failures the way a default on short-term debt could.

Our proposal, then, is for a new system of regulation that protects the systemically relevant obligations of large financial institutions — making sure they would be repaid by the institution (not by taxpayers) in the case of bankruptcy — but leaves open the possibility that non-systemically relevant obligations will not be protected.

Under this new system, banks would be required to hold two layers of capital to protect their systemically relevant obligations. The first layer would be basic equity — not much different from today's standard capital requirement, except for the fact that the amount of equity required would be determined not by an accounting formula, but by a market assessment of the risk contained in the second layer.

That second layer would consist of so-called "junior long-term debt." Being explicitly labeled "junior" means this debt would be repaid only after the institution has made good on its other debt, and so also means that it would involve more risk for those who buy it (therefore offering higher rates of return). Such debt would provide an added layer of protection to basic equity because, in the event the institution defaulted, the junior long-term debt could be paid back only after other (more systemically relevant) obligations have been repaid. Perhaps most important, because this layer of debt would be traded without the assumption that it would always be protected by federal bailouts, it would make possible a genuine market assessment of its value and risk — and therefore of those of the financial institution itself.

This is the crucial innovation of the approach we propose. The required second layer of capital would allow for a market-based trigger to signal that a firm's equity cushion is thinning, that its long-term debt is potentially in danger, and therefore that the financial institution is taking on too much risk. If that warning mechanism provides accurate signals, and if the regulator intervenes in time, even the junior long-term debt will be paid in full. If either of these two conditions is not met, the institution may burn through some of the junior-debt layer—but its systemically relevant obligations will generally still be secure. In this case, the firm may suffer, but the larger financial system will be kept safe.

This remedy would work more or less as a margin-call system does in the stock market. When an investor buys stocks on margin, he puts down only part of the cost; as a result, he must show that he has enough collateral to cover the risk his broker is taking in lending him the money to make up the difference. If the stock price drops below an agreed-upon level, that risk increases. The broker then issues a "margin call"—which means the buyer must either provide additional collateral or sell his stocks to pay back the broker in full. The system of financial regulation we are proposing would treat large banks the same way: They would have to show the regulator that they have enough collateral (in the form of equity) to ensure that all of their debt—not just the systemically relevant part—could be paid in full. And if declines in the value of their underlying assets put the banks' debt at greater risk, they would face a kind of margin call from the regulator, forcing them to either post additional capital or submit to liquidation—allowing their debt to be repaid either way.

The success of this system rests, of course, on the timely intervention of the regulator tasked with making that "margin call." If the intervention were too slow in coming, the bank's long-term creditors could be at risk (though as long as the delay was not too severe, the systemic obligations would still be shielded). Thus, it is essential to have an effective mechanism that assesses risk and triggers a response—operating as both a warning to the regulator and a means of compelling him to act swiftly.

### A MARKET-BASED TRIGGER

In a normal margin account, a broker considers the total value of the investment—which is easily determined, since all assets are traded—and compares the value of the collateral his client has posted with the likely risk of loss. If the collateral is insufficient to cover a plausible decline in the stock's value, he calls for more collateral. In the system we propose, of course, the value of the "investments" (that is, the value of the financial institution's assets) is not as easy to determine, because the assets—commercial loans and home-equity lines, for example—are not standardized and not frequently traded; they do not have a clear price. It is therefore difficult to tell when the equity the bank has posted is too thin to protect the existing debt—and so difficult to know when the bank has taken on too much risk. In addition, debt holders are often dispersed, and incapable of coordinating a margin call. If a margin-call approach is to be followed, then, it requires an easily observable, automatic trigger.

Ideally, such a trigger would be market based—i.e., tied to the price of some traded security. This means it would incorporate and reflect all the information available in the market, which traders gather because it is profitable for them to know it. The breadth and diversity of the market also mean that such a signal would be hard to corrupt, and not subject to political pressures like those that can be focused upon a single credit-rating agency or government regulator.

To avoid unnecessary fluctuations and false alarms, the trigger should also be a security traded in a market with a lot of liquidity, and therefore stability. And its price should be closely linked to the financial event we want information about: in this case, the fact that an institution's long-term debt is at risk.

Equity prices, for instance, fail to satisfy this final criterion. As long as there is the possibility of a significant upside, equity prices will stay relatively high even when the company is close to bankruptcy and the debt is at risk of not being paid in full.

The price of the junior long-term debt would be a better place to look. When the equity cushion is running thin, that long-term debt becomes endangered and will start trading below par. This option, though, fails to meet another criterion: The bond market, where such debt might be traded, is highly segmented and illiquid; bond prices are therefore unreliable signals.

There is, however, a security that is linked to bond prices but remains very liquid: the credit default swap. A credit default swap is essentially an insurance claim that pays off if the underlying entity fails and creditors are not paid in full. The buyer of a CDS for a bank's debt, for instance, makes periodic payments to the seller (which is a third party, not the bank itself) and receives a payoff if the bank defaults on that debt. (A CDS differs from insurance, however, in that the buyer need not actually own the underlying security—e.g., the bank's debt.)

Since a CDS is basically a bet on the odds of a particular firm's failure, the CDS price reflects the market's assessment of how likely it is that the firm's debt will not be repaid in full. It thus offers exactly the instrument we seek. Under our system, the CDS price for a bank's long-term debt would be used to gauge the risk of the equity cushion's being devoured by losses. If the CDS price were to rise above a critical threshold—thereby flagging imminent danger—the regulator would force the institution in question to issue equity (that is, to offer new stock for sale) until the CDS price moved back below the threshold. If the price did not fall below that threshold within a predetermined period of time, the regulator would intervene.

Credit default swaps have developed a bad reputation lately, as they are often cited as one of the causes of the financial crisis. The problem, though, was not with credit default swaps as such, but with the way they were traded. To profit from the higher margins available in an opaque market, large banks lobbied heavily against requiring credit default swaps to be traded in an open exchange and to be properly collateralized. A seller in the futures market, for instance, has to update his collateral position daily, which protects the buyer against the risk of the seller's default. But the CDS market before the crisis required no such protections—allowing AIG, for example, to sell enormous amounts of "insurance" without posting the proper collateral. When the risk increased and the buyers asked for the collateral, AIG had to be rescued. So credit default swaps are not bad per se; they can be dangerous only to the extent that they are not properly collateralized. When traded in an organized exchange, the CDS is a very useful instrument for reducing the exposure to credit risk—and its price offers just the signal upon which our system relies. Fortunately, there is now a clear trend toward moving credit default swaps onto exchanges, which will naturally require better collateralization to protect the exchanges' members. Thus it seems likely that CDS prices will become increasingly reliable.

Another benefit of this transparent, market-based signal is that it helps to address two major risks posed by regulatory intervention in the financial system. One is that a regulator could arbitrarily close down well-functioning financial institutions for political reasons. The other is that a regulator, under intense lobbying by the regulated, can be too soft—a phenomenon known in the banking literature as "regulatory forbearance" (and a contributing factor to the 2008 crisis). Our mechanism removes most of the regulator's discretion to make either error: The regulator cannot intervene if market prices do not signal distress, and yet it would be difficult for the regulator to avoid intervening when the market *does* signal — to everyone — that a firm is in trouble. As added incentive, we would allow bondholders in a regulated institution to sue the regulator if the trigger were clearly set off without any action being taken. Since the required subsequent intervention would stabilize the value of the bonds, bondholders would have a legitimate cause of action.

And just what form should the regulator's intervention take? Here, too, we think the presence of a market-based trigger for action makes it possible to adopt targeted, prudent measures that avert both overreaction and under-response.

If the trigger were to be set off by a too-high CDS price, the regulator would be required to carry out a "stress test" on the financial institution to determine if it is indeed at risk. In a stress test, regulators use sophisticated algorithms to run "what if" scenarios that examine whether a financial institution has sufficient assets to survive serious financial shocks. A stress test should precede any other action, so that extraneous panic is not allowed to bring down financial institutions unnecessarily. If, for instance, a few significant hedge funds or other investors lost confidence in a bank on the basis of a rumor or misperception about its strength, and began to buy credit default swaps as protection against its failure, the CDS price would rise and might trigger regulatory action. It is important that the regulator first test the validity of the concern before acting on it.

If the bank passed the test and showed the regulator that the CDS price was not accurate, the regulator would then declare the company adequately capitalized. But if the bank failed the test, the debt was found to be at risk, and issuing equity did not improve its situation, the regulator would replace the institution's CEO with a receiver or trustee. This person would be required to recapitalize and sell the company, guaranteeing in the process that shareholders were wiped out and creditors — while not wiped out — received a "haircut," meaning that the value of what they were owed would be reduced by some set percentage. That haircut is crucial in ensuring that the market prices credit default swaps in a way that takes regulator interventions seriously — showing that creditors will pay a price for an institution's failure — and so makes the trigger more reliable.

This regulatory receivership would be similar to a mild form of bankruptcy. But while it would achieve the chief goals of bankruptcy—imposing discipline on investors and management—it would avoid bankruptcy's worst cost: the possibility that one firm's failure could take down the entire financial system.

A potential risk of this proposal is that the news that a regulator is performing a stress test on a bank might scare off the short-term creditors and induce a run on the bank. This problem can easily be fixed by having the regulator temporarily guarantee the bank's senior debt for the brief period of the stress test itself. With our early-warning system and double layer of protection, the systemic obligations (which in our mechanism are all "senior" debt) will essentially always be paid. So the government is not assuming real risk; it is only defusing the risk of a run. This guarantee can then be lifted when the bank is deemed well capitalized (and more junior debt is issued) or, if the bank is put into receivership, when it emerges from receivership.

## THE CONCEPT IN PRACTICE

In addition to setting out the conceptual case for the trigger and the form of intervention, putting this approach into practice requires us to specify two parameters: the particular size of the junior-debt cushion financial institutions should be required to have, and the particular threshold CDS price for triggering regulatory action.

The best way to estimate both is to try to apply our proposal to the financial crisis of 2008. When we do, the first thing we learn is that the CDS rate is in fact a powerful predictor of the fate of large financial institutions in a crisis. Table 1 shows the one-year CDS rates for the nation's largest financial institutions throughout the crisis in basis points per year. (A CDS rate of 11 basis points means that it costs $11 to insure a $10,000 debt against default for a year.) The dates we have chosen are what is now taken to be approximately the beginning of the crisis, the end of 2007, the date of the rescue of Bear Stearns, and the date the initial TARP proposal was rejected by Congress.

While it is true that the CDS market did not anticipate any problem until the summer of 2007, after that point the market provided a remarkably accurate indicator of the eventual fate of the major financial institutions. As the table makes clear, the market early on singled out Washington Mutual and Bear Stearns as the two most problematic institutions. In fact, if one had to predict in August 2007 the five institutions that would go under first on the basis of their CDS rates, one would be correct in four out of five cases. By the end of 2007, the data showed a decisive worsening of the situations of the investment banks and Washington Mutual. In late December, the market put the probability of Washington Mutual's defaulting within a year at 10%. By March 2008, that estimate had risen to 30%—and yet the regulator waited until September 25 to take over the bank.

TABLE I: ONE-YEAR CDS RATES OF THE MAJOR FINANCIAL INSTITUTIONS AT KEY DATES DURING THE CRISIS

| Financial Institution | 8/15/2007 | 12/31/2007 | 3/14/2008 | 9/29/2008 |
|---|---|---|---|---|
| Bank of America | 11 | 29 | 93 | 124 |
| Wells Fargo | 23 | 45 | 113 | 113 |
| J.P. Morgan | 19 | 32 | 141 | 103 |
| Citigroup | 15 | 62 | 225 | 462 |
| Wachovia | 14 | 73 | 229 | 527 |
| Washington Mutual | 44 | 422 | 1,181 | 3,305 |
| Goldman Sachs | 28 | 78 | 262 | 715 |
| Morgan Stanley | 31 | 129 | 403 | 1,748 |
| Merrill Lynch | 29 | 159 | 410 | 666 |
| Lehman Brothers | 38 | 100 | 572 | 1,128 |
| Bear Stearns | 113 | 224 | 1,264 | 118 |
| AIG | 31 | 59 | 289 | 821 |

All figures are in basis points per year.

This history of the crisis read through the lens of CDS rates can also help us see approximately where and when the CDS-rate trigger should be set. If our goal is to intervene between, say, six and nine months in advance of a genuine failure, we can go back and see how high the CDS rates of failed institutions were six to nine months before the failures occurred. We can then determine the false positive rate by looking at how many stable institutions the trigger mechanism would have flagged as questionable.

Table 2 presents a one-month average of one-year CDS rates six months and nine months before the "failures" of major institutions. We use failure here loosely, because Bear Stearns, Merrill Lynch, AIG, and Citigroup did not fail—they were of course rescued by the government, either through a shotgun wedding or a direct taxpayer bailout. The classification "surviving" is also open to debate, since Goldman Sachs and Morgan Stanley could also be said to have been saved by the government. But these labels generally correspond to how the practical fate of these institutions has been understood.

### TABLE 2: TRIGGER RULE SIMULATIONS

| "Failed" Institution | Date of "Failure" | Average CDS Six Months Prior | Average CDS Nine Months Prior |
|---|---|---|---|
| Bear Stearns | 3/14/2008 | 121 | 10 |
| Lehman Brothers | 9/15/2008 | 288 | 106 |
| Washington Mutual | 9/25/2008 | 957 | 430 |
| Wachovia | 9/30/2008 | 176 | 45 |
| Merrill Lynch | 9/15/2008 | 282 | 177 |
| AIG | 9/16/2008 | 234 | 70 |
| Citigroup | 9/30/2008 | 162 | 44 |

All figures are in basis points per year.

As the table demonstrates, all the "failed" institutions had CDS rates above 100 basis points six months before collapsing; only Lehman Brothers and Washington Mutual had CDS rates above 100 nine months before they went under. With the exception of Bear Stearns, though, all of the institutions had CDS rates above 40 nine months before their respective failures.

In Table 3 we look at the false positives; that is, when the institutions that did not fail would have first set off our market-based trigger.

### TABLE 3: FALSE POSITIVE SIMULATIONS

| "Surviving" Institution | False Positive Date with Trigger at 100 | False Positive Date with Trigger at 40 |
|---|---|---|
| Bank of America | 9/22/2008 | 1/22/2008 |
| Wells Fargo | 9/18/2008 | 11/23/2007 |
| J.P. Morgan | 9/29/2008 | 2/15/2008 |
| Goldman Sachs | 2/14/2008 | 8/20/2007 |
| Morgan Stanley | 11/13/2007 | 8/22/2007 |

All figures are in basis points per year.

For the commercial banks—Bank of America, J.P. Morgan Chase, and Wells Fargo—the 100 basis points threshold would have been crossed only after the Lehman failure that sent the financial industry into a panic. For the two investment banks—Goldman Sachs and

Morgan Stanley—it would have been crossed in February 2008 and in November 2007, respectively. It is unclear, though, whether these are really false positives: One could easily argue in retrospect that these two institutions did in fact need more capital back then. The 40 basis points threshold, by contrast, definitely seems to generate too many false positives—since it would have triggered an intervention in Wells Fargo back in November 2007. A trigger at 100 basis points therefore seems roughly appropriate.

With the benefit of this information, we can also consider the appropriate size of the junior-debt cushion. Given our trigger rule and the potential delays in a regulator's response, the junior-debt layer should be thick enough to fully protect the systemically relevant debt. Suppose we wanted to make sure each institution had a sufficient cushion to endure a delay of six months: It would be reasonable for us to set the rules such that after an institution has exhausted its equity layer, the probability of its running through the junior-debt layer in six months is less than 5%. If asset volatility is around 8% per year, our calculations suggest that maintaining a layer of junior long-term debt worth roughly 11% of assets will offer the necessary protection. By today's standards, this figure is hardly high: For the eight largest banks, the long-term debt-to-asset ratio in September 2008 was 19%. A new regulatory system that required a CDS rate below 100 and a long-term debt layer of at least 11% would therefore not be a great burden for the major banks today.

The key to our proposal is not the toughness of the initial rules, but rather the promptness of the corrective action triggered by a market signal. This lack of a harsh crackdown means the transition to our system would be relatively painless for the banks. Our approach would also have several other significant advantages over today's regulatory system, not to mention most of the ideas for reform now being proposed and debated. For one thing, it would be quite simple, and not very different from the system of capital requirements currently in place. Second, it would be easily applicable to diverse financial institutions—such as hedge funds and insurance companies, as well as banks—if policymakers wanted to expand its reach. Many mechanisms designed explicitly for banks would be difficult to adapt to other financial institutions, but our system is based on three simple concepts that are easily portable: an equity cushion, a junior-debt cushion, and a CDS trigger. Third, this approach would overcome the natural tendency of regulators to forbear by introducing a trigger determined not by one person but by the whole market. Last, but surely not least, our mechanism would not rely on significant amounts of taxpayer money.

### BEYOND TOO BIG TO FAIL

The financial crisis of 2008 resulted from a series of misguided policies, failures of regulation, and missed signals. Unfortunately, much of the conversation about regulatory reform since has revolved around ideas that would only extend and exacerbate all three. Even worse, the actions taken in the aftermath of the crisis — and the remedies now being proposed — seem likely to further solidify the dangerous perception that some institutions are just too big to fail.

That perception dulls competition and distorts the allocation of capital — favoring excessive risk-taking, and sowing the field for the next crisis. What we need instead is a means of curbing reckless risk-taking, and especially the incentives that drive it, while making sure not to unduly constrain economic activity, investment, and growth.

The combination of a new capital requirement for large financial institutions with a new market trigger for regulatory action would offer just that balance. It could be introduced today without causing any serious hardship to financial institutions or the larger economy, without costing taxpayers much (if anything at all), and without requiring much in the way of new legislation. Our proposal would also offer a means of averting future bailouts, of re-establishing some confidence and order in the system, and of allowing once again for genuine competition in the world of finance. It would offer an opportunity to apply the lessons of the financial crisis without overreacting — and, most important, to protect the dynamism of American capitalism without neglecting the government's responsibility to protect the American public.

*Originally published as "Curbing Risk on Wall Street" in the Spring 2010 issue of* National Affairs.

# How to Regulate Bank Capital

## Charles W. Calomiris

*WINTER 2012*

I N MARCH 2009, at a hearing of the House Financial Services Committee, Treasury Secretary Timothy Geithner was asked what steps the regulators of our banking system should take to avoid another financial crisis. His answer captured the basic thinking of regulators around the world:

> [T]he most simple way to frame it is capital, capital, capital. Capital sets the amount of risk you can take overall. Capital assures you have big enough cushions to absorb extreme shocks. You want capital requirements to be designed so that, given how uncertain we are about the future of the world, given how much ignorance we fundamentally have about some elements of risk, that there is a much greater cushion to absorb loss and to save us from the consequences of mistakes in judgment and uncertainty in the world.

Clearly, one of the lessons of the 2008 financial crisis was that large financial institutions need to be subjected to more effective capital requirements. But precisely what kinds of requirements, and just how to structure them, have been subjects of heated debate ever since—and with good reason.

Bank capital requirements are rules that force a firm to maintain some minimum ratio of capital (such as the bank's equity or preferred stock) to assets (such as the securities and loans it holds). The purpose is to ensure that banks can sustain significant unexpected losses in the values of the assets they hold while still honoring withdrawals and other

CHARLES W. CALOMIRIS *is the Henry Kaufman Professor of Financial Institutions at Columbia Business School.*

essential obligations. The Basel Committee on Banking Supervision, established in 1974 by the central banks of the G-10 countries, has sought to standardize capital requirements in the world's major economies. Under the committee's recommendations (which have been adopted with minor modifications throughout the developed world), regulators weigh the risks involved in the different kinds of assets banks hold — assigning no risk to cash holdings, for instance, and incrementally higher risk to interbank loans, mortgages, and ordinary loans — and require a ratio of capital to these risk-weighted assets.

Before the global financial crisis of '08, the minimum capital ratio for banks under these rules was generally around 8%, with higher requirements for institutions with riskier holdings. But the crisis persuaded regulators and policymakers that these standards were insufficient. Thus politicians and regulators the world over are now crafting new rules to set higher capital-ratio requirements, especially for large banks (or so-called "systemically important financial institutions").

The Basel Committee has recommended significantly stricter requirements, including a 2.5% increase in the minimum capital ratio of the 30 or so most systemically important institutions around the world (a list that includes eight American banks — Bank of America, Bank of New York Mellon, Citigroup, Goldman Sachs, JPMorgan Chase, Morgan Stanley, State Street, and Wells Fargo — as well as European, Japanese, and Chinese banks). European leaders, now confronting the very real prospect of another banking crisis, are pushing their banks to implement much higher capital ratios immediately, and to structure capital mainly in the form of equity (common stock) claims rather than in riskier and more complex forms. But bankers, both in America and in Europe, are arguing that imposing higher capital requirements will result in a collapse of bank credit and lending, which will fuel economic decline and only further weaken the financial system.

There is a great deal at stake in this debate. The stability of the global financial system depends on effective and adequate capital requirements for financial institutions, and the 2008 crisis did reveal serious problems with the existing requirements. But the prospects for economic recovery, both in the United States and in the rest of world, depend on a steady flow of credit and lending. And the available evidence suggests that a dramatic increase in capital requirements would indeed result in a serious credit crunch.

Can capital requirements be improved without undermining economic growth? Although it is impossible to avoid some adverse consequences when implementing necessary increases in bank capital requirements, stability and growth are best seen as complementary outcomes of a proper capital standard—not as alternatives to be balanced against each other. Both a healthy economy and a reliable supply of bank credit can be achieved if policymakers understand just what it was about the old rules that failed in 2008, and just what risks are involved in the reforms they are now considering. Such an understanding could point us toward an alternative to today's proposed reforms—one that would maximize the prudential effectiveness of capital requirements while also minimizing the resulting short-term contraction in the credit supply.

## WHY REGULATE BANK CAPITAL?

For banks, as for other companies, capital may be best understood as a loss absorber in bad times. When the value of a bank's assets falls unexpectedly and the bank experiences sharp losses, having a sufficient amount of capital allows the bank to continue honoring withdrawals and other obligations, and so to avoid collapse. Capital therefore generally includes "unprotected" sources of financing for the bank, meaning that, in times of distress, these obligations do not have to be paid off until after the bank has paid off its other, more pressing obligations. The bank can thus draw on these financing sources as needed to address shortfalls caused by a sharp decline in asset values, providing security against a default. And the larger the ratio between these financing sources and the bank's overall assets, the better the bank is able to weather losses from loans or other risky activities.

Generally, these unprotected financing sources take three forms. The first is equity, or common stock, which is an ownership share in the bank and can therefore be drawn upon to cover losses in the event of financial trouble. The second is preferred stock, which is a fixed-income obligation of the bank; it must be paid before common stock is paid off, but after the bank's debts, and a failure to pay it does not result in a bankruptcy. Preferred stock is therefore also available to cover losses in times of financial trouble. The third form is unprotected debt, such as contingent convertibles, often called CoCos, which are essentially bonds that automatically convert to equity in times of economic distress. When some pre-established trigger is reached (like when the company's stocks reach a certain low price, or when its ratio of equity to debt reaches a certain low level), a CoCo conversion automatically occurs. Thus CoCos, too, are available to offset losses in a crisis.

All companies need to maintain adequate capital to help them survive financial distress, so why do banks — unlike other firms — have formal capital requirements imposed by government regulators? For most companies, the market is the regulator that encourages them to maintain adequate capital: Firms that choose too low a capital ratio will pay higher interest on their debts, as the holders of those debts judge them to be riskier investments because their capital might prove inadequate in a time of financial difficulty. This used to be true of banks as well, but has not been since at least the middle of the 20th century, thanks in part to several government policies implemented in response to the Great Depression. As a consequence of government deposit insurance (like that provided in the United States by the Federal Deposit Insurance Corporation) and other government policies that protect debt holders from losses, bank-debt holders in most countries today typically do not bear losses when the banks they have invested in (or deposited in) fail. That removes the incentive for debt holders to charge higher interest rates for the higher default risk assumed when banks maintain inadequate capital. The assumption that large banks in particular will be bailed out by their governments if they approach failure — an assumption confirmed by prominent rescues over the past few decades, and of course by more recent events — has further reduced the market's incentive to discipline banks through higher interest rates.

For these reasons, investors do not monitor or attempt to discipline banks as they do other kinds of companies. Regulators must therefore step in and do the job, and minimum capital ratios are among their most important tools of oversight.

In this environment, capital-ratio requirements, if enforced properly, are extremely important in limiting the potential for bank distress and failure, and in giving banks effective incentives to continuously manage risk. Because a properly capitalized bank's stockholders (among whom are often the bank's managers), rather than taxpayers, will bear the costs of asset losses, the bank's managers have every reason to keep the risks they take in check.

Recent studies of the financial crisis have highlighted the importance of such ongoing risk management. Perhaps surprisingly, on average, the banks that suffered the most in 2007-2009 had somewhat higher capital ratios in 2006 than other banks. Why did they fail? Because those higher initial capital ratios diminished as losses mounted. If the failed banks had begun with higher levels of capital and, even more important, had been required to *maintain* those capital ratios by replacing lost capital in a timely fashion, they would not have failed.

Regulating the adequacy of bank capital is thus necessary both for limiting the costs of distress and for improving banks' incentives to manage risk. But establishing effective capital requirements is not merely a matter of setting the required ratio high enough. It also requires a disciplined regulator, a reliable way to measure capital, and a clear understanding of the purpose of the rules. It was a set of failures on these fronts, as much as an inadequate minimum ratio, that made the recent financial crisis possible.

### REGULATORY FAILURE

Regulatory capital requirements are not all equally effective, mainly because of two important pitfalls to which they are susceptible: the familiar problem of discretionary bailouts by government, and discretionary loss recognition by both banks and regulators.

Discretionary loss recognition involves the use of accounting practices that distort the meaning of capital. Rather than using market-based concepts (like the price of bank stock) to measure risk and establish the need for capital, regulators rely on accounting concepts: They look at a bank's books, not at the market's assessment of the value of what the firm holds. Regulatory capital is thus a so-called accounting residual: It is defined as the difference between the accounting value of assets and the accounting value of debts.

Of course, accountants' book values are subject to strict legal requirements. But those requirements provide both banks and regulators with a great deal of discretion, particularly with regard to timing, allowing them to choose when to report losses and therefore allowing them to delay acknowledging problems and acting to address them. And neither bankers nor regulators tend to fully recognize losses during bad economic times. Bankers often prefer the delay tactic of "evergreening"—that is, re-lending money to delinquent borrowers so that those borrowers can repay ballooning debt-service costs with yet more debts to mask their troubles (and therefore the bank's troubles). For their part, bank regulators—always craving stability in the system—often prefer "forbearance": In order to avoid precipitating or worsening a crisis, they find ways to use their allotted discretion to pretend that losses are smaller than they are so that banks do not have to replace lost capital.

When these practices are carried out on a large scale, the results can be disastrous. In the buildup to the crisis of 2008, for instance, the combination of these two practices led to a failure to replace lost bank capital in a timely fashion, which intensified the eventual meltdown. The large financial institutions that failed or were bailed out did not deplete their capital overnight: Many months passed between the initial financial shocks of the crisis—the first revelations of trouble in the spring of 2007, the August 2007 run on asset-backed commercial paper, the Bear Stearns bailout of March 2008—and the systemic collapse of mid-September 2008. Nor were the markets for raising capital closed in that period: During the year or so leading up to the systemic collapse, roughly $450 billion of capital was raised by global financial institutions. Clearly, global capital markets were open, and there were many willing investors, especially hedge funds and private equity funds, as well as wealthy individuals willing to invest in banks. But many of the financial institutions most deeply affected by the crisis prior to September 2008, despite persistent and significant declines in the *market* values of their equity relative to assets, chose not to raise sufficient capital.

They were able to avoid doing so because the *accounting* values of their equity and assets did not fall as sharply. For instance, Citibank—which eventually received a large government bailout—had a capital ratio (according to the accounting values used by regulators) of 11.8% at roughly its low point in December 2008, when the stock-market capitalization of Citibank's holding company was about 2% of its total assets. All of the banks that required bailouts in the crisis reported high (and obviously exaggerated) levels of capital in the period before the intervention.

A top executive at a crisis-troubled institution confessed to me during the summer of 2008 that, despite the need to replace lost equity, the price of his stock was too low at that point to consider offering new equity into the market. Issuing significant equity in the summer of 2008 would have substantially diluted existing stockholders (including management), driving down share values as new stock was issued and priced by the market. So he preferred to wait it out, assuming either that conditions would improve (causing asset prices to rise again) or that, if the situation deteriorated sufficiently, the government would step in. On balance, the best strategy was to wait and hope for the best.

The temptation of forbearance remains a constant challenge for regulators, who often find themselves under political pressure to delay bank-loss recognition. Those pressures often lead them to play for time rather than to enforce capital-adequacy requirements. Britain's Financial Services Authority, which was widely regarded as one of the most effective and forward-looking regulators in the world, provided a particularly egregious example of forbearance with its oversight of Northern Rock—a British bank that collapsed in the early stages of the global crisis, in 2007. Just a few months before the bank collapsed, the supervisors authorized it to adopt the Advanced Measurements Approach to risk-weighting its mortgages, which reduced its required capital by 30%.

Recent actions in Japan show that, even after a decade of economic stagnation (worsened by the postponed recognition of losses in Japan's banks), politicians still pressure regulators to forbear whenever they see a short-term political advantage. In 2008, in an effort to assist banks and small- and medium-sized companies, Japan passed a law saying that delinquent loans from banks to such companies did not have to be considered delinquent for regulatory accounting purposes (thus avoiding recognition of lost capital) so long as the delinquent company had a plan to cure the delinquency. In 2009, that law was revised to allow forbearance on delinquent loans so long as the borrower had a plan to have a plan.

Beyond explicit (and often mutual) decisions by banks and regulators to understate losses, bankers can be very creative in their use of complex transactions to disguise losses on securities. Regulatory supervisors face serious challenges in detecting and preventing manipulation of accountants' book values through so-called "gains trading"—the common practice of recognizing capital gains on positions that are held at book value, while deferring the recognition of losses. The bankruptcy of Lehman Brothers revealed another device for circumventing capital-adequacy measures—the so-called "Repo 105" or "Repo 108" transactions that disguised repurchase agreements (a kind of loan in which the borrower sells the lender a security with an agreement to buy it back at a later time for a higher price) as removals of assets. This was basically a way to report a loan as though it were a sale of assets, and therefore a reduction in the size of the balance sheet (and in the level of assets counted in the capital-to-asset ratio).

Banks have enormous financial incentives to engage in such gimmickry, and their agility in doing so makes it unlikely that regulators will ever be able to keep up. Thus, while capital requirements are essential, their design matters enormously. Regulators must therefore find ways to structure these requirements so that they minimize the incentive for avoiding the recognition of losses, while also creating powerful incentives against gaming the system.

### THE COSTS OF CAPITAL REQUIREMENTS

Effectively designed capital requirements must not only overcome the inadequacies of existing rules: They must also take account of the social costs involved in raising such requirements, and find ways to minimize them.

The costs of higher capital requirements come primarily in the form of reduced banking activity—especially reduced lending (in other words, a "credit crunch") that can result from a large, sudden increase in capital requirements. After all, a capital requirement is a ratio of capital to assets, which means that a higher ratio can be achieved both by increasing the amount of capital in the numerator of the ratio and by *reducing* the quantity of assets in the denominator—that is, by reducing lending.

Some economists argue that banks will not forego profitable lending just because they have to meet higher capital-ratio requirements. That argument begins with a theoretical proposition known as the Modigliani-Miller (M&M) theorem, which states that a firm's activities should be invariant to its financing structure. In other words, regardless of how a bank is financed, the degree of its lending should be driven by its understanding of market conditions and incentives. This suggests that it should not matter to banks whether they raise money by issuing stocks or by issuing debt. This theorem needs qualifying, of course, when debt and equity finance are treated differently for tax purposes—since equity finance is more costly than debt finance, as a result of the deductibility of interest on debt.

But different tax treatment is not the only reason the M&M theorem turns out to be inaccurate. The theorem assumes that investors in debt and in equity can observe the value and the riskiness of the assets of the bank—but the past 30 years of theory and evidence regarding the financial structure of banks have shown that this assumption does not hold. Equity finance is relatively disadvantaged by the fact that it is difficult for investors to properly assess the value of a bank, so it tends to be harder for banks to sell equity than to raise debt finance. An important consequence of this reality is that banks tend to respond to higher required capital ratios mainly by curtailing their lending rather than by raising new capital. Thus, despite the benefits of banking-system stability that may accompany higher capital requirements, there are significant downsides in the associated contraction in the supply of bank credit.

There is a great deal of empirical evidence supporting this view. The literature on bank "capital crunches" demonstrates that shocks to bank-equity capital, holding constant the required capital ratio, have large contractionary effects on the supply of lending. In other words, capital is costly to replace when it is lost. Other studies show that, for a constant amount of capital, an increase in capital requirements leads to a contraction in lending. Some of those studies analyze banks' lending behavior around the time of system-wide regulatory changes, while others analyze cross-sectional differences in lending by banks that differ according to their regulatory circumstances. All, however, point to the same conclusion.

Two recent studies exploit features of the regulatory regimes of the United Kingdom and Spain, using individual bank data to identify how banks react to changes in bank-specific capital requirements. Like other countries' banks, U.K. banks are subject to minimum capital-ratio requirements of around 8% of risk-weighted assets. But to ensure an adequate buffer against losses related to credit risk, British regulators have at times added further capital requirements relating to their perceptions of the interest-rate risk exposures or operational risks (like poor managerial practices) of individual banks. This has resulted in substantial variation in capital-ratio requirements above the 8% level among British banks.

In a 2011 paper, using a sample of banks from 1998 to 2007, Shekhar Aiyar, Tomasz Wieladek, and I examined British banks' reactions to capital-requirement changes, taking into account variation in loan demand and other influences that could affect credit-supply contraction. We found that increases in bank-specific capital-ratio requirements resulted in large contractions in credit supply: A 10% increase in the capital-ratio requirement (say, from a 10% requirement to an 11% requirement) resulted in a 9% contraction in the supply of bank credit.

Another 2011 study, by Gabriel Jiménez, Jesús Saurina, Steven Ongena, and José-Luis Peydró, examined the consequences of increases in capital requirements using data from the recent experience of Spain.

This study, too, was able to isolate the effects of loan demand, and found similarly dramatic effects on the supply of bank credit. The study found that increases in dynamic-provisioning requirements — essentially, requirements that banks increase their regulatory reserves for loan losses, which is akin to, but less costly to banks than, an increase in capital-ratio requirements — showed responses roughly half the size of those observed in the study of the United Kingdom. That smaller magnitude is consistent with the findings for the U.K., since an increase in a capital-ratio requirement should have a larger effect than a similarly sized increase in a dynamic-provisioning requirement.

The implication of these studies is that increases in capital requirements, even if they are carried out carefully and well, are not cost-free. But this fact does not in turn imply that increases in capital requirements should be avoided. The empirical literature on banking crises uniformly suggests that allowing banks to operate without adequate capital is even more costly for limiting bank-credit growth than an increase in capital-ratio requirements. The combination of government protection and undercapitalized banking tends to result in excessive risk-taking and systemic banking collapses — both of which have far worse consequences for the supply of credit over the medium and long terms, as well as for economic growth, than the more modest, and more predictable, contractions of credit that result from requiring adequate capital. The key, then, is to properly understand the nature of the credit-supply costs of increasing capital requirements, so that policy decisions about the structure and timing of capital-requirement increases can take those costs into account.

### A BETTER WAY

What would an approach to regulating bank capital that took these various concerns into account look like? Such an approach would have to involve three crucial elements: establishing an appropriate structure and level of required capital; implementing complementary measures to strengthen or reinforce the requirement; and phasing in the new requirement predictably and gradually to avoid sudden disruptions of bank-credit supply.

The approach I propose for achieving these goals is quite different from the one endorsed by the Basel Committee and by American regulators charged with enforcing the Dodd-Frank bill enacted in 2010. Both of these plans continue to rely on failed accounting measures of capital, inadequate minimum capital ratios, and regulatory enforcement protocols that allow banks to delay replacing lost capital until it is too late.

To their credit, the latest Basel proposals — the so-called Basel III reforms, intended to take effect over the next few years and set to be implemented alongside Dodd-Frank in the United States — do propose to raise overall capital requirements modestly. Under this general requirement, the rules also specify an increase in the amount of required equity capital, especially for "systemically important" financial institutions (although the precise size of those increases remains uncertain). These reforms also introduce "macro-prudential" variations in the size of capital-ratio requirements — that is, rules that change in response to the business cycle so as to limit credit growth during booms and relax constraints on credit growth during recessions. Basel III also introduces new liquidity requirements intended to reduce banks' exposure to liquidity risk (potential problems that banks can face in rolling over debts backed by illiquid assets).

While increases in the quantity and quality of required bank capital ratios are a welcome improvement in prudential regulation — and while enhancing bank liquidity is an important complement to capital regulation — the Basel-Dodd-Frank approach does nothing to encourage timely loss recognition, and does not sufficiently incentivize banks to improve their risk-management practices. Furthermore, the liquidity-regulation aspects of Basel III are based on complex and opaque criteria, and are intended to reduce systemic liquidity risk; they do not address the more fundamental problem of bank-default risk.

To better meet the goals of effective and prudential bank regulation, policymakers should start by reconsidering the basic *form* of capital requirements. Form matters because it can affect cost as well as efficacy. As already noted, equity capital is a very useful form of finance in bad times, since it is sold with the understanding that it is unprotected. But it is also the most costly form of capital for banks to raise.

To significantly increase the capital available in a crisis while minimizing the increase in cost — and therefore the likelihood of a credit crunch — regulators should seek to combine equity capital with a less expensive, but still reliable, form of capital. The contingent convertible is an obvious candidate: Sold as debt, it is cheaper for banks than raising equity capital in normal times; because it converts into equity in times of financial distress, however, it provides a capital cushion if trouble hits. Requiring a combination of equity capital and CoCos — if that combination is properly designed — can provide a large and credible buffer against loss, while also reducing the costs of raising capital. I suggest the imposition of a 20% capital-ratio requirement, consisting half of equity and half of CoCos.

The key to the use of CoCos as part of such a capital requirement is not simply that they would convert to equity if the risk of insolvency loomed (and thus play the same role as additional equity capital). Rather, in a properly designed regulatory system, using CoCos would create a powerful financial incentive for the bank to issue more equity capital long *before* a financial failure that would trigger the conversion of CoCos into equity. The threat of triggering a large conversion of CoCos — thereby severely diluting the value of the common stock held by shareholders, often including bank officials themselves — would provide institutions with a powerful motive to strengthen risk management and take remedial measures to raise equity well in advance of a crisis, rather than masking losses and colluding with regulators to delay action. (In a 2011 paper, Richard Herring and I provide the details of a CoCo requirement that would achieve this objective.)

To produce the strongest incentive for banks to issue equity preemptively, the size of the CoCo requirement should be large; the trigger should be credibly and observably based on market prices and set at a high trigger ratio of equity to assets (one that would be reached long before serious concerns about insolvency arose); and the conversion ratio (that is, the amount of value in new equity that the holders of CoCos would receive for the bonds they surrendered) should be sufficiently dilutive of existing common shareholders. This last requirement is key, as the CoCo conversion ratio needs to be painful enough that it makes the prospective dilution from issuing pre-emptive equity into the market appear very desirable by comparison. A CoCo requirement of 10% would be large enough to have this effect, particularly if combined with a conversion ratio that ensured that holders of CoCos were left with at least as much value in new equity as the principal of the bonds they surrendered. At the same time, however, it would minimize the up-front costs to the banks, and therefore minimize the danger of a severe credit crunch.

The trigger for the conversion of CoCos to equity should be based on the market's valuation of a bank's debt-to-equity ratio — which is a more reliable measure of the bank's financial condition than the accounting measures now used by regulators. For example, the trigger could be set so that CoCos would convert from debt to equity if the ratio of the market value of the bank's equity relative to the sum of the market value of its equity plus its debt fell to an average of, say, 9% over a 90-day period. (The ratio should be measured as a 90-day average to avoid the risk of investors forcing a CoCo conversion through a coordinated bear run on the bank's stock.)

Such a combination of a large CoCo requirement, a market-based trigger, and a painful conversion ratio would result in a greater dilution of common stockholders than the alternative pre-emptive stock offering. Under these conditions, a large financial institution experiencing significant losses and approaching the neighborhood of dilutive conversion would choose to issue equity into the market, thereby avoiding the even more costly conversion trigger and also avoiding a significant risk of insolvency or regulatory intervention.

As an added benefit, CoCos designed to result in substantial dilution upon conversion would have an enormous practical advantage as *debt* instruments: The strong incentives for management to avoid conversion would mean that CoCos would be likely to almost never convert, and thus to trade more like fixed-income instruments than like ordinary convertible securities. They could be sold more like relatively stable debt (bonds) than like comparatively volatile equity (stocks). Thus coupons paid on CoCos that follow the design features outlined here should qualify for tax deductibility; furthermore, apart from tax considerations, CoCos would likely hold greater appeal to institutional investors, such as pension funds, which tend to prefer low-risk debt instruments.

Under these circumstances, CoCo conversion would be a bank CEO's nightmare. Not only would existing stockholders who were diluted by the conversion be calling for his head: He would also face an onslaught of sophisticated new holders of stock (such as the institutional investors who were formerly CoCo holders) who would likely be eager to sack senior management for its demonstrated incompetence. This threat would only add to the incentive for management to pre-emptively issue equity to avoid conversion, as well as to maintain high initial ratios of capital to assets, accurate measures of risk, and effective controls on risk. Such powerful financial incentives would be much more effective than a set of rules that banks can circumvent with clever financial instruments, to say nothing of requirements that both regulators and financial institutions can easily put on hold when the rules prove inconvenient.

This new capital requirement would overcome many of the problems that have bedeviled such attempts at regulation in the past, but it needs further policy reinforcement. Though capital regulation is an important mechanism for ensuring the stability of our financial system, it cannot succeed by itself. Indeed, in recent times, regulators' excessive reliance on capital requirements has caused them to neglect other prudential tools that can be even more effective.

The most obvious and historically important of these additional prudential tools is the cash-reserve requirement, under which banks must maintain actual cash reserves at some minimum fraction of deposits or assets. Over the past three decades in the United States and many other developed economies, however, this requirement has fallen by the wayside. The Basel Committee has recommended new liquidity requirements (requiring banks to maintain stocks of "high-quality liquid assets" sufficient to cover their net cash outflows for 30 days), but these are complex, opaque, and not linked to observable and predictable holdings of cash by banks.

Instead, a portion of bank assets should be required to take the form of cash deposited in a nation's central bank, earning interest. Cash deposited in a central bank is continuously observable, and therefore not subject to the danger of so-called "window dressing": the use of accounting practices to create the appearance of cash assets at particular dates — like just before public quarterly reports are due to regulators — without having actually invested in cash (as happened in the recent MF Global collapse).

Cash and capital offer complementary means of insulating government-protected deposits from the losses that arise from risky, non-cash assets. Capital absorbs losses, while investments in cash reduce losses by cutting the share of risky assets financed by deposits. But cash is not an equal alternative to capital on the asset side of the balance sheet: Unlike capital (the value of which depends on accurate measurement of the value of risky assets), the value of cash reserves held at the central bank is continuously and accurately known. That makes cash a more credible buffer against loss than capital. Furthermore, as Florian Heider, Marie Hoerova, and I show in a new study, because cash is essentially riskless and not subject to manipulation, requiring a significant amount of cash to be held as a fraction of assets improves bank executives' incentives to better manage the risks that banks take on, particularly in the wake of losses on risky assets, as during a recession.

A cash requirement, like the proposed CoCo requirement, would improve incentives for good risk management, because cash holdings dull bankers' incentives to game the regulatory system. In essence, more cash holdings have the effect of increasing the downside risk exposure borne by bank stockholders: They will have more to lose if things go wrong. Combining minimum required ratios of cash and capital relative to assets would more credibly limit bank risks than would relying on capital alone.

Although there are no "magic numbers" for just the right ratios to require, based on a review of successfully regulated banking systems of the present and the past, I believe a "20-20" combination of minimum requirements—requiring at least 20% of risk-weighted assets to be financed by capital (half in equity and half in CoCos), and requiring at least 20% of risk-weighted assets to be held in interest-bearing cash reserves—would be an excellent starting point for enabling an effective, prudential regulatory system.

Such requirements would have to be gradually phased in, to avoid cost shocks that might set off a credit crunch. The most costly feature of this plan, in terms of its likely consequences for credit supply, would be the 10% equity-capital requirement. Because banks already hold substantial Treasury securities and reserves, the cash requirement would affect the *composition* of those assets more than the amount. CoCos would be priced and treated much like debt, limiting the costs of compliance with this new requirement. But raising substantial new equity would be costly, particularly in today's highly uncertain environment.

For that reason, the implementation of this approach should not be too sudden, and should ensure predictability, so that banks can plan their affairs accordingly. Allowing banks to phase in the new requirements over, say, a five-year period (rising evenly each year over five years) should properly balance the need for credibility with the desire to avoid a collapse of credit supply.

## SMARTER RULES

Before banks' debts were protected by government deposit insurance and bailouts, markets ensured that banks maintained adequate amounts of capital and cash assets, and rewarded bankers who engaged in better risk management with lower costs for raising funds. In today's world, however, government protection has removed the incentives for market participants to play that role. Prudential regulators, therefore, have had to devise rules for capital and cash adequacy to ensure that bank owners, rather than taxpayers, absorb losses related to the risks banks take.

But the regulatory system that was developed over the past several decades, in the U.S. and in many other countries, has failed repeatedly to provide effective, prudential regulations that limit taxpayer financing of bank losses. The recent financial crisis of 2007-2009 is just the latest (and most severe) in a long line of episodes that demonstrate the terrible costs of combining government protection of banks with ineffectual regulation. Since 1980, more than 100 countries have experienced banking crises (defined as episodes in which the negative net worth of failed banks exceeds 1% of annual gross domestic product); across those episodes, the negative net worth of failed banks averaged 16% of GDP. Such frequency and severity of bank loss are historically unprecedented, and are clearly consequences of the brave new world of government protection of bank debts. Consider that, a century earlier, from 1874 to 1913, banks were at least as important to the financing of trade and industry—and yet I have been able to identify only four episodes of bank-insolvency crises worldwide during those years, with an average negative net worth of 6% of GDP.

Existing regimes for regulating capital—and the reforms of those regimes that have been enacted thus far by the Basel III system and the Dodd-Frank bill in the United States—not only require too little capital, but also fail to provide bank officials with incentives to manage their risks and to act in advance of bank failures. And these policies persist in protecting banks from the consequences of their own recklessness, essentially enabling and formalizing the practices that made the recent crisis possible.

A proper understanding of the dynamics of the recent crisis—of how rules interacted with incentives to make excessive risk far too attractive and to give bankers no reason to behave responsibly—can point us toward a set of rules that offer far better protection at relatively low cost to all involved.

Of course, moving to such a system would not be entirely without costs, especially since the supply of bank credit today is already meager and higher capital requirements will further limit short-term credit growth. But as we have learned all too painfully, allowing banks to expand credit on an inadequate base of capital delivers short-term credit growth at the expense of medium-term credit collapse and economic disaster. It is time to recognize at last that rules that fail to account for financial incentives are bound to fail, and that harnessing the disciplining power of markets — rather than replacing it with the supposed cleverness of regulators — is the only way to prudently keep our banks in check while also enabling economic growth.

*Originally published as "How to Regulate Bank Capital" in the Winter 2012 issue of* National Affairs.

# How to Reform Monetary Policy

## *Scott Sumner*

FALL 2011

T HE QUARTER-CENTURY THAT PRECEDED the financial crisis of 2008 was
a period of low inflation and relatively stable growth, interrupted
by just two relatively mild recessions. Economists call it "the Great
Moderation," and many of them argue that it was made possible in large
part by the fact that, during those years, the Federal Reserve (and many
of the world's other central banks) adopted stable regimes of inflation targeting: deciding on a preferred inflation rate and steering the economy
toward it, generally by lowering interest rates when inflation fell below
the target and raising interest rates when inflation exceeded the target.
By sticking to such an approach throughout the Great Moderation, the
common argument goes, the Fed effectively balanced a commitment to
growth with a determination to keep prices stable.

But that era ended with a bang. In 2008 and 2009, we suffered the most
severe recession since the Great Depression, and in its wake we continue to
experience high unemployment and weak growth. Most people think they
know the proximate cause of this calamity: There was a housing bubble of
unprecedented size, which burst in 2006 and led to a severe financial crisis
in 2008, which greatly intensified a recession that had begun in December
2007. All of that put together, they believe, was enough to overwhelm the
Fed's inflation targeting; there was little the central bank could do to avert
the crash, and it has done what it could since to respond to the crisis.

The available evidence, however, does not quite support this familiar
narrative. For one thing, the housing crash did not lead directly to a recession or high unemployment. More than two-thirds of the decline in
housing construction occurred between January 2006 and April 2008,
and yet, during that 27-month period, the unemployment rate rose only
slightly, from 4.7% to just 4.9%. Most of the workers who lost jobs in

*SCOTT SUMNER is a professor of economics at Bentley University.*

211

housing construction were re-employed in commercial construction, exports, and services. It wasn't until October 2009 that unemployment soared to 10.1%, as job losses spread across almost all sectors of the economy. The financial crisis (which of course had roots in the housing bubble) and its associated shocks to the system clearly had much to do with that timing, yet somehow this looming crisis did not set off alarm bells at the Fed until remarkably late in the process. Monetary-policy officials simply failed to see the problem coming and did not react nearly quickly enough; even now, the Fed seems to be flailing.

In other words, the economic crisis not only overwhelmed the Fed's inflation-targeting methods, but showed them to be deeply inadequate. Given the consequences of that failure, America's policymakers now need to ask: Could the Fed have done better?

It could have, had it set its sights not on inflation but on nominal gross domestic product — the sum of all current-dollar (non-inflation-adjusted) spending in the American economy. NGDP growth, which is made up of the inflation rate plus "real" (or inflation-adjusted) GDP growth, would have been a better indicator of the severity of the crisis. Between 2008 and 2009, NGDP declined at the fastest rate since 1938, while inflation (at least the "core" inflation rate, which excludes food and gas prices and which the Fed uses as its key inflation measure) raised no red flags. Because inflation cannot quickly adjust to such sudden drops in spending, this decline in nominal GDP brought about a sharp decline in real GDP — thus, a severe recession.

In an important sense, the sharp drop in NGDP *precipitated* the crisis: It was the proximate cause, even if the housing crisis was the ultimate cause. This suggests that NGDP is useful not only as a predictor and indicator of trouble, but as a target for monetary policy. Setting a goal in terms of nominal GDP could provide a superior alternative to the Fed's current inflation targets.

Why, then, do economists not place greater emphasis on nominal GDP, even as they focus intently on its two components — real GDP growth and inflation? Indeed, even the basic data are surprisingly hard to find: When quarterly GDP figures are announced by the federal government, the press generally reports real GDP growth, but almost never mentions nominal growth. The same is true in the field of macroeconomics, where professional economists frequently work with real GDP (or "output") and prices, but rarely model NGDP.

The reasons for this behavior have as much to do with the politics of inflation as they do with economics. This suggests that the monetary-policy failure of 2008 reflected not so much a failure of technical macroeconomics as an inability of professional economists to understand how their ideas are filtered through our highly politicized policy arena. As we shall see, inflation targeting can work, but only in a world in which policies explicitly aimed at *raising* the inflation rate are non-controversial. Obviously, we don't live in that world; in the universe we occupy, a nominal GDP target would be more effective.

By considering the past few years through the lens of nominal GDP data, we can both gain a greater understanding of the crisis from which we are still recovering and see our way to a superior approach to monetary policy.

### INFLATION AND GROWTH

Although the term "nominal GDP growth" appears infrequently in the economics literature, its two components — inflation and real growth — underlie much of conventional macroeconomics. Studying the interactions of these factors provides a unique window into the movements of our economy, in both the short and the long term.

Over the long term, real GDP growth has been highly regular, averaging roughly 3% a year for more than a century in the United States. Inflation, however, has been quite variable: Between 1972 and 1981, for instance, nominal GDP growth averaged about 11% due to roughly 8% inflation. That inflation rate was universally deemed to be unacceptably high, and, under Paul Volcker's leadership, the Federal Reserve was able to gradually reduce inflation (and thus NGDP growth). Between 1990 and 2007 — the bulk of the Great Moderation period — the economy generated fairly steady NGDP growth, at just over 5% a year, with inflation at just over 2% and real growth continuing to average about 3%. Thus, over the long term, nominal GDP and inflation have tended to move together while real GDP has been stable.

But in the short term, through the ups and downs of the business cycle, things look quite different. In the short term, nominal and real GDP tend to move together, while inflation is, in the parlance of economists, relatively "sticky" — meaning slow to move. People's choices about spending can change on a dime, but their wages cannot, and neither can prices throughout the economy. That means that a sudden widespread change in spending decisions (which economists call a "nominal shock") will drag real GDP along with it, while inflation lags behind.

So, for instance, between mid-2008 and mid-2009, NGDP fell about 4% (and thus, at -4%, was 9% below its trend rate of 5% growth) as real output fell sharply while inflation remained fairly stable. The same effect can be achieved in a positive direction in the short term—a spike in nominal GDP (achieved, for instance, by monetary or fiscal stimulus) can push real GDP up, though not for long. Almost no one believes that boosting nominal GDP will permanently raise real output: If it could, then a poor country could develop its economy by simply printing more money. Zimbabwe would be the wealthiest country in the world. But for a little while, nominal and real GDP do move together.

These relationships among real GDP, nominal GDP, and inflation yield a standard model of macroeconomics. To recover from a nominal shock, the government can boost nominal spending (or "aggregate demand") through deficit spending or monetary stimulus, and the boost will lead to higher output and, in time, to higher prices. In the long run, however, only the effect on prices will last: Again, it is not possible to make a country permanently richer by printing money. Stimulus is thus short-term medicine, aimed at giving the economy a chance to stabilize and recover from a slowdown.

To avoid nominal shocks in the first place, the government should seek a steady level of nominal GDP growth. It should do this, most economists argue, by using monetary policy to keep output (that is, real GDP) growing steadily and, above all, to keep inflation close to about 2%. Why 2%? Such low inflation is desirable because high inflation rates are believed to hurt the economy. But economists do not believe that inflation is harmful for the reason that most non-economists would cite—the impact of rising prices on consumers. After all, when prices rise, incomes usually rise as well. Instead, many economists would argue that high inflation is a sort of tax on capital: Our tax system punishes savers during high-inflation periods like the 1970s, as people must pay taxes on capital earnings that merely reflect price increases driven by inflation. The result is reduced saving and investment.

So if inflation is harmful, why not aim for a target below 2%, say zero inflation? The country that has come closest to such "price stability" in recent years is Japan, where the Consumer Price Index inflation rate has been at almost zero for more than a decade. Many economists believe this extremely low inflation has hurt Japan in two different ways. First, it is the primary reason that Japan has had almost 15 years of near-zero interest rates on short-term government bonds—a situation often called a "liquidity trap." Such a "trap" makes conventional monetary policy almost impossible: The Bank of Japan is unable to lower rates to spur demand in a downturn. It can resort to some tools other than interest rates, like quantitative easing, but central banks are often reluctant to use such non-conventional policy tools.

The second problem is so-called "wage stickiness." In a competitive market economy, some wages need to fall relative to others. In an economy with mild inflation (which causes all wages to gradually rise), relative wage adjustments can take the form of some workers getting smaller pay increases than others. But if inflation is near zero, it may become necessary to give genuine nominal wage cuts to a significant fraction of workers—and of course workers strongly resist cuts in the current dollar (or yen) amount of their pay.

An inflation rate around 2% is believed to be low enough to avoid most of the downsides of inflation but high enough to avoid the liquidity trap and the challenge of wage stickiness. Inflation at roughly that rate has therefore been considered the ideal target of monetary policy.

Of course, the Federal Reserve cares about more than just inflation. Its "dual mandate" is to provide stable prices and high rates of employment. During the Great Moderation, the Fed carried out this mandate by raising interest rates (tightening policy) when inflation or real output (or both) rose above the Fed's target, and by cutting interest rates when either or both fell below the target—a policy referred to as the "Taylor Rule," after its chief exponent, Stanford's John Taylor. But although this approach takes in elements of both inflation and real GDP, it is still essentially an inflation-targeting mechanism—or what economists call "flexible inflation targeting." Under the Taylor Rule, for instance, the short-term interest rate is adjusted by one and a half times changes in the inflation rate plus half the so-called "GDP gap" (the difference between measured real GDP and the estimated maximum amount the economy could produce while maintaining reasonable price stability). This policy insures relatively stable inflation, and also moderates the business cycle.

So although it pursues a dual mandate, the Federal Reserve views the manipulation of inflation through interest rates as the key role of the central bank. And this approach seemed to work for a long period of time. What, then, went so spectacularly wrong in 2008?

### THE CRISIS RECONSIDERED

The Federal Reserve made two crucial and revealing errors in its response to the recession and economic crisis of 2008 and 2009. First, it failed to "target the forecast" — that is, to implement policies that could be expected to actually produce the results the Fed wanted to achieve. This was the consequence not of a failed attempt to use the Fed's power, but rather of an explicit reluctance to use that power at all.

Consider the following analogy. Suppose a passenger is chatting with the captain of a ship that is scheduled to reach New York in two days. The captain mentions that, due to wind and currents, he expects to make landfall in Boston, not New York. The passenger might ask why the captain doesn't adjust the steering, so that the city he expects to reach (the forecast) is the same as the city he had initially hoped to reach (the target). To most people, this would seem like common sense. Thus one might be surprised to learn that, while a few prominent economists (like Lars Svensson of Princeton University) have advocated a policy by which the Federal Reserve would similarly embrace and adjust policies as needed to reach its forecast, most economists take a kind of "wait and see" approach. When the economy drifts off course, the Fed makes an adjustment — but not necessarily one that is expected to lead to on-target nominal growth. Rather, the Fed waits and sees how its policy moves affect the economy, and then makes further adjustments as needed, in an effort to avoid overreacting to short-term data.

In late 2008, this incremental approach produced a very weak and ineffectual policy response to a rapid and deep decline in nominal spending — a policy response that was clearly understood by the markets to be grossly inadequate in a fast-changing economic environment. Although we have no futures market for NGDP expectations, the sharp and simultaneous plunge in stock prices, commodity prices, and Treasury-bond yields provides a strong indication that investors foresaw a sharp slowdown in spending.

But this was not the Fed's only, or greatest, error. The central bank's sluggish response to early indications of trouble might help account for the severity of the decline in economic activity in late 2008, but it can't really explain why the economy remains in the doldrums nearly three years later.

Before considering what went wrong, it would be helpful to compare the current recovery to the recovery from the other post-war recession that featured double-digit unemployment: the recession of the early 1980s. That recession was really two related slowdowns—one in the first six months of 1980, and then another in the 16 months from July 1981 to November 1982. Six of the 12 quarters in that period saw negative real GDP growth (including -7.9% in the second quarter of 1980 and -6.4% in the first quarter of 1982, two of the worst quarterly performances since the Great Depression). Unemployment also spiked higher than it had at any time since the Depression, reaching a peak of 10.8% in November 1982. But that recession was followed by an equally strong rebound: During the first six quarters of the "Volcker recovery," starting at the end of 1982, NGDP rose at 11%, RGDP rose at 7.7%, and (therefore) inflation was about 3.3%.

The recession of 2007-09 was of a roughly similar magnitude, featuring five quarters of negative real GDP growth, including an astounding contraction of 8.9% in the fourth quarter of 2008. As noted earlier, unemployment during this downturn peaked at 10.1%, in October 2009. But the recovery from this latest recession has been nowhere near as impressive as that of the early 1980s. During the first six quarters of our current "recovery," NGDP rose at a rate of 4.3%, RGDP rose at 3.0%, and inflation ran at about 1.3%. In the first two quarters of this year, NGDP growth slowed even further, to 3.4%. Our "jobless recovery" is thus no mystery: Unemployment remains high because the economy is not really recovering at all. Real GDP growth is roughly equal to trend, and hence we are not closing the output gap created by the severe decline of 2008 and 2009. We fell into a deep hole, and we started digging sideways.

Also less than mysterious is the reason for that slow real GDP growth: Nominal growth has been much slower in the past few years than during the 1983-84 recovery. It is almost inconceivable that the economy could grow at the 7.7% real rate of 1983-84 with nominal spending growing at only 4.3%, which is below even the trend rate of nominal GDP growth during the Great Moderation. There is an ongoing debate about whether the current problem is a matter of demand (i.e., not enough nominal spending) or whether it is "structural" (i.e., workers' lacking the right skills for the available jobs). But we will never find out until we actually see the sort of nominal spending that would be required to ignite a robust recovery.

This is something that should be kept in mind by those who argue that our problems are "structural." Advocates of the structural view sometimes lose sight of the fact that we do not have enough nominal spending to launch a real recovery *even if the economy had no structural problems at all*. Whatever our long-term problem, our immediate problem is poor NGDP growth. Just as a sharp drop in NGDP was the proximate cause of the crisis, persistently low NGDP is the proximate cause of our slow recovery. Monetary policy that focused directly on nominal growth rather than viewing it only indirectly through the lens of inflation would identify this problem more clearly, and would thus be better positioned to address it. The Fed's second error, in other words, is that it has been focused on the wrong problem.

Many economists would contest this description of the policy failure, on two different grounds. First, they would argue, prominent macro-economists did understand that there was a demand shortfall in 2008, but did not think that monetary policy was capable of fixing the problem, especially once short-term interest rates approached zero, leaving the Fed "out of ammunition." This is the "liquidity trap" view.

But the Fed itself never claimed to be "out of ammunition," even after rates hit zero. Indeed, Chairman Ben Bernanke has repeatedly stressed that the Fed still has many options for boosting demand, and he has proved the point with two rounds of "quantitative easing." Indeed, it is hard to see how a fiat-money central bank would ever be left unable to boost nominal spending. That would logically imply it was unable to raise the rate of inflation — that is, to "debase the currency," which it can always do. There is no example in history of any fiat-money central bank that tried to create inflation and failed. In 1933, for instance, Franklin Roosevelt was able to create substantial inflation by devaluing the dollar against gold, despite near-zero interest rates. Some economists (most notably Paul Krugman) cite the example of the Bank of Japan over the past decade and more to suggest that a central bank can try and fail to raise inflation. But the Japanese twice *tightened* monetary policy in an environment of zero inflation (in 2000 and 2006), so it would be hard to claim that they were trying to create inflation.

Indeed, by just *hinting* at quantitative easing in a series of speeches last year, Fed officials were able to drive up stock prices, elevate inflation expectations, and lift commodity prices. After the past few years, there can no longer be any serious disagreement about whether monetary policy can be effective once rates hit zero. Clearly, it can be. The only questions are how the Fed understands its goals and how aggressive it is willing to be in pursuing them.

Second, some critics might argue that the policy of inflation targeting should have been able to address the demand shortfall in 2008-'09 yet failed to do so, and that it is therefore not clear why nominal GDP targeting would have done any better. This of course raises the question of why inflation targeting itself did not succeed. A substantial decline in aggregate demand will tend to reduce both inflation and output to below the central bank's targets—so if the Fed uses a flexible inflation target like the Taylor Rule, such reductions should trigger monetary stimulus, which would eventually help put the economy back on track. We have seen above that this policy was not sufficiently forward-looking in late 2008, and that the Fed was too slow to react and not aggressive enough in targeting its goals. But what is the problem today? Why is inflation targeting not producing a more aggressive Fed policy now? And is there reason to think that NGDP targeting would do any better?

## THE LIMITS OF INFLATION TARGETING

The Federal Reserve's continuing failure to address our economy's woes points toward four major problems with inflation targeting itself.

The first problem is well understood by macroeconomists: The optimal policy response to inflation depends on whether price increases are caused by greater aggregate demand (that is, an increase in nominal spending) or by an adverse supply shock (such as a suddenly reduced supply of food or oil due to a natural disaster or war). Policymakers generally try to "accommodate" temporary changes in food and oil prices, as these don't reflect changes in aggregate demand and so generally don't result in persistent changes in the rate of inflation. For instance, inflation in mid-2008 was quite high due to rising oil prices, but by early 2009 the CPI was actually falling for the first time in more than half a century. The Fed understands this distinction and generally directs its attention to "core inflation," which excludes food and energy prices.

By itself, however, the problem of supply shocks should not result in the sort of policy failures that we have witnessed since 2008. After all, during 2009 and 2010, real output and core inflation were both below the Fed's implicit targets, yet the central bank still did not act aggressively enough to address the problem. The Fed's wait-and-see approach was part of the reason, but the remaining flaws of inflation targeting—which are frequently overlooked by macroeconomists—were crucial factors.

The second major problem with inflation targeting has to do with how the Consumer Price Index, which is the standard measure of inflation, is calculated—a problem brought into stark relief by the housing crisis of the past few years. As of mid-2009, the rate of NGDP growth over the previous 12 months was about -4%, as noted above. In contrast, core inflation was running about 1.5%, only slightly below the Fed's (implicit) 2% target. In fact, between mid-2008 and mid-2009, the housing component of the CPI rose even faster than the overall index. That's right: During the greatest housing-price crash in American history, government data showed the cost of housing *rising*, even relative to other goods.

This is largely because the government relies on a flawed "rental equivalent" estimate for housing costs, which in turn distorts the entire CPI measure. Until 1983, the Bureau of Labor Statistics measured housing prices based on direct ownership costs like home purchase values, mortgage-interest rates, and property taxes. But because interest rates and housing values were changing rapidly, the BLS became concerned that this measure was providing an inaccurate measure of inflation—making inflation seem more jerky and uneven than it was. And because a home is a long-term investment as well as a consumer good, the agency also worried that it was giving too much weight to considerations tied to the investment component—factors that did not relate to the immediate state of prices in the real economy. Thus it sought to separate the investment component of housing from the consumption component through a calculation of the rental value of homes; it has since measured the prices of homes based on what the cost of renting them would be. This has meant that the CPI and home values have grown increasingly disconnected. And because housing inflation accounts for 39% of the core CPI, the official inflation rate fell much less during the housing crash than the actual decline of prices in the economy—because the cost of renting homes stayed relatively flat, even as their resale values plummeted. So the Fed did have its eye on inflation, but was receiving faulty inflation signals. During a period of rapidly declining aggregate demand, NGDP would have provided far more timely and accurate data on the need for monetary stimulus than price indices composed mostly of sticky prices.

By mid-2010, however, it was clear that the recovery was faltering. Even the inflation indicator was providing a relatively clear signal of the need for more stimulus, as the core CPI inflation fell to 0.6%, far below the Fed's implicit target. Beginning in late August 2010, Fed officials started sending signals that additional stimulus was coming, and in early November the Fed announced a new round of quantitative easing (which came to be known as QE2). But even before the announcement, the prospect of QE2 generated a great deal of controversy. Many people seemed bewildered by news stories that Ben Bernanke thought inflation was too low and was trying to engineer an increase in the "cost of living." The typical American tends to see inflation as a problem, not a solution, so the policy became a lightning rod for criticism — and pressure to end it was growing before QE2 had even begun.

This episode exposed the third fatal flaw in inflation targeting: the politics of inflation. In principle, an inflation target means that, while the Fed will sometimes need to restrain inflation to keep it under control, the rest of the time it will need to boost inflation to keep it from falling below the target. Indeed, if its errors are "unbiased," the Fed should spend about half of its time trying to increase the inflation rate. But clearly the American public has not bought into this view of the matter. Americans view inflation as a process that reduces their living standards, because they take their own nominal incomes as a given when thinking about the impact of higher prices. Inflation is thus highly unpopular.

Yet according to standard macroeconomics, only supply-side inflation (caused by shortages or other supply shocks) reduces living standards; inflation generated by the Fed actually *raises* living standards. Consider an example: As noted above, NGDP has been rising at about 4.3% during this slow recovery. If the Fed were able to boost NGDP growth to, say, 6.3%, then part of the extra nominal spending would show up as inflation and part would show up as higher real GDP, or real output — since stimulus can't move inflation as quickly as it can move output. Therefore, with real output growing, more people would have jobs and those already working would be able to work more hours. Income from capital would also increase.

Now suppose that, instead of saying inflation was too low in mid-2010, Bernanke had announced that we needed to boost the incomes of Americans in order to have a healthy recovery — and that the Fed would therefore try to boost the growth rate of national income from 4.3% to 6.3%. This message would have sounded much more appealing to the average voter than a call for higher inflation.

One might object that there is something disreputable about the Fed's trying to deceive the public by working to engineer higher inflation under the guise of "more income." A call for boosting income, however, would have been not only more popular but also more truthful. Ben Bernanke does not really want higher inflation; it would be more accurate to say that he wants more aggregate demand and expects such higher demand to result in somewhat higher inflation rates. Unfortunately, however, the Fed has chosen a language to communicate its intentions that is both deeply unpopular and profoundly misleading. Inflation targeting gives the public the wrong impression, and the resulting political reaction impedes the Fed's ability to carry out its work.

If we stopped talking about inflation targeting and started talking about NGDP targeting, we could greatly simplify the policy debate. Do we want more demand, or not? Most Americans surely think that more demand would be a good thing right now, but very few people want to see more inflation. To the Federal Reserve, these two effects are simply two sides of the same coin. But because the Fed expresses its aims in terms of inflation, its work is understood as a matter of managing inflation, and therefore Fed policies aimed at boosting inflation are politically problematic.

This dynamic contributes to the fourth flaw in inflation targeting—that it creates the strong impression that the job of the central bank is to control inflation while the job of *fiscal* stimulus is to produce economic growth and more employment. This view is a function of economic ignorance, but it is encouraged by the way the Fed defines its role, and it contributes to profound confusion about economic policy.

Almost any article on monetary stimulus will cite someone discussing the policy's impact on inflation. And almost any discussion of fiscal stimulus will include someone weighing the benefits of growth against the problems of deficits. There is a popular misconception that we should talk about fiscal and monetary stimulus using completely different terms and concepts, but from an economic perspective, there is no justification for the divide.

The standard economic model says that both fiscal and monetary stimulus boost aggregate demand (nominal spending). Whether that shows up in the form of higher inflation or more real growth depends on supply-side factors — like whether there are large numbers of unemployed workers or factories sitting idle that might respond to greater demand, or whether there is little such "slack" (such that new demand would lead mostly to higher wages and prices). If there is a difference between the two policy tools, it is that fiscal stimulus would actually be the *more* inflationary policy, because it consists of government spending (which is often less efficient, and hence may reduce aggregate supply and create shortages that boost prices), while monetary stimulus enables more private-sector spending. Indeed, free-market economists should be especially partial to monetary stimulus on these grounds.

Recent events in Britain provide a perfect example of the confusion generated by drawing this sort of false dichotomy between monetary and fiscal policy. The government of Prime Minister David Cameron has been sharply criticized for its policy of fiscal austerity. The recovery from the recent recession has been even weaker in Britain than in the United States, and there are fears that budget cuts will lead to a double-dip recession. At the same time, the press has been highly critical of the Bank of England for allowing inflation to rise far above the 2% target. But these criticisms cannot both be correct: Either Britain needs more aggregate demand or it does not. If it needs more, then the inflation rate in Britain needs to rise even higher, because the Bank of England needs to provide even more monetary stimulus. If inflation is too high and Britain needs less aggregate demand, then Britons should desire fiscal austerity that would slow the economy. The press seems to believe in some sort of policy magic whereby fiscal stimulus can create growth without inflation and monetary tightening can reduce inflation without affecting growth.

The way to clear up this muddle is to stop talking about the effect of monetary stimulus on inflation and the effect of fiscal stimulus on growth, and to start talking about how each affects nominal spending. Then we can focus on the fundamental issue: Does Britain need more NGDP growth or not? Most observers would agree that Britain needs both *more* NGDP growth (because its recovery from the last recession has been anemic) and *less* government spending (because its deficits and debt threaten its credit and potential for growth). The only way to achieve both goals is to combine monetary stimulus with fiscal austerity. And that can occur only if the Bank of England is free to focus on NGDP growth, rather than on inflation.

It is likely that Britain faces very unpleasant short-term tradeoffs, regardless of what happens with nominal spending. Monetary policy cannot solve real structural problems, and massive growth in government over the past decade has hurt the supply side of the British economy. Britain is likely to end up with an unfavorable inflation-to-output split regardless of what monetary policy it chooses — but at least NGDP targeting can provide a stable spending environment in which the Cameron government can pursue fiscal reforms. As those reforms reduce government spending, private spending will need to increase. Under this approach, the key is to remember that, if the Cameron government tries to shrink the state at the same time the Bank of England is trying to reduce aggregate demand, the British may end up with a double-dip recession that discredits the policy of fiscal austerity.

Indeed, monetary policy has always been the Achilles heel of conservative economics. Conservatives tend to favor low inflation, which is generally a laudable goal. But as we saw in America during the 1930s and in Argentina during the late 1990s, tight money can discredit free-market policies and open the door to left-wing governments if it is disconnected from an understanding of the proper aims of monetary and fiscal policy. There are times when higher inflation is necessary, and if it does not materialize, the public may choose an explosive growth of government instead. To discern such circumstances, we need to look not at inflation but at nominal spending. NGDP targeting is a way of making the world safe for laissez-faire capitalism. It becomes much easier to say we will not bail out General Motors if we have a monetary policy that assures that the failure of GM will not reduce aggregate spending, but will instead result in resources being re-allocated to other parts of the economy. It is easier to shed jobs in declining sectors if jobs are being created just as rapidly in booming sectors.

The knee-jerk opposition of many conservatives to monetary stimulus — and to inflation under any circumstances — arises from the confusion created by inflation targeting. It is a risky attitude, and one especially ill-suited to this moment. Explicitly targeting nominal GDP rather than inflation would greatly alleviate that confusion, and help make for a political environment friendlier to a more effective monetary policy.

### FINDING THE TARGET

Given these theoretical advantages of nominal GDP targeting, how ought it to be implemented in practice?

Most simply, the Federal Reserve should begin by adopting an approach of "level targeting" of nominal GDP. This doesn't mean keeping NGDP level, but rather targeting a specified trajectory, such as a 5% NGDP growth path, and committing to make up for any near-term shortfalls or excesses. Thus, if NGDP grew by 4% one year, the central bank would cut rates or engage in quantitative easing until its models yielded an expectation of 6% NGDP growth for the following year.

Level targeting is especially important when the economy is beset by severe shocks, as in late 2008. If markets had understood that any near-term shortfalls in NGDP growth would be made up for over the following several years, then asset prices (stocks, real estate, etc.) would have declined much less sharply, which would have moderated the decline in late 2008. Promising stable NGDP growth in later years along a pre-determined trajectory would actually make near-term NGDP much less unstable.

Another approach—which would be more radical, but perhaps also more effective—would limit the Fed's role to setting the NGDP target, and would leave the markets to determine the money supply and interest rates. This would mitigate the "central planning" aspect of the Federal Reserve's current role, which has rightly come under criticism from many conservatives. To give a simplified overview, the Fed would create NGDP futures contracts and peg them at a price that would rise at 5% per year. If investors expected NGDP growth above 5%, they would buy these contracts from the Fed. This would be an "open market sale," which would automatically tighten the money supply and raise interest rates. The Fed's role would be passive, merely offering to buy or sell the contracts at the specified target price, and settling the contracts a year later. Market participants would buy and sell these contracts until they no longer saw profit opportunities, i.e., until the money supply and interest rates adjusted to the point where NGDP was expected by the market to grow at the target rate.

It might be helpful to compare this idea to the old international gold standard. Under that system, the U.S. government agreed to buy and sell unlimited gold at $20.67 per ounce. This kept gold prices stable, and the money supply adjusted automatically. Unfortunately, however, stable gold prices did not always mean a stable macroeconomic environment. Putting NGDP futures contracts on the market along a similar model would likewise create a stable price for those contracts, hence stabilizing expected NGDP growth. And stable NGDP growth would be more conducive to macroeconomic stability than a stable price of gold, especially in a world in which rapidly growing demand from Asia might distort the relative price of gold.

Some critics might argue that NGDP targeting would be too easy on inflation. And it is true that looking at nominal GDP targeting through the prism of the past few years might make such targeting seem less "hawkish" than inflation targeting—a backdoor method of allowing excessive inflation. But the argument cuts both ways. Nominal GDP targeting would produce *lower* than average inflation during a productivity boom. Indeed, one criticism of inflation targeting is that, because central banks focus on consumer prices, they allow asset bubbles to form, which eventually destabilizes the economy. Nominal GDP targeting cannot completely eliminate this problem, but it can impose more monetary restraint during periods of high-output growth than can inflation targeting.

Others might acknowledge that NGDP targeting could help stabilize output, but would nonetheless point to a serious cost: greater inflation variability. In fact, however, many of the problems generally associated with inflation are actually linked to NGDP volatility. For instance, inflation is said to raise the effective tax rate on capital, as most tax systems don't index taxes on interest and dividends to inflation. But the nominal interest rate may be more closely correlated with NGDP growth than with inflation, meaning that the tax distortion is better explained by high NGDP growth than by high inflation. Or, to take another example, deflation is often blamed for high unemployment—but, once again, the problem is actually caused by falling NGDP growth, as lower inflation resulting from productivity gains does not create unemployment. Low inflation, meanwhile, is often thought to make a liquidity trap more likely; in fact, it is low NGDP growth that best accounts for the risk of hitting the zero-rate bound. Interest rates fell to zero when Japan experienced mild deflation, but not when China experienced mild deflation. The difference was NGDP growth: It has been near zero for Japan since 1993, while Chinese nominal growth has not fallen below the 5% to 10% range, even during the East Asian crisis of the late 1990s.

Moreover, George Selgin has shown that, contrary to conventional wisdom, unexpected inflation is not unfair to lenders as long as NGDP growth is on target. If inflation were to rise sharply during a period of stable NGDP growth, it would mean that a real shock had depressed the economy. When real shocks occur, it is only fair that debtors and creditors share the loss. Suppose lenders made lots of foolish loans to the housing sector, leading to a subsequent fall in real GDP as housing construction plummeted and workers had to be retrained for other sectors. In that case, NGDP targeting would lead to a period of above-normal inflation, and lenders would bear some of the burden for this misallocation of capital, even in the absence of outright defaults. That would be appropriate.

So the idea that NGDP targeting might allow for higher inflation and thus fail to prevent the problems caused by inflation is mistaken. In fact, many of the problems we associate with inflation are actually caused by fluctuations of nominal GDP, and would be better addressed by a policy aimed at keeping NGDP at some pre-determined target.

### POLICY AND POLITICS

In the end, there is no escaping the fact that the Federal Reserve is a political institution. For most of the 20th century, the politicization of monetary policy meant easier money and thus more inflation. In the current policy environment, the politicization of the Fed means tighter money, and so lower inflation; for all the complaints about easy money, especially on the right, we have a policy that is actually too tight to maintain even 2% core inflation. Either way, though, the inevitable politicization of monetary policy has combined with the Fed's overly narrow focus on inflation to produce monetary policy that is not well suited to produce the kind of consistent growth our economy needs.

Nominal GDP targeting is, of course, not the only possible solution to the problems bedeviling monetary policy today. But the solution that offers the most economically plausible alternative—a higher inflation target, between 3% and 4%—is not politically viable. Nominal GDP targeting, on the other hand, offers both a politically *and* economically sensible alternative, which would be far better equipped to advance stable growth, to overcome the politics of inflation, and to help the Fed avoid discrediting itself. It offers a single target that effectively combines both facets of the Fed's dual mandate, and so should be attractive to those on both the left and the right who argue that the requirement to simultaneously address inflation and unemployment makes it impossible for the Fed to tackle either very well.

This does not mean, of course, that NGDP targeting can address our broader economic predicament. Monetary policy is not an answer to structural policy problems. It cannot make up for a failure to control the growth of public spending or the explosion of entitlement costs. But it can do a great deal to help create a stable environment of consistent growth, and thus make the difficult structural reforms ahead both more effective and easier to tolerate. At the moment, our monetary policy risks making the hard task facing fiscal reformers all the more challenging. A Federal Reserve with its eyes firmly set on the right target would greatly ease their way.

*Originally published as "Re-Targeting the Fed" in the Fall 2011 issue of* National Affairs.

# v. Education Reform

# How to Modernize Our School System

## Chester E. Finn, Jr.

FALL 2011

To anyone concerned with the state of America's schools, one of the more alarming experiences of the past few decades has been the sight of waves of innovative reforms crashing upon the rocks of our education system. Charter schools have popped up all over the landscape; vouchers are being implemented in more and more places; massive federal initiatives like No Child Left Behind and Race to the Top have invested billions of dollars in fixing our schools. And yet the results remain dismal: Millions of children still cannot read satisfactorily, do math at an acceptable level, or perform the other skills needed for jobs in the modern economy.

Why this persistent failure? One major cause is clearly our deeply flawed system for organizing and operating public schools. Currently, our approach to school management is a confused and tangled web, involving the federal government, the states, and local school districts — each with ill-defined responsibilities and often conflicting interests. As a result, over the past 50 years, obsolescence, clumsiness, and misalignment have come to define the governance of public education. This development is not anyone's fault, per se: It is simply what happens when opportunities and needs change, but structures don't. The system of schooling we have today is the legacy of the 19th century — and hopelessly outmoded in the 21st.

But given that our method of school governance is so significantly responsible for what ails American education today, it has received surprisingly little attention. Efforts to address the problem elicit either boredom — governance is passé in the reform world, especially compared to hotter fads like vouchers, tenure, and merit pay — or eye-rolling,

CHESTER E. FINN, JR., is president of the Thomas B. Fordham Institute and a senior fellow at Stanford's Hoover Institution.

as many argue that, even if school-system structure and governance pose problems, trying to fix them is politically futile.

Yet to fail to confront these malfunctions is to accept the glum fact that even the most urgent and earnest of other reform efforts cannot make meaningful improvements to public education. And we cannot afford such complacency. Only by seeking to understand how we came to operate schools in such a haphazard way, what particularly ails our governance structures now, and how they might be reformed can we restore sanity and efficiency to America's public schools.

## THE SCHOOL DISTRICT AND ITS ORIGINS

The main structures of modern American public education generally date to the 19<sup>th</sup> century (and in some cases even earlier), when individual towns and families paid essentially all the costs of operating whatever schools they had. Indeed, education in the early days was an entirely local affair, and so quite varied: Some towns had schools, others didn't; some paid for them with taxes, others with bushels of wheat, church tithes, or tuition charges levied on parents. Just as individual communities decided whether and how to operate schools, so did individual families determine which, if any, of their sons and daughters would attend school (and for how long). If a child was poor, he ordinarily got little or no schooling unless someone took pity on him and paid for his education.

This started to change in the mid-19th century, when states began requiring children to attend school, at least for a few primary grades. Massachusetts led the way in 1852, and New York followed a year later. By 1918, every state had some sort of "compulsory attendance" law on its books. With such requirements came an obligation on the state's part to ensure that schools were available so that these requirements could be fulfilled. This demand drew states into both the financing and governance of primary and, in time, secondary education.

The deepest imprint on today's school-governance structures, however, may have been left by the Progressive Era — when it was deemed important to "keep politics out of education" so as to avoid the taint of patronage and party. According to the prevailing wisdom, it was better to entrust the supervision of public education to expert professionals and independent, non-partisan boards that would attract disinterested community leaders to tend to this vital civic function. Mayors and aldermen were to be kept at bay, lest public education grow entwined with other government functions and agencies, and thus become contaminated.

At the state level, too, the governance structures devised for education were meant to serve as a buffer from conventional politics. Most states established their own boards of education, some with members appointed by the governor to fixed terms, some elected. Each of these boards then hired a "commissioner" or "superintendent" of education, ordinarily a career professional, to head the education department—a state agency, to be sure, but seldom part of the governor's "cabinet" and rarely subject to his direct control.

A few of these state-level structures pre-dated the Progressives. For instance, the New York State Board of Regents—with members chosen by the legislature—was launched in 1784 (though its mandate at the outset was limited to higher education). Massachusetts created its state board of education—focused on primary and secondary schooling—in 1837. Its establishment was a response to Governor Edward Everett's admonition to lawmakers that, while locally operated "common" schools were well and good,

> The school houses might, in many cases, be rendered more commodious. Provision ought to be made for affording the advantages of education, throughout the whole year, to all of a proper age to receive it. Teachers well qualified to give elementary instruction in all the branches of useful knowledge, should be employed; and small school libraries, maps, globes, and requisite scientific apparatus should be furnished. I submit to the Legislature, whether the creation of a board of commissioners of schools, to serve without salary, with authority to appoint a secretary, on a reasonable compensation, to be paid from the school fund, would not be of great utility.

The very first secretary of that "board of commissioners" was Horace Mann, often termed the father of public education in the United States.

In the years that followed, as state constitutions were written and rewritten, they included provisions that explicitly tasked the states with the responsibility of educating their own citizens. The wording of these clauses varies considerably; typical examples are Ohio's charge to its legislature to "secure a thorough and efficient system of common schools throughout the state" and Texas's assignment to its lawmakers to "establish and make suitable provision for the support and maintenance of an efficient system of public free schools." Whatever the phrasing, every state constitution now includes some provision to this effect.

But though states bear formal responsibility for public education, all save Hawaii have opted to deliver schooling through "local education agencies" (LEAs), also known as school districts. The states did not create LEAs out of whole cloth: They inherited them from the earlier era of community-based, locally financed education. And their configurations vary just as greatly as our communities. In some states, they coincide with counties, while in others they are coterminous with cities or townships. Rarely, however, are LEAs actually governed directly by these political entities.

Because of this history, and owing to differences among states, LEAs vary greatly in size and number. Today, Illinois has 1,100 of them, Maryland just 25. LEAs have also been shaped by decades of consolidation. In 1930, for instance, the United States contained a staggering 130,000 LEAs, many responsible for just one school each. Today, we have only one-tenth that number: There were 13,809 LEAs in 2008, responsible for 98,706 schools. This would suggest that, on average, each district in America is responsible for seven schools. But in another instance of the unevenness of LEAs, this figure is deeply deceptive, as some school systems (mostly in large cities) enroll more than 200,000 students each while 80% of America's LEAs educate fewer than 1,000 students apiece.

Save for charter schools, a few specialized schools run directly by states, and a handful of federally operated schools for military children and Native Americans, LEAs administer America's public schools. They do so via a "central office" presided over by a superintendent — almost always a career educator — and his staff, which usually functions as a typical public-sector bureaucracy with one unit in charge of transportation, another responsible for personnel, and so on. Except in a dozen or so cities where the superintendent reports to the mayor, or the mayor appoints the governing board, the LEA's administrative team is answerable to an elected board of education or school committee. Typically, school boards consist of seven or nine members; there are some 100,000 such officials nationwide.

The powers of these boards vary from place to place. Part of this variation stems from the fact that some states are more prescriptive than others when it comes to public education; it is also the result of differing approaches to revenue-raising. School boards in some jurisdictions have their own authority to levy taxes and issue bonds, though in many cases school budgets and the local taxes that support them are subject to approval either by other local bodies — such as city councils and county supervisors — or by voters in referenda.

Because today's LEA and school-board structures arose organically from 18th- and 19th-century arrangements — and because these entities are thoroughly familiar and ubiquitous — their utility is rarely questioned. We hardly ever bother to ask how well this system is working, much less whether children, taxpayers, and the cause of American competitiveness might be better served by a different set-up. We just take for granted that this is how public education works.

### ROADBLOCKS TO REFORM

Such complacency, however, is deeply harmful. Today, this system produces ever more failure; indeed, it is telling that the national education agenda has shifted from *running* schools to *reforming* them. In the course of that historic shift, the customary governance structures have emerged as major obstacles. Upon reflection, though, it should hardly be surprising that the governing bodies that produced the current dysfunction are none too eager — or competent — when the time comes to make significant changes.

Examples of how current school-governance structures hinder reform abound. Consider, for instance, the emerging practice of "distance learning." Information and communications technologies are transforming the development and delivery of education; already, dozens of "cyber schools" have opened — some as charters, some operated as franchises of national for-profit firms, some (like the Florida Virtual School) run as integral parts of the state education system. The biggest of these schools operate throughout the states in which they are located — but they could just as easily be operated inter-state or nationwide. After all, political borders do not constrain the delivery of online courses into children's homes, day-care centers, churches, or brick-and-mortar schools.

But which government would write the ground rules for cyber-schooling and hold its vendors to account for their results? Who would set distance learning's academic requirements and assessments? And who would pay for kids to attend them or — in an even more complicated scenario — to take separate courses from several of them, in order to assemble a curriculum tailored to each student? Districts? States? The federal government? Encumbered by the old LEA model, we have no governance mechanism well suited to answering these questions — certainly not local school boards with geographically bounded jurisdictions. Thus the potential for distance learning as an alternative to underperforming schools remains barely tapped, and its financing and rule-making remain absurdly complicated.

Or consider the challenges of teacher preparation. Today, states "certify" teachers, but districts and individual charter schools employ them. Washington, meanwhile, superimposes rules of its own — federal law requires a "highly qualified" teacher in every classroom — while national non-profits like Teach for America recruit and place instructors all over the country. Graduates of our roughly 1,200 teacher-training programs move around, too — but the state in which each program is located sets its own curriculum, meaning that graduates of such programs may not in fact be fully prepared for the teaching jobs they will ultimately hold. Further confusing matters is the fact that most of these programs are "accredited" by a national organization (the National Council for Accreditation of Teacher Education) — except for those that opt for other accreditors or get by with none at all. And that's before adding the new complexities of "virtual" teacher-preparation programs, such as those operating under the aegis of the University of Southern California or Kaplan University (a for-profit enterprise). Because of our patchwork governance system, there is little uniformity in teacher preparation, dubious quality control, and limited portability of credentials and skills.

Another example is school financing. Several promising reform proposals focus on how schools are funded — such as those hoping to force accountability and improve incentives by tying dollars to students and then allowing the money to go where the students do. But complicating such proposals is the fact that school funding today is hopelessly tangled. Nationwide, state taxes generate about 47 cents of the public-school dollar, local taxes (mostly levied on property) yield about 43 cents, and Uncle Sam kicks in the remaining dime. This distribution varies greatly, however; there are places where the state portion is only about one-third (such as in Florida, Missouri, Nebraska, and South Dakota), while other states (like New Mexico, Vermont, and Hawaii) cover more than 70%. Funding amounts vary even more widely *within* states: The public schools of Beachwood, Ohio, spend about $20,000 per pupil; 70 miles down the highway, the Strasburg schools spend less than half as much. Despite round after round of "equity lawsuits" (many of them successful), the financing of schools across the country is woefully uneven and confused.

Current governance structures also pose an obstacle to charter schooling. These independently operated public schools are meant to provide alternatives to district schools, and in most places are designed to function as their competitors—giving choices to families, offering an escape hatch to kids trapped in dreadful schools, and creating at least a partial marketplace within what has long been a near-monopoly. Yet more than half of America's charter schools owe their very licenses to operate to the school systems they are supposed to compete with. In many states, would-be charter operators have nowhere else to turn for such licenses. Unsurprisingly, most school-district bureaucracies abhor these upstart rivals; using their power and influence over local and state politicians, they do all they can to contain the growth of charters and, where possible, to eradicate them.

Even the signature education-reform effort of the past two decades—the imposition of rigorous academic standards and accountability for meeting them—has been stymied by our dysfunctional approach to school governance. This structure makes it almost impossible to address the question of what happens to school districts that fail to meet the higher standards, and the further challenge of especially bad schools—"dropout factories" that fail completely in their most basic mission. After all, whose responsibility is it to fix them? The federal government's? That has already been tried with the No Child Left Behind law, which will certainly fail to meet its goal of establishing universal student proficiency by 2014. So are states responsible? The same districts that allowed these schools to fail in the first place, sometimes year after year? What reason is there to believe that these districts would now know how to set things right?

Given these obstacles, it is no accident that all the major education reforms of the past quarter-century have come from outside of the traditional governance structures. Whether one looks at the development of academic standards, the imposition of testing-and-accountability regimes, the spread of school choice in its many variants, or major changes in how teachers are evaluated and compensated, the impetus has almost never originated with state or local boards of education or the people who work for them. Rather, such initiatives have come from governors and business leaders, from mayors and national commissions, from private foundations, and even from the White House.

Putting those bold reforms into practice, however, generally depends on the traditional management structures of public education. And that is where the momentum slows to a creep. These traditional structures are lethargic, bureaucratic, and set in their ways; while people within them may have experience managing schools and complying with rules, they seldom have the capacity to innovate, to make judgments about matters beyond their customary duties, or to stage successful interventions in failing districts and schools. Moreover, many of these people fiercely oppose the policies they are asked to implement. It thus seems that, regardless of the innovative solutions emerging from foundations and think tanks — and no matter how many promising policies are propagated from Washington and state capitals — our current approach to operating schools will remain an all-but-insurmountable roadblock to reform.

### ADULT INTERESTS

Making matters worse is the fact that these traditional structures — theoretically designed to advance the educational interests of children — now exist principally to serve the material interests of adults. Many of these adult interest groups derive enormous benefit from the status quo, and are thus extremely hostile to changes that disrupt it.

Teachers' unions head the list of such organizations, but by no means complete it. School custodians, too, have unions. So do school principals: Even though one might expect these educators to be classified as "management," the principals' contracts in cities like Las Vegas and Baltimore clearly treat them as employees allowed to organize. And behind the unions are queued more rent-seekers: Textbook publishers, tutoring firms, uniform manufacturers, bus companies, food-service and building-security businesses, as well as all manner of data-processing, information technology, and communications outfits have longstanding contracts with public-school systems. Colleges of education, local universities, and civil rights organizations all have stakes in how those systems work, whom they employ, and where they obtain guidance and expertise.

What gives these adult interests traction? Often it is habit, bureaucratic routine, multi-year contracts, and regulatory regimes that limit the options from which LEAs can select, thereby reducing the threat of competition.

But with mounting frequency—particularly in the case of teachers' unions—traction comes from political clout. This is achieved by helping union-friendly individuals get elected to school boards, a feat made easier in the many jurisdictions where such elections are non-partisan, often un-contested, and conducted on random dates that don't coincide with other elections and thus draw few voters. In such circumstances, any organized interest group that can mobilize its members and supporters has an ex-cellent chance of prevailing at the polls. Time after time, we have seen examples—in the District of Columbia, Los Angeles, San Diego, Houston, and elsewhere—of unions mustering their members and their allies to ensure the electoral defeat of board members and superintendents who pressed aggressively for reforms that the groups found objectionable.

Much the same thing happens at the state level. Through the use of savvy candidate recruitment, campaign contributions, shoe leather, publicity, and voter mobilization, it is often possible for unions (and, occasionally, other interest groups) to sway key legislative elections. This king-making power then intimidates both incumbent and aspiring lawmakers, steering them toward policies the unions favor. The unions frequently fend off, defeat, or marginalize those who defy their interests. Though most recipients of such help are Democrats, in jurisdictions where Republicans wield long-term influence in the state house, the unions have found ways to befriend—or defang—some of them, too.

Still, state-level politics can be difficult to influence: Those elections generally *are* contested, partisan, and held on regular election days when voter turnout is strong. Local school boards are thus easier to manipu-late. And nowhere is this more true than in urban America.

The nation's urban school districts are located within enormous, bureaucratic, and often highly politicized municipalities. These cit-ies are demographically and economically heterogeneous, containing many different "communities" with conflicting priorities, needs, and dreams—especially when it comes to the education of children. And a large proportion of the nation's children are educated within such systems: 35% of American students are enrolled in the 281 districts with 25,000 or more pupils, and a majority of all students (54%)—includ-ing the overwhelming majority of poor and minority students—are accounted for by fewer than 900 districts. This means that about 7,000 individual school-board members are responsible for the education of more than half the country's children.

And what are these urban school-board members like? Generally speaking, our cities have already abandoned the Progressive ideal of having board members interested only in the welfare of children and the community, free of the stain of politics, and able to rise above party and patronage in order to advance the public interest.

In urban America, well-educated, civic-minded, and reasonably prosperous people—of all races—find district-level politics daunting and painful. Many have foresworn the city school system itself, moving to the suburbs, enrolling their kids in private or charter schools, or busying themselves with other kinds of community service—service that is less onerous, and more likely to result in gratitude than in hostility. Particularly in large districts, school-board service has grown demanding—according to 70% of the board members in such districts, it consumes more than 25 hours a month—and poorly compensated. Though a slight majority of large U.S. school systems pay board members a stipend, few stipends exceed $10,000 a year. Serving on such boards can also bring unpleasantness: long, boring evenings listening to public testimony; onerous (and costly) election campaigns; the risk of name-calling, picketing, and racial acrimony; painful responsibilities like closing and "reconstituting" neighborhood schools; and agendas laden with micromanagerial issues but short on decisions about fundamental policy and direction. And even if a school-board member feels that fundamental policy needs to be addressed, he likely knows that to make waves is to risk being booted out of office.

Under these circumstances, who wants to serve on a school board? A look at many big-district boards provides the answer: aspiring politicians, union puppets, individuals with some cause or scheme they yearn to inflict on everyone's kids, and ex-employees of the system with scores to settle. As a result, able, well-meaning, even reform-minded superintendents with commendable plans to improve their schools are often undermined by their own board members. Is it any wonder that the average tenure of urban superintendents is just 3.6 years? And this frequent turnover exacerbates yet another challenge to school reform: the tendency of any bureaucratic system to "wait out" the latest attempt to fix it, mindful that in a year or two that plan's author will move on—and that life will then revert to the old modus operandi, or that yet another reform notion will be tried only to prove similarly short-lived.

Even where there is a decent board and a competent superintendent, the ability to alter the system in any meaningful way is limited. The neediest youngsters will likely require additional help from other agencies that answer to the mayor or city manager, not to the school system. Pre-schools, if there are any, answer to their own organizations or shareholders. A multi-state consortium decides what the academic standards will contain, what assessments will be used, and what makes for an acceptable level of achievement. And if local universities and employers don't like what comes out of the public high schools, they are under no obligation to admit or employ them.

From start to finish, schooling is produced by disparate and far-flung participants, often working against one another; no one figure or organization in a student's community "owns" responsibility for the outcome of his education. In many school systems, particularly the largest, children thus fall through the cracks, and local control fails to establish real accountability. What exactly is "local" about the Los Angeles Unified School District, the Houston Independent School District, or, for that matter, the Fairfax County (Virginia) Public Schools, serving vast territories and enrolling hundreds of thousands of children of every conceivable background in hundreds of schools? Or, at the other end of the demographic spectrum, how "local" is the Park County, Colorado, school system, serving just 678 students scattered over 1,721 square miles—with a mountain range down the middle and school-bus routes that sometimes exceed 50 miles?

Stuck with the corrupted remains of old governance structures, such places are losing the spirit, if not the forms, of "local control" of their public schools. Put another way, our rigid adherence to the "local education agency" approach to school management now undermines the very principles that gave rise to the approach in the first place.

## RECLAIMING "LOCAL" EDUCATION

There is clearly a need to restore a true sense of local education, in which families and communities—more knowledgeable about their own desires and their children's needs—make crucial decisions about how to educate children, rather than leaving those choices to distant, scattered, self-concerned bureaucrats and adult interest groups. The good news, however, is that, while all of this dysfunction has depleted the traditional version of "local control" in American public education, new forms of local control have started to take root.

The most conspicuous of these efforts involve turning over management of the school system to someone else. In several major cities—most prominently New York, Boston, Chicago, Cleveland, and the District of Columbia—the mayor is now in charge; the superintendent (or chancellor) reports directly to him. In Newark, Philadelphia, Detroit, and a handful of other disastrous (or bankrupt) districts, the state has simply seized control.

Less visible, but far more widespread, is the quiet re-invention of local control—alternatives that move away from the traditional LEA model while advancing the aims of decentralization and increased parental influence and choice. Typically, this re-invention takes three forms.

The first is the right in most states of parents, educators, and organizations to form and run their own charter schools. This is a limited tool, to be sure, subject to myriad requirements and political risks (including, in too many places, the power of the existing school bureaucracy to veto a charter plan). But these charter schools—5,000 of them and counting—are essentially self-governing, not unlike private schools. The potential for charters is enormous, and the charter laws of many states are flexible enough to be used for diverse ends. Indeed, in the aforementioned Park County, Colorado, district, two tiny towns took the charter route to effectively "secede" from the distant central office and reclaim control over their own schools.

Second, as other forms of schooling arise and various choice programs confer more options on more parents in more places, the district monopoly is starting to fracture. Charter schools are just the beginning: There are also Science, Technology, Engineering, and Mathematics (STEM) schools, magnet schools, "governor's schools," virtual schools, regional vocational schools, "tech-prep" and "early-college" programs, not to mention access to schools in other neighborhoods, in the next district, and even, in places with voucher programs, to private schools at public expense. And all of this choice is available without making the decision to move home and hearth in order to reside near a better "neighborhood" school. When one adds this "real-estate choice" to all of these other choice options, it can accurately be said that slightly more than half of all American students today attend schools that they or their parents selected.

Third, outside of the schools themselves, technology is combining with prosperity—and in some cases with religious faith or strongly held preferences about instructional methods—to lead parents to pursue educational alternatives for their kids. Full-time "home schooling" is the most extreme version, and close to 3% of all American children are now educated in this manner. In some places, students — particularly high schoolers — may be able to split their education, spending part of their time in a traditional brick-and-mortar school and the rest being taught at home or in a "parent collaborative" that functions much like the one-room school houses of yore. More widespread and accessible still is the supplementation of children's regular schooling with software and high-quality online programs, after-school programs, summer school, and education-focused camps, as well as plain old books and their electronic clones. These developments are not a formal change of school governance — but they do allow "local control" of education to be brought right into parents' homes.

It is in this direction that the future of American education should point. The aim should not be to abolish local control or to devise more clumsy "work-arounds," but rather to re-invent "local control" altogether. Empowering families, volunteer groups, education organizations, and even neighborhoods to create and run their schools is what "local control" should mean — a meaning not so very different from the one it had a century ago, when the United States had a smaller and less mobile population, much of it spread across rural areas and small towns, and when we had about 130,000 school systems rather than nearly 14,000.

Under this re-definition of "local control," what ought day-to-day education look like? Self-governing, charter-style schools should become the norm, not the exception. These schools of choice could vary dramatically in size, staffing, calendar, curricular and pedagogical focus, and in their uses of technology. Some would be operated by regional and national firms; others would be "virtual." Many would likely band together in order to share services and pursue greater efficiency. Some might join integrated "feeder school" networks, which allow a child to remain part of a coherent institutional sequence from kindergarten (or earlier) through 12th grade (or later). Others would be local franchises of brand-name charter schools — such as Core Knowledge or the Knowledge Is Power Program.

For this arrangement to work, however, the heavy burden of reform would have to fall on the states. For instance, in order for such a system to maintain a semblance of order and equality, states would need to both increase and shrink their roles in school governance and finance. The state or its reliable agents would "authorize" every school and hold it accountable — for academic results, for complying with essential rules, for properly handling public dollars, and so forth. Those state authorizers would, in effect, license schools to operate, determine whether they are functioning properly, and gauge when and how to intervene in cases of malfunction. The authorizer would also watch over the governance of "its" schools and perhaps sign off on the selection of their principals. Authorizers could take many forms, as they do under current charter laws. Ultimately, the state and its authorizers would need to ensure the existence of enough approved schools to accommodate all children, regardless of the students' educational circumstances. This might also involve operating (or outsourcing) a placement service to help match students and families with public schools that are accessible and best suited to meeting children's needs.

In a related function, states would also need to set suitable academic standards, assess student and school performance, and report the re-sults—much as they do today. Those results would be presented as data capable of being sliced and compared in hundreds of ways, enabling improved education policy and practice. States could make this respon-sibility simpler and the results more readily comparable by signing up for newly minted (and generally sound) "common" standards as well as for shared assessments, which are still in development. Crucially, however, as states took on greater responsibility for setting the broad outlines of education policy, they would have to back off from their cus-tomary micromanagement and regulation of the K-12 space—instead entrusting the responsibility for personnel, curriculum, budget, and several other functions to individual schools, where it belongs.

An added burden for the states—but an essential one, if this new structure is to work properly—would be shouldering almost total re-sponsibility for raising and disbursing the public dollars that flow to schools. (And in this case, "states" must mean the governor and legisla-ture—not a quasi-independent body without direct accountability to parents, voters, and taxpayers.) The optimal way to channel those public dollars is through "weighted student funding," whereby the amount of money devoted to a child's education varies with his needs and educa-tional circumstances and accompanies that child to the school of his choice. States would use whatever revenue sources they favored—taxes, lotteries, riverboat gambling—to raise these funds, but the "local share" as we know it would vanish. Individual schools might want to "top up" their state funding with locally raised money; whether they would be allowed to do so is a decision each state should make for itself.

In this new system, what would happen to the LEA? Its fate would likely come to resemble that of its counterparts in England, known there as "local education authorities." Over the past quarter-century, these governing bodies have been marginalized; the decisions, controls, and authorities that they once wielded have moved both up (to London) and down (to individual schools and their "governors"). The LEAs still exist—but they don't have much to do.

On this side of the ocean, it would of course be cleaner to erase LEAs altogether. If states wanted to, most could accomplish this through legislation; in only a few, such as Colorado, are the LEAs themselves enshrined in the state constitutions. But such all-out elimination doesn't seem likely and may not be necessary: Some LEAs would naturally wither away. Some—perhaps the large and reasonably well-functioning agencies like the one in Montgomery County, Maryland—might seek to play a version of the state role as outlined above. (Indeed, having existing local districts take on the aforementioned state functions could be a useful "trial run" before full statewide re-invention.) Other enterprising districts might become vendors of goods and services in their locales: Schools that wanted to cluster together for a range of purposes—from sports leagues to shared facilities, building maintenance, pupil transportation, information technology, group purchasing, business management, special education, advanced calculus, or fifth-year Japanese—might find the LEA to be the most convenient and efficient provider or consolidator. The key, however, is that the schools would choose to work with the LEA—a far cry from having the LEA run the schools.

### A TIME FOR CHOOSING

Naturally, the picture sketched above may seem radical, and is of course incomplete. Filling it in will require altering the federal government's role in education, too. And getting even partway to this goal may require some states to amend their constitutions—an inevitably contentious proposition, sure to be resisted by the same adult interests that so fiercely obstruct reform today.

But the challenges that this course poses are no excuse not to embark upon it. The first step toward reform is to openly acknowledge that our inherited arrangements for governing education are archaic and dysfunctional—and that to continue to take them for granted is to consign almost all of today's other education reforms to stagnation and failure.

The next step is to seriously consider who should be in charge of America's system of education. After decades of leaving its management to self-serving contractors, bureaucracies, and unions, the results are bitterly disappointing. The new approach outlined above, however, would dramatically shift this responsibility, placing it with governors and legislatures, individual schools and their own governing bodies, and, ultimately, parents and taxpayers.

And it is with taxpayers and parents that the responsibility for educating our children should ultimately lie. The original principle behind our local governance system was that the people who had the most invested in their schools and the most to gain from them — as well as the best, most direct knowledge of whom those schools needed to serve and what services they needed to provide — should govern them. Over the past century and a half, we have drifted far away from that original aim — to the detriment of America's students. For their benefit, and for the nation's, we must now endeavor to make education local again.

*Originally published as "Beyond the School District" in the Fall 2011 issue of* National Affairs.

# How to Think About School Choice

## Frederick M. Hess

FALL 2010

T HESE WOULD SEEM TO BE DARK DAYS for the school-choice
movement, as several early champions of choice have publicly
expressed their disillusionment. A few years ago, the Manhattan Institute's
Sol Stern — author of *Breaking Free: Public School Lessons and the Imperative
of School Choice* — caused a stir when he backed away from his once-ardent
support. Howard Fuller, an architect of Milwaukee's school-voucher plan
and the godfather of the school-choice movement, has wryly observed, "I
think that any honest assessment would have to say that there hasn't been
the deep, wholesale improvement in [Milwaukee Public Schools] that we
would have thought." Earlier this year, historian Diane Ravitch made
waves when she retracted her once staunch support for school choice in
*The Death and Life of the Great American School System.* "I just wish that
choice proponents would stop promising that charters and vouchers
will bring us closer to that date when 100 percent of all children reach
proficiency," she opined in her blog. "If evidence mattered, they would
tone down their rhetoric." Harvard professor and iconic school-voucher
proponent Paul Peterson has characterized the voucher movement
as "stalled," in part by the fact that many "new voucher schools were
badly run, both fiscally and educationally," and in part because results in
Milwaukee were not "as startlingly positive as advocates originally hoped."
Likewise, Peterson argues, "the jury on charter schools is still out."

To many who hold out hope that choice can help fix what ails
America's schools, these hedges and reversals have been startling. And
yet, looking back, it is hard to see how they were not inevitable. For
decades, school-choice advocates have seemed bent on producing this
hour of disappointment.

FREDERICK M. HESS *is director of educational-policy studies at the American Enterprise
Institute.*

There has been, for instance, a tendency to vastly overpromise. In 1990, the same year that Milwaukee's tiny voucher program launched the school-choice debate, scholars John Chubb and Terry Moe argued in their seminal volume, *Politics, Markets, and America's Schools*: "Without being too literal about it, we think reformers would do well to entertain the notion that choice is a panacea...It has the capacity all by itself to bring about the kind of transformation that, for years, reformers have been seeking to engineer in myriad other ways." Chubb and Moe are gifted thinkers, and their book was a tour de force, but this may have been some of the worst advice that school reformers ever got.

The search for that panacea, and the insistence that it must be just around the corner, have been destructive distractions. They have led champions of market-oriented reforms—and so also allowed skeptics—to adopt a ludicrous standard for judging whether school choice "works." Since reformers have suggested that the mere presence of choice will bring about dramatic improvement in schools, the expectation has been that the simple fact of having an alternative—even inadequately funded vouchers, or charter schools hog-tied by regulation—should yield demonstrable gains in academic achievement. And so, for the past 20 years, the question of whether school choice "works" has been understood to mean simply whether a school-choice program boosted reading and math test scores in a given year.

The need to answer this question with an unequivocal "yes" has forced choice advocates into bizarre contortions and short-sighted thinking. The same can be said of opponents, whose insistence, in the face of all evidence, that school choice is harmful has led them to ignore its real achievements.

Particularly problematic is how this way of thinking has caused school-choice proponents to ignore crucial questions of market design and implementation—especially the extent to which reforms have, or have not, created a real market dynamic in education. The chief promise of choice, after all, was that it would displace ossified, monopolistic school bureaucracies or at least inject into them a degree of flexibility, competition, and quality control. The question education reformers should be asking, then, is not simply whether choice "works"—because choice is neither the sole end of nor a sufficient means for bringing about successful market-based reform.

The questions to focus on are when, how, and why deregulation and monopoly-busting improve the quality and cost effectiveness of goods and services—and whether they can do the same for K-12 schooling. What would a vibrant market in K-12 education look like? To what degree has it really been tried? What needs to change in order to bring about such a market, and how would we assess whether it is in fact improving the education received by children in America's schools?

Before answering these crucial questions, however, it is important to understand how reformers came to paint themselves into a corner.

## A LEGACY OF OVERPROMISING

Educational choice is hardly a modern innovation. In some ways, it dates back at least as far as ancient Athens with its marketplace of sophists and philosophers. In the Anglo-American context, explicit proposals for state-funded arrangements that would let parents choose how their children would be educated can be traced to the writings of Thomas Paine in the late 18th century, and of John Stuart Mill in the 19th century. Both men thought it appropriate for the state to ensure that young people were given at least a basic level of education—but both also felt that this aim should be advanced through private arrangements, rejecting the notion of state educational monopolies.

School choice as we think of it today originated with an essay penned in 1955 by economist Milton Friedman. Friedman's argument was that a voucher system of education—one in which the government's role would be limited to providing funding and setting basic standards for "approved" educational institutions, while parents would retain the right to determine which of these institutions could best educate their children—would promote both equitable and efficient schooling. The first substantial effort to translate the concept into policy took shape in President Lyndon Johnson's Office of Economic Opportunity, where a cluster of social scientists toyed with vouchers as a politically viable and promising alternative to school busing. The efforts of the OEO wonks resulted in a tiny, dead-end "school voucher" pilot program in Alum Rock, California; the experiment, which ultimately looked a lot more like a magnet-school program than anything we would today call a "voucher" system, resulted in little besides a mammoth-yet-banal study by the RAND Corporation.

The modern school-choice movement did not begin in earnest until the 1980s, when it grew out of the overlapping efforts of four distinct champions. One was Ronald Reagan, who had reached out in 1979 and

1980 to disaffected Catholics who were dismayed by judicial assaults on school prayer, and were seeking assistance with parochial-school tuition. Another was an ascendant Republican Party, seeking a proactive, market-friendly agenda. The third was legendary American Federation of Teachers president Al Shanker—who was pitching "charter" schools as a way for teachers to establish schools in which they would have heightened autonomy, and in which they could insulate themselves from district bureaucracy. And the fourth was a group of frustrated African-American leaders seeking good, safe schools for urban children stuck in horrendously mismanaged districts.

The most politically marketable of these advocates were the urban black leaders—and so, before long, the various parties found common ground in emphasizing the language of empathy and rights. The case for school choice was thus not argued in terms of efficiency or deregulation, but instead presented as a moral imperative—an obligation to give poor, black inner-city parents the kinds of educational choices taken for granted by suburban home owners. This "social justice" rhetoric was the mantra of the school-choice movement when Wisconsin enacted the Milwaukee voucher program in 1990; it has been the reigning justification ever since.

This approach helps explain why choice advocates—inclined to approach choice-based reform not as a regulatory question, but as one of justice and rights—have spent so much less time considering the dynamics of deregulation than have pro-market reformers in sectors like transportation, telecommunications, and cable television. Because education reformers have approached choice not as a matter of political economy but as a moral crusade, they have favored grand, sweeping claims over empirical reality.

For example, in a celebrated 1999 article in the *New Republic*, author and former Al Gore advisor David Osborne boldly declared, "Those who invented charter schools...wanted to improve all 88,000 public schools in the country [and]...empirical studies have demonstrated that, indeed, competition works just as the reformers predicted." In remarks that proved unduly optimistic, Wisconsin governor Tommy Thompson declared in his 2001 "State of the State" address: "Nowhere in America does a parent have more choices than in Milwaukee, Wisconsin. And it's making all the difference...There is no doubt in my mind that Milwaukee will become the national model for renewing urban education in America within a few years." Such rosy assessments ensured that more realistic appraisals would inevitably disappoint.

Another consequence of the empathy-and-rights approach has been that the few education economists sympathetic to market-based reforms have felt compelled to devote their energies to demonstrating the superiority of choice-based systems, rather than to exploring and explaining the complexities of market-based reform. They have devoted limited attention to studying the political economy of K-12 education or potential sources of market failure.

Meanwhile, with a few exceptions — most notably the NewSchools Venture Fund and the Center for Reinventing Public Education — earnest reform advocates focus on selling the appealing promise that choice "works" rather than on the more arduous task of tackling K-12 education as a serious deregulatory project.

As a result, crucial questions have received scant attention — including regulatory and licensure chokepoints; the tendency of successful non-profit charter organizations to grow slowly; the dearth of information regarding the quality of providers; a third-party financing system that gives consumers no reason to weigh cost considerations; when and why private schools add new capacity in response to voucher programs; and the way in which statutes and collective-bargaining agreements limit how school districts respond to competition.

In any other deregulation project, such questions would be front and center. But in the effort to establish a genuine marketplace in education, they have been largely ignored.

### THE DATA ON CHOICE

This is not to say, of course, that straightforward evaluations of student achievement should not play a central role in assessing market-oriented reforms. But it is unwise to interpret these data without a broader appreciation of how markets work.

To a frustrating degree, the conclusions one draws from the educational-performance evidence depend on which experts one trusts. And different credentialed, respected scholars have offered very different takes. For instance, Jay Greene — chair of the University of Arkansas's Department of Education Reform, and a widely recognized authority on school choice — argues that research shows unambiguously that "vouchers have positive effects for students who receive them." The only question, Greene adds, "is in regard to the magnitude of vouchers' benefits." On the other hand, Princeton economist Cecilia Rouse and Chicago Federal Reserve economist Lisa Barrow characterize the evidence rather differently; last year, they concluded that most of the small gains made by voucher students "are not statistically significant from zero."

More recent studies have mostly added to the ambiguity. In 2009, the Center for Research on Educational Outcomes (CREDO) — generally regarded as a pro-school-choice organization — issued a controversial study of charter-school performance in 15 states and the District of Columbia. The study found that 17% of charter schools outperformed local district schools, 46% performed similarly, and 37% performed worse than local district schools. CREDO's conclusion was that the overall picture shows "wide variation in performance."

Earlier this year, University of Arkansas professor Patrick Wolf — principal investigator on a major study of school-voucher effects in Milwaukee — reported that there were no significant differences in achievement between students who received vouchers and those who did not. Wolf summarized, "At this point the voucher students are showing average rates of achievement gain similar to their public school peers."

And this summer, two long-awaited studies on school vouchers and charter schooling issued their final analyses. In July, the Institute of Education Sciences released the multi-year "Evaluation of Charter School Impacts" study, which examined student performance in 36 charter middle schools across 15 states. The study found that, on average, the charter schools were "neither more nor less successful than traditional public schools in improving student achievement, behavior, and school progress" (though admission to a charter did "consistently improve both students' and parents' satisfaction with school"). The study also found that "charter schools serving more low income or low achieving students had statistically significant positive effects on math test scores, while charter schools serving more advantaged students — those with higher income and prior achievement — had significant negative effects on math test scores." It is worth noting, too, that in order to participate in the study, the charter schools needed to have enough excess demand to require an admissions lottery — meaning that the charters evaluated were those that parents most wanted their children to attend.

If oversubscribed schools are typically better than charters with available seats — which seems a perfectly plausible assumption — then the study may actually overstate charter-school quality.

In June, the federally mandated study of the Washington, D.C., Opportunity Scholarship Program — another evaluation led by Patrick Wolf — also issued its final report. Established in 2004, the Washington scholarship program provided vouchers for up to $7,500 per child per year, which could be applied to tuition, transportation, and other fees required to attend the participating private school of a family's choice. Supporting between 1,700 and 2,000 low-income D.C. children a year, this was the first federally funded voucher program in the nation.

Wolf's team tracked educational outcomes over four or five years for 2,300 public-school students who applied for the scholarships, which were awarded by lottery. The researchers found that the reading and math scores of lottery winners were not statistically different from those of the control group at the conventionally recognized 95% confidence level (though their reading scores were higher at a 94% confidence level). As Wolf has explained, "A reasonable person would conclude that the voucher students made small gains in reading due to the program... [even if the] gains were modest and somewhat fragile." On a more upbeat note, students who won the lottery and used the vouchers to attend private schools were more likely — by 21 percentage points — to receive a high-school diploma than were students who lost the lottery.

The mixed findings suggest that simply legislating "school choice" programs, or enrolling a child in a charter school, will have no obvious short-term impact on achievement. But choice does consistently increase parental satisfaction, and there is evidence that carefully designed choice programs — like Washington's voucher program — may modestly bolster achievement and substantially boost graduation rates. Indeed, a fair-minded observer could read the middle-school and D.C. studies and conclude that choice "works" — almost by definition — if the goal is to get low-income children out of terrible urban school systems and into high-quality private schools where they can learn safely and increase their odds of getting high-school diplomas. Even the most determined choice skeptic should be able to acknowledge this as an improvement over the status quo.

This case was laid out most forcefully by Paul Peterson, the University of Chicago's William Howell, and two colleagues in their invaluable

2002 book *The Education Gap.* Reporting findings from randomized-control trials in New York City, Washington, D.C., and Dayton, Ohio, the authors found that attending a private school through a voucher program had a significant positive effect on the achievement scores of African-American students (though not on those of other students). Families who won the lotteries to attend these schools were also much more satisfied with their schools, and found them far safer, than families who lost the lotteries. While Princeton economist Alan Krueger later made the case that the achievement effects in New York City could be washed away with enough data manipulation, the straightforward and plausible conclusion is that students stuck in failing urban schools often benefit from moving to high-quality private schools.

More recent research has similarly found clear academic benefits for students attending choice schools. In 2009, Stanford University economist Caroline Hoxby examined the gains made by New York City students who won admission to charter schools from 2000 to 2007, and compared them to those of students who did not. Hoxby found that a student who attended a charter school from kindergarten through eighth grade would substantially outperform his district-school counterparts; on average, African-American students who enrolled in charters closed 86% of the black-white achievement gap in math and 66% in reading. And in another 2009 study, Harvard University economist Thomas Kane found "large positive effects for charter schools" for Boston students in both middle school and high school. Charter students, Kane discovered, had larger gains in reading and much larger gains in math than their peers in district schools. The largest observed gains were in middle-school math, where the effects of charter-school enrollment amounted to half of a standard deviation. These effects were large enough to lift a student from the 50th percentile of performance to the 69th percentile in a single year.

In a 2010 study, Mathematica Policy Research examined student achievement in the nation's most prominent charter-school network: the Knowledge Is Power Program, or KIPP. A non-profit founded in 1994, KIPP operates a national network of 99 schools serving mostly low-income children. KIPP schools feature strict discipline, high expectations, a longer school year, and a school day that runs from 7:30 A.M. until 5 P.M. (typically including Saturday classes). KIPP middle schools begin in fifth grade—and the Mathematica study showed that, by seventh grade, half of the KIPP schools evaluated showed growth in math scores equal to an additional 1.2 years of schooling. KIPP reading gains reflected an additional three-quarters of a year of growth. In general, Mathematica reported that middle-school students in KIPP academies significantly outperformed similar public-school students in both reading and math.

The positive findings from New York, Boston, and KIPP should not be too surprising. Students who switch from troubled schools to high-quality charter alternatives are likely to benefit—especially in cities like Boston and New York, where caps on charter schooling and an abundance of talented charter operators have produced a rich crop of terrific schools. By the same token, however, proponents of market-based school reform should not be surprised that the results may look very different in other environments. Only by stepping back from the notion that "choice" itself is a panacea, and instead embracing the contingent nature of choice's impact, can we make sense of when and why choice "works."

### THE COMPETITION QUESTION

A key feature of genuine markets is, of course, competition. In evaluating whether choice "works," what matters is not only whether escape routes to private or charter schools offer some students better educational alternatives, but also whether school-choice programs make traditional district schools better.

Any observer who takes market theory seriously would probably respond, "Of course they do." But because of the peculiarities of American education, the answer is hardly so obvious. After all, market dynamics depend upon consumer behavior, regulatory frameworks, labor-market considerations, and incentives and consequences for producers and consumers. Competition matters only when it pinches, and the reality is that competition in K-12 education has not yet been given a robust test.

Still, there is some evidence that districts and schools may respond to even the mild competitive pressures that choice currently exerts. In 2003, Jay Greene examined Florida's A+ voucher program and reported that those low-performing schools that risked having their students granted vouchers to attend private alternatives were improving "in direct proportion to the challenge they face[d] from voucher competition." In 2005, scholars Paul Peterson and Martin West reported similar findings. Under the accountability standards imposed by Florida in 2002, students at public schools that received "F" performance grades became subject to the threat of vouchers if they continued to perform poorly; Peterson and West concluded that students at schools put under the gun "performed at a higher level in the subsequent year than did students at similar schools not so threatened."

More recent research confirms the same patterns. After the Florida Supreme Court ruled in 2006 that the portion of the A+ program that funded private-school vouchers was unconstitutional, the state created an alternative program (which relies on private funding incentivized by tax credits to corporations). In June of this year, economist David Figlio released a study of the new voucher program reporting that students in Florida public schools with a diverse array of private schools in close proximity showed slightly larger achievement gains than students in public schools with fewer nearby alternatives. Figlio also determined that student gains were larger in those schools at risk of losing state funds tied to the proportion of low-income students they enroll. Figlio concluded that the public schools' response to competition was real, although limited: "What we find is certainly positive and statistically strong," he explained, "but it's not like public schools are revolutionizing overnight because of this."

One challenge in interpreting these results is gauging whether the market-induced improvements reflect attempts to fundamentally rethink or re-engineer a school or district, or merely a re-allocation of effort and resources from untested activities to tested ones. This matters a lot, because quick-fix measures—like, say, shifting time from science or art to reading instruction—may improve student test performance (and thus answer a competitive threat) without signifying any attempt to boost productivity or overhaul cost structures, staffing, operations, or management. Moreover, in most cases, district responses to choice-induced competition have primarily been changes in marketing and outreach—such as the distribution of t-shirts and ads on local billboards intended to persuade parents to keep their children in their local public schools. Choice advocates have historically erred in reading these developments as signs of bigger changes to come.

It has been a mistake, in other words, to expect public schools to behave like the private sector—where competition, investor demand, and personal consequences for success or failure drive executives to press on productivity and the bottom line, and where executives have substantial leeway to remove, reward, and otherwise recognize employees based on their contributions to organizational improvement. In systems choked by politics, bureaucracy, collective-bargaining agreements, and institutionalized timidity, there is little incentive or opportunity to react to competition in these ways.

To get schools to respond more meaningfully to competitive pressure, incentives and rules must be changed in order to ensure that the competitive pressure is actually felt. Consider that today's charter schools get about 75 cents for every dollar that district schools receive, and that the per-pupil funding levels of the voucher programs in Washington, D.C., and Milwaukee amount to less than 50% of district per-pupil spending. This funding disparity prevents public-school alternatives from mounting serious challenges to traditional district schools.

Moreover, the D.C. voucher program capped enrollment at about 3% of the District of Columbia's student population, and there was no risk of monetary loss to the school district if students departed for private schools. Indeed, the compromise that allowed the voucher-program legislation to pass required that D.C. public schools receive additional funding, even as they would no longer bear the expense of educating the voucher students. The initial sum was an extra $13 million a year; this figure was eventually boosted to $40 million per year after Democrats took control of Congress in 2007.

Milwaukee's public schools have been similarly insulated from the consequences of losing students to the Milwaukee Parental Choice Program: Even as the tiny pilot grew from 337 participants in 1990 into a program that enrolls 20,000 students today, the Milwaukee public-school system has remained largely unscathed. Since 1990, while enrollment has dipped, the district has boosted per-pupil spending by more than 80% (from $6,200 to more than $11,700), and increased the teacher work force (from 5,554 to 5,768). This is choice without consequences — competition as soft political slogan rather than hard economic reality.

As a result, despite hopes that school choice could "all by itself" bring about the other changes reformers have battled for, choice has not necessarily changed incentives or dynamics. Imagine a private-sector manager who knows that gaining or losing customers will have little or no impact on his salary, performance evaluations, or job security. Bizarre as it seems, this is exactly how "competition" generally works in K-12 education today. When a principal loses dozens of students, her evaluations, job prospects, and salary remain unaffected. And a principal who competes successfully is typically rewarded with nothing more than the joys of a more crowded cafeteria.

Of course, none of this is an indictment of school choice or of market-oriented reforms; rather, it suggests that much of our policy-making to date has tended to reflect impassioned hopes instead of cool calculations. If every dollar spent on a student followed him when he changed schools—a state of affairs that exists nowhere in this country today—the verdict on choice-inspired competition would likely be quite different. That difference would be sharper still if the laws and contracts that protect teacher and administrator jobs and salaries, and that handcuff managers, were changed—or if changes in school enrollment became a significant criterion for evaluating superintendents and principals.

The fiscal crunch in which many state and local governments now find themselves, or the moves in some jurisdictions to reform teacher tenure and pay, may make it possible to remove some of the insulation that has protected educators for so long. And because school districts are political entities, an exodus of students has the potential to spur useful change by altering the local political calculus. The departure of one-third of students to charter schools over the previous decade, for instance, helped create the conditions that led Washington, D.C., mayor Adrian Fenty to appoint the hard-charging Michelle Rhee as schools chancellor in 2007. For now, however, competition does not appear to much perturb most public-school administrators—especially as many superintendents and school boards seem perfectly content to run slightly smaller districts with proportionally fewer dollars.

The biggest mistake pro-market school reformers have made can thus be put simply: They have mistaken choice for competition. The conviction that school choice constitutes, by itself, a market solution has too often led reformers to skip past the hard work necessary to take advantage of the opportunities that choice-based reform can provide. Choice is merely part of the market equation; equally crucial are the requirements that market conditions permit high-quality or cost-effective suppliers to flourish, that regulation not smother new entrants, and that rules not require inefficient practices or subsidize also-rans.

Note that reformers rarely focus on "choice" when promoting market-based improvements to other sectors; in earlier decades, reformers didn't speak of "telecommunications choice" or "airline choice." Rather, they talked of "deregulation." Implicit was the understanding that deregulation involves more than the mere proliferation of options, that dynamic markets require much more than customers' choosing among government-operated programs and a handful of non-profits, and that vacuums in a particular sector will not naturally or necessarily be filled by competent or virtuous actors. Whether dealing with nascent markets in Eastern Europe in the 1990s or the vagaries of energy deregulation, reformers have struggled to nurture the institutions, incentives, and practices that characterize healthy markets. Markets are a product of laws, norms, talent, information, and capital, and the absence of these can readily yield market failures—not because markets do not work, but because markets are not a magical salve.

Just as school improvement does not miraculously happen without attention to instruction, curriculum, and school leadership, so a rule-laden, risk-averse sector dominated by entrenched bureaucracies, industrial-style collective-bargaining agreements, and hoary colleges of education will not casually remake itself just because students have the right to switch schools. Happily, in recent years, a growing number of thoughtful scholars—like Andrew Coulson, John Merrifield, Terry Moe, Jay Greene, Patrick Wolf, and Paul Hill—have paid increasing attention to these questions of market structure and design. But such thinking remains the exception, not the rule.

### MAKING CHOICE WORK

So, taking account of all of this, does school choice "work"? The question needs to be answered in three parts. First, for poor parents trapped in dangerous and underperforming urban school systems, it is pretty clear that school choice works. The evidence is reasonably persuasive that access to private schools and charter schools increases the likelihood that their children will fare well on reading and math tests or graduate from high school. And even if those results do not materialize, the parents are more likely to be satisfied with their children's schools and to regard them as safe.

Second, school choice *can* help make possible more coherent, focused schools. When families and teachers are assigned to schools based upon geography or bureaucratic formulas, it becomes difficult to forge the kind of agreement needed to establish strong discipline or clear expectations. The opportunities that choice creates for school leaders to recruit like-minded teachers and families — and then to set clear norms around conduct, learning, and pedagogy — can be a powerful tool. Still, their impact ultimately depends on effective use by savvy school leaders — as these opportunities in themselves surely will not automatically yield better schools.

Third, it is far from clear that school choice will necessarily offer broad, systemic benefits. Choice has not inspired hordes of charter-school operators to develop outstanding alternatives; there is no evidence that charter schools, on average across the nation, are better than district schools. Moreover, there is (at best) only very modest evidence that choice programs, in and of themselves, prompt school districts to become more productive or cost effective. There is, however, fairly clear evidence that school districts do respond under sufficient duress and that high-quality charter schools will emerge under the right conditions.

The path forward requires that choice advocates overcome the legacy of their inflated expectations and promises. The insistence that school choice simply "works" helped put a saleable, amiable face on the tough medicine that champions of school reforms sought to deliver — but often at the cost of silencing discussion about how to make choice-based reform work *well*. In fact, to even question the claim that "choice works" has frequently been deemed a betrayal by choice advocates; this has left the field to a coterie of enthusiasts eager to talk about moral urgency, but disinclined to address incentives or market dynamics.

On one level, the benefits of such smiley-face advocacy are plain to see. One need only look at the raft of strong-willed, pro-charter-school Democrats — figures like New York City schools chancellor Joel Klein or Colorado state senator Michael Johnston — to see how the choice mantra has helped to broaden and deepen the support for transformative change. It is also true that there has not been a major pull-back in any place where choice has gained a foothold. Outside of the Obama administration's move to end the D.C. voucher program — a change imposed on the school district from the outside — nowhere have charter schooling, school-voucher programs, or tuition tax credits been implemented and then lost favor.

At the same time, however, there has been little attention paid to the innate limitations of the "social justice" case for choice, even as a *political* strategy. For one thing, this approach immediately signals to the three-fourths of American parents whose children are not enrolled in inner-city schools that this debate is not about them. And given that only about one household in five even contains school-age children, choice proponents are pushing an agenda sure to seem disconnected from or even threatening to the vast majority of Americans.

Like the architects of the Great Society nearly half a century ago, choice advocates have an unfortunate habit of dismissing or denigrating middle-class voters who do not share their moral zeal. They ignore the genuine, practical worry that choice-based measures may adversely affect the property values of suburbanites who paid a premium to purchase homes in good districts or school zones, and the concerns of these home owners that their children may find themselves crowded out of popular schools.

Perhaps not coincidentally, in roughly two dozen referenda across the country over the past few decades, voucher advocates have yet to record a single win. In fact, the annual poll in the Hoover Institution's choice-friendly journal *Education Next* has shown that popular support for vouchers declined by a third, from 45% to 31%, between 2007 and 2010.

Proponents can (and do) rightfully place much of the blame for this track record on ferocious opposition from teachers' unions, but they have also blithely ignored basic political reality and prudence. They need to stop hectoring suburbanites, ease up on the moral indignation, and start promoting reform that will credibly improve the quality and cost effectiveness of American education for more than a small slice of households.

If advocates of market-oriented school reform accept this diagnosis, they can take a number of steps to improve their practical and political prospects.

First, they should get serious about markets as a way to promote cost efficiency. Given the fiscal straits school systems now face — and given that the country has just been through a monumental health-care debate that focused on the problems with third-party purchasing and the lack of incentives for consumers to think about costs — it is peculiar that the power of markets to engender price competition remains so unexplored in education. School spending entails no direct contribution from parents, and parents currently gain nothing from choosing a more cost-effective school; as a result, administrators in charter, district, and private schools have less reason to take tough steps to adopt cost-saving technologies or practices. And yet the choice agenda neglects mechanisms that could reward price-conscious parents by permitting them to save dollars for other educational expenditures (such as college or tutoring) if they chose lower-cost school options.

Second, reformers should broaden the educational-choice discussion beyond "school" choice. The narrow vocabulary of school choice made more sense 20 years ago, when online tutoring and virtual schooling were the stuff of science fiction, and when home schooling was still a curiosity. But in 2010, this language is profoundly limiting. In the health-care debate, even the most ardent single-payer enthusiasts believed that patients should be free to make a series of choices among physicians and providers of care. Yet in education, the most expansive vision of choice asks parents to decide among schools A, B, and C. This kind of choice may appeal to urban parents eager to escape awful schools; it does little, however, for suburban parents who generally like their schools but would like to take advantage of customized or higher-quality math or foreign-language instruction. A promising solution would be to permit families to redirect a portion of the dollars spent on their children through the educational equivalent of a health savings account. Such a mechanism would help families address children's unmet needs (such as extra tutoring in difficult subjects, or advanced instruction in areas of particular aptitude); it would also allow niche providers to emerge, would foster price competition for particular services, and would make educational choice relevant to many more families.

Third, champions of market-based reform should stop downplaying the role of for-profit educators. The Obama administration has been particularly guilty on this count, enthusiastically championing charter-school expansion even as its Department of Education radiates hostility toward for-profits in K-12 and higher education. The result is entrenched funding arrangements, policies, and political currents that stifle for-profit operators — organizations such as National Heritage Academies, which operates 67 charter schools in eight states, or EdisonLearning, which operates schools and provides supplemental education services across the United States and overseas. If choice-based reform is to yield more than boutique solutions, for-profits are a critical piece of the puzzle.

Consider that it has taken the celebrated KIPP program — an organization lauded for its aggressive expansion — 16 years to grow to 99 schools serving fewer than 27,000 students. This is longer than it took Microsoft, Subway, and Amazon to grow from start-ups to global brands. For-profits find it easier to tap private equity; they have self-interested reasons to aggressively seek cost efficiencies and to grow rapidly; and their focus on the bottom line can make them more willing to re-allocate resources when circumstances warrant a change. Of course, these same incentives can translate into corner-cutting and compromising quality; still, no one should imagine that non-profits can readily match the dexterity, capacity for rapid growth and massive scale, and aggressive cost-cutting that are hallmarks of the for-profit sector.

Fourth, reformers should foster genuine competition by arranging markets so that there are real consequences for competitive failure or success. One simple step would be to ensure that all of the dollars spent on students follow children when they change schools (the notion implicit in efforts to promote "weighted student funding" systems). Such a reform would entail stripping school districts of their hefty subsidies and of their monopolies over local school facilities. It would mean overhauling contracts and statutes that protect teacher jobs and seniority-driven pay scales — practices that leave school and district leaders without the tools needed to reward good teachers and penalize mediocrity. Real consequences for enrollment loss could help push educational leaders to start taking enrollment and parental preferences seriously when evaluating employees and doling out bonuses. And, because school districts are politically governed entities, it would enable reformers to leverage student flight — as they have in Washington, D.C. — to create the pressure and political cover that public officials need to pursue painful, but essential, reforms.

Fifth, markets are predicated on the assumption that consumers have the ability to make informed choices. It is not essential for every single consumer to have the knowledge or inclination to make savvy decisions — but providers do need to expect that the quality of their performance will be known, and will matter. Today, unfortunately, it is enormously difficult for parents in most communities to get useful information on school quality. Simple test scores generally tell parents at least as much about the students attending the school in question as they do about the quality of instruction. Reliable measures of how much students learn during a year (i.e., the school's "value added") are infinitely more use-ful, but they are as yet available in only a handful of places for a limited number of schools, grades, and subjects. Similarly, it is difficult for parents to find comparable or trustworthy data on school safety, arts instruction, programs for high achievers, or the fate of former students. There is a gap-ing need for third parties to step up and play the role of a Zagat's guide or *Consumer Reports*, providing accessible, independent information on K-12 schools. As these examples make clear, there is absolutely value in having multiple providers, perhaps focusing on different educational concerns or kinds of schools. This area presents a vast opportunity for philanthro-pists or civic-minded enterprises, especially as promising but primitive information-distribution efforts already exist in cities like New Orleans, Milwaukee, and New Haven, Connecticut.

Finally, reformers should recognize that dynamic markets require vi-brant entrepreneurial ecosystems. What has made Silicon Valley a locus of entrepreneurship is not that it has a "freer" marketplace than other American cities, but that it has attracted over decades the investors, researchers, and networked expertise necessary to develop and sustain high-quality ventures. Experience has made clear that such ecosystems don't necessarily spring into being unbidden, and that they some-times need to be consciously cultivated. Even in choice hotbeds like Milwaukee and Washington, we still do not see many growth-oriented providers or savvy investors screening potential new entrants and nur-turing those with the most promise. Meanwhile, too little is being done to help new education providers find facilities, negotiate politi-cal obstacles, or leverage labor-saving technologies. Ventures like New Schools for New Orleans and The Mind Trust in Indianapolis represent pioneering efforts to clear bureaucratic obstacles, attract talent, and cul-tivate networks. Such efforts are multiplying across the land, spurred by supporters like the Gates Foundation and the NewSchools Venture Fund, and aided by federal policies like the Race to the Top program. These are promising developments—and they deserve more attention and care from reformers.

## MAKING MARKETS

It would seem, then, that school choice "works" in some respects and in some instances—but that choice alone could never work as well as many of its champions have expected, and promised. It is time for those who would like to transform America's schools to let go of the dream that choice by itself is any kind of "solution." The goal ought to be a much more serious agenda of school deregulation and re-invention.

Choice advocates still routinely invoke iconic market thinkers, particularly Milton Friedman, in asserting that "school choice works." It might be time for them to take another look at their Friedman, and their Friedrich Hayek. It was Friedman who admonished that the market "is not a cow to be milked." And it was Hayek who, in collecting his Nobel Prize, encouraged policymakers to think of themselves as gardeners — creating the conditions in which enterprise could flourish. Neither Friedman nor Hayek believed that markets were self-sustaining or failsafe. Their approach to market-based reform was not the enthusiastic cheerleading of the choice movement; it was a far sterner, grittier charge. And as school choice now enters its third decade, its champions would be wise to take the counsel of Friedman and Hayek to heart.

*Originally published as "Does School Choice 'Work'?" in the Fall 2010 issue of* National Affairs.

# vi. Reforming State Finances

# How to Address the State Fiscal Crisis

## *John Hood*

WINTER 2011

OVER THE PAST THREE YEARS, the news out of state capitals has been dire. From Albany to Sacramento, economic shocks have reduced states' tax revenues, even as the downturn has required states to spend more on welfare for the struggling and newly jobless. The Great Recession has thus torn gaping holes in state budgets—holes that governors and state legislatures are now desperately trying to close.

That effort has been painful for state officials. When Arizona cut state funding for kindergartens, educators and parents cried foul. When New York raised tuition at its state universities, students protested. When California, North Carolina, Oregon, and Connecticut raised their income taxes, angry taxpayers flocked to Tea Party protests and expressed their displeasure through buzzing phone lines and clogged inboxes. With every attempt to fix state budgets, an acceptable solution has seemed ever more out of reach.

But alarming as these recent developments have been, the states' fiscal calamity is not simply a function of the recession. Their shaky financial foundations were in fact set long ago—through unsustainable obligations like retirement benefits for public employees, excessive borrowing, and deferred maintenance of public buildings and infrastructure. The result has been a long-building budget imbalance now estimated in the trillions of dollars.

The nightmare that governors and state legislators are living through will therefore not end when the effects of the recession do. Even as state officials address large short-term operating deficits, they must confront the more troublesome structural gaps between current state revenue projections and massive future liabilities. And the tools that these state

JOHN HOOD *is president of the John Locke Foundation, a state-policy think tank based in North Carolina, and the author of, among other books,* Investor Politics.

officials have at their disposal to deal with the crisis are limited. Many state constitutions require the repayment of bonds to take priority over almost all other state spending. Others require state-employee pensions to be paid out at the promised terms no matter what, making it almost impossible to negotiate those liabilities down. States, unlike municipalities, do not have the legal option of declaring bankruptcy. At some point, if some states approach default, just meeting these debt obligations will consume all of their revenues — leaving no money for basic functions like maintaining a state police force, operating roads and other transit infrastructure, or educating children.

If these states fail to find their way out of their current predicament, their only option may be to beg for federal bailouts. And the states would not be the only losers if this comes to pass. If the federal government were to refuse a bailout request, it would risk a disastrous crisis in the bond markets — as investors who had always assumed state debt to be safe (in part because they assumed it would have federal backing in a crisis) would suddenly rethink all their state-bond investments. On the other hand, if the federal government were to grant a bailout to any one state, the other 49 would certainly expect assistance as well. This would put our federalist system to an unprecedented test. It would also require an enormous amount of money from federal coffers that are themselves perilously hollow.

It is in everyone's interest, at all levels of government, to avoid such a collapse. Gratifying as it may be to scream about the various Armageddon scenarios facing the states, it is far more useful to consider how those problems might be solved through our everyday political and policy processes — precisely to avoid truly extreme measures. Policymakers can start by getting a better handle on the problem: Just how big is the crisis? What caused it? And if America's elected leaders and voters are serious about reform, what exactly should they do to pull the states back from the brink?

## THE FISCAL CRISIS

The first step in getting a better handle on the crisis is to understand why the Great Recession has been so brutal to state budgets. The main reason is that the recent lean years were preceded by several fat ones, in which state politicians oversaw massive increases in state spending. Following a pattern reaching back decades, policymakers chose to use times of relative prosperity and growth to irresponsibly expand the size and scope of government services. When tax revenues declined precipitously as a result of the 2008 financial crisis, state officials' optimistic budgeting crashed into cold, hard reality.

As a result, the scale of the fiscal challenge facing most state governments today is immense. State tax revenues were 8.4% lower in 2009 than in 2008, and a further 3.1% lower in 2010. The demand for many state services, meanwhile, has increased as a result of the economic downturn. Medicaid enrollment (and with it state spending on the program) grew by more than 13% between the end of 2007 and the end of 2009. As unemployment spiked, unemployment insurance and welfare payments ballooned. The states thus faced a combined budget shortfall of nearly $200 billion — or almost 30% of their combined total budgets — in 2010. Most expect shortfalls nearly as great in the next fiscal year.

Beyond its startling magnitude, the crisis is also widespread. A few states with oil or mineral wealth (Alaska, Montana, and New Mexico in particular) weathered the recession relatively well at first, though even they have not avoided budget shortfalls. Most everywhere else, the combination of declining tax revenues and rising unemployment has produced a painful budget squeeze. The two charts that follow show each state's revenue shortfall as a percentage of its budget (the first chart lists the worst-performing states, and the second the best-performing states).

With the exception of Vermont, every state is required by its laws or constitution to balance its budget (though many of these requirements are quite flexible in their definitions of "balance," as discussed below). State governments have thus been unable to carry huge deficits from one year to the next, and have been forced to find ways to immediately close their immense budget gaps.

Many states have found relief in the form of substantial federal aid: The 2009 stimulus bill provided about $140 billion to the states over three fiscal years, largely through increased Medicaid dollars and a "State Fiscal Stabilization Fund," which states have used to fill other gaps. The "jobs bill" enacted in August 2010 gave the states another injection of Medicaid dollars, and added another $10 billion to the stabilization fund. Of course, federal assistance of this magnitude will probably not be available in the coming years. For now, however, these federal dollars have helped fill about 35% of the total combined deficit in state budgets.

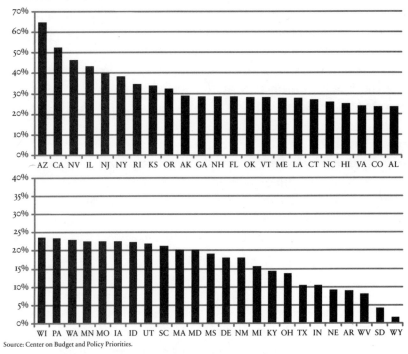

REVENUE SHORTFALL AS PERCENTAGE OF 2010 STATE BUDGET

Source: Center on Budget and Policy Priorities.

Yet even that aid has left states far short—so most have also had to take serious steps to curb spending or raise revenues. In fact, since 2008, 46 states have cut services to residents: According to the Center on Budget and Policy Priorities, 31 states have cut health-care funding, 29 have cut services to the elderly and disabled, 34 have cut K-12 education funding, and 43 have cut higher-education funding. More than 30 states, meanwhile, have increased taxes in the past three years—13 states have raised personal income taxes; 17 have raised sales taxes; 22 have increased taxes on tobacco, alcohol, or gasoline; and 17 have increased business taxes. Most individual changes in tax rates have been modest, but their combined effects have been significant, adding up to almost $30 billion in 2009 (almost 4% of total state revenues).

As grim as these indicators are, they do not even capture the whole picture—for it is impossible to study the finances of state governments across the country without taking into account the finances of *local* governments as well. In most states, the two levels of government are legally and practically interrelated: Counties and municipalities are not independent constituents of federations, the way the states relate to the federal government; rather, they are creations of states, designed to carry out state functions.

Moreover, the division of labor among the levels of government differs from state to state. In some places, public-school teachers are classified as state employees; their salaries and benefits are therefore funded primarily by state income or sales taxes, and show up on the state's books. In other states, teachers are classified as district employees — and their expenses are paid from local property or sales taxes. Similar differences exist in other budgeting categories, such as law enforcement, social services, and transportation. As a result, the most accurate method of examining state finances — and the cleanest way to compare them across state lines — is to combine state and local expenditures.

When we do, what does the spending picture look like? According to the most recent official data from the Census Bureau, for the 2008 fiscal year, states and localities spent about $2.8 trillion. (The spending was funded through revenue from state and local taxes and fees, as well as through federal grants, loans, and trust funds.) Of that amount, some $2.4 trillion was classified as "direct general expenditure" — the major programs and services that attract most of the attention of state policymakers and citizens. About a quarter of these "direct general expenditures" went to public K-12 schools; higher education, public safety, and transportation each claimed about 10% of the total. Public-assistance programs — including Medicaid, cash welfare, and housing subsidies funded mostly by Washington — made up about 30%. The remaining 15% or so funded smaller programs such as parks, the management of natural resources, or business recruitment, as well as general administration. As a share of the national economy, such state and local spending has roughly doubled over the past 50 years — from 11.56% of GDP in 1959 to 21.79% today.

In assessing this incredible growth, it is essential to take into account the influence federal spending has over state spending. Indeed, since much of the revenue that makes state spending possible comes from federal transfers, it is impossible to disentangle the two. For example, the biggest jump in state and local spending occurred in the decade after President Lyndon Johnson implemented his Great Society programs: From 1965 to 1975, state and local spending went from 12% to nearly 17% of GDP. By far the most important cause of that spending explosion was the creation of Medicaid, which combines federal and state dollars to provide a package of acute and long-term health care for the poor and disabled. This structure offers perverse incentives for policymakers to constantly expand the program: State and local officials benefit from providing ever more generous benefits without having to shoulder a proportional share of the financial cost, since the federal government pays most of the bill. Likewise, any effort to contain costs by cutting benefits harms state and local officials immensely, and in exchange, most of the savings go to the federal government. Consequently, ever since Medicaid was created, it has been one of the largest and most relentless drivers of state budget growth.

Another major driver is education, the largest single category of state and local spending. Both K-12 and higher-education spending have grown during the past two decades — by 10% and 3%, respectively, as a share of GDP — as states have raised teacher pay and benefits, hired more teachers to reduce class sizes, built more expensive facilities, and added large numbers of administrators and support staff. In most jurisdictions, per-pupil spending in elementary and secondary schools now approaches or exceeds $10,000 (for comparison, the average annual tuition charged by private schools across all grade levels, according to the most recent data from the National Center for Education Statistics, is $8,549). In the case of higher education, some governors and legislatures have recently begun to reduce the subsidies provided to public universities; there are still many states, however, where most of the cost of a public undergraduate education is funded by taxpayers, not the student's tuition.

Other familiar state and local services, such as transportation and law enforcement, have actually experienced little real growth in spending over the past two decades. For example, despite increases in the federal and state taxes on motor fuels — revenues that fund much of the nation's spending on roads and bridges — increases in the average fuel efficiency of the cars traversing America's highways have pushed actual revenue collections per mile traveled *down*. The result? Less money to maintain, repair, and expand our primary system of surface transportation — which means more roads that are crumbling and congested.

This funding shortage for America's roads may seem surprising, given the astronomical amounts of government money spent on transportation. The reason is that a large — and egregiously wasteful — chunk of state and local transportation budgets is devoted to obsolete transit and rail programs, which seek to apply the leading technologies of 1900 to the mobility needs of 2011. Because much of the money for these projects ultimately comes from the federal government — in the form of highway bills and other pork-laden legislation—the funding dynamic that governs transportation is similar to the one that obtains with Medicaid. The fact that only a fraction of the money comes from locally raised taxes gives state and local politicians significant incentive to pursue transportation projects that would make no sense in the absence of federal largesse. But in order to get the federal money for transit projects, state and local authorities must invest *some* of their own revenues—often in significant amounts. So the lure of federal money for rail programs often ratchets up state and local transit spending.

A recent example of this phenomenon is the situation surrounding New Jersey governor Chris Christie's decision to cancel a rail-tunnel project that would have provided an additional link between the Garden State and New York City. Much of the opposition to the governor's decision stemmed from the argument that New Jersey would lose out on federal backing—the federal government and the Port Authority of New York and New Jersey were to provide $3 billion each for the project, and the state of New Jersey was on the hook for $2.7 billion, plus any cost overruns. It was when those overruns were projected to be between $1 billion and $5 billion that Christie pulled the plug, arguing that the burden was too much for the state to bear.

When all of this wasteful spending is combined with the recent budget shortfalls caused by the recession, the states face a total projected deficit of $130 billion in the coming fiscal year. But unfortunately, this is only the beginning: Most observers do not expect to see state revenue collections return to pre-recession levels until 2014, at the earliest. And even when the recession does pass, the massive long-term budget imbalances will still be there—poised to bring in a new, and far more difficult, set of fiscal challenges. The bill for decades of reckless promising and spending is about to come due.

## UNFUNDED LIABILITIES

High on the list of reckless expenditures and promises are unfunded government pensions. When Wall Street tumbled in 2008, it drove down the values of many state retirement funds—leaving policymakers with far less time than they thought they had to bridge huge gaps between saved resources and promised benefits. But state and local lawmakers were not simply the victims of bad timing and bad luck—they were the perpetrators of bad planning and bad policy.

At the heart of this problem lies the fact that government pension plans do not function the way most private retirement plans do. Americans with jobs in the private sector are likely most familiar with "defined contribution" retirement programs—like 401(k) accounts—which involve a set contribution (generally some percentage of one's pay). This contribution, made over the course of a person's working years, is channeled into a savings account that accrues interest; upon retirement, that account begins to pay out benefits. An individual can generally choose how to invest the money in his account to improve its rate of return; he can also buy an annuity when he retires to insure against an old age that outlasts the account's reserves. Such a retirement plan cannot be underfunded, since it pays out in benefits only what one contributes over the course of one's working life.

Most government pension plans, by contrast, are "defined benefit" programs. These plans, as the name suggests, guarantee a particular annual benefit to each retiree (generally based on the income he earned while he was working, the number of years he worked, and some cost-of-living adjustment). Instead of disbursing payments based on the amount of money collected over time in a savings account, defined-benefit programs work backwards: They first determine the benefits they will provide, and then try to calculate how to collect enough money to meet those obligations. The accuracy of that calculation depends on correctly predicting the rate of return that the retirement funds will be able to draw over the years—which makes defined-benefit programs extremely vulnerable to fluctuations in the stock market (and the economy more generally).

The structure of defined-benefit programs also strips away the safeguards that protect defined-contribution programs from being underfunded. If a defined-benefit plan promises excessively generous payouts, or fails to collect enough money to meet its financial pledges to retirees, the result will be a massive accumulation of debt as large numbers of workers begin to retire. Of course, many states have done both. Forty-eight states (Alaska and Michigan are the only exceptions), as well as a great many local governments, provide defined-benefit retirement plans to their employees. And even before the recent financial crisis caused the stock market to tumble, many of these plans were seriously underfunded.

Just how short are these retirement plans? According to a recent report from the Pew Center on the States, state governments face an unfunded liability of $1 trillion for retirement benefits promised to public employees. This figure, which remains the most accurate available assessment of the problem, is based on FY 2008 data—that is, *before* the financial markets and economy really tanked. More recent estimates, calculated by Northwestern University economist Joshua Rauh and his colleagues, have suggested a figure closer to $3 trillion in unfunded state liabilities (the shortfall in city pensions totaled an additional $574 billion).

Yet alarming as the recent headlines about underfunded *pension* funds may be, pensions are not in fact the primary reason that states are facing a meltdown in their retirement funds. Indeed, according to the Pew study, state pension systems as a whole had accrued about 84% of the assets needed to pay projected benefits as of 2008; the long-term pension hole came to about $450 billion. The states' greater challenge is paying out promised benefits *other* than cash pensions—benefits for which the states have, astonishingly, set aside virtually no money at all. The most problematic of these obligations is of course health care—specifically, the coverage above and beyond Medicare that many state and local governments have promised to their retirees. That unfunded liability came to about $550 billion—which, when combined with the $450 billion pension hole, produced what Pew called the "Trillion Dollar Gap." The charts below break down this sum by state, showing the dollar amounts (in billions) of each state's pension and other (principally health-care) retirement liabilities.

TOTAL UNFUNDED LIABILITIES (IN BILLIONS OF DOLLARS)

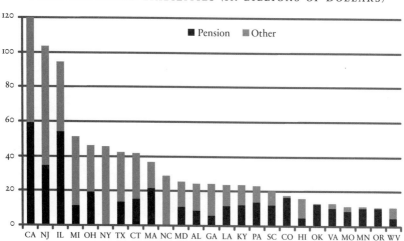

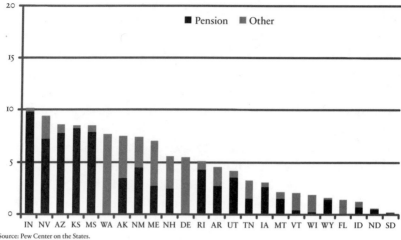

Source: Pew Center on the States.
*Nebraska did not provide data on health-care liabilities, and so is not included.

Of course, the populations of the states and the sizes of their budgets vary enormously—which means that the sheer dollar amount of a state's unfunded liability may not always be the best measure of the severity of its fiscal crunch. So while these figures offer a sense of which states would require the most money—either from Washington bailouts or their own tax coffers—to make their underfunded retirement programs whole, they do not necessarily tell us which states have done the worst job of managing their liabilities. It is therefore useful to consider exactly what portion of each state's total retirement liability is unfunded.

As the following charts demonstrate, there is wide variation in how the states have managed their pension obligations. As of 2008, Connecticut, the worst offender, had no money set aside to pay for a staggering 62% of its total retirement liability. At the other extreme, Florida had a small surplus in its pension system and only modest health-care obligations—making it the best-funded state retirement system in the nation.

By examining the data presented in both of these sets of charts—both the sheer size of a state's unfunded liability, as well as the portion of its total retirement liability for which no money has been saved—one gets a sense of the severity of each state's fiscal troubles. California, for instance, ranks near the middle of the pack in terms of the portion of its retirement obligations that is unfunded. But because of the enormous size of both its population and state work force, the Golden State's total unfunded liability amounts to more than $120 billion—making

UNFUNDED PORTION OF TOTAL RETIREMENT LIABILITIES

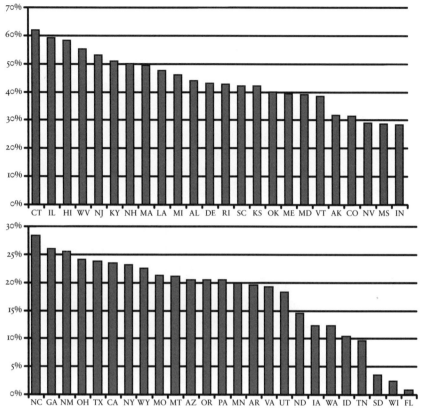

Source: Pew Center on the States.
*Nebraska did not provide data on health-care liabilities, and so is not included.

California's predicament far more grave in real terms than the woes of some states that have failed to fund even larger portions of their projected liabilities. The states that rank near the top of both dishonor rolls — most notably Connecticut (62% of its liability unfunded, for a total unfunded obligation of almost $42 billion), Illinois (59% of its liability unfunded, for a total unfunded obligation of $94 billion), and New Jersey (53% of its liability unfunded, for a total unfunded obligation of $103 billion) — are in the worst trouble of all.

Unfunded liabilities for retirement benefits are both outrageously irresponsible and completely avoidable — and yet wholly unsurprising. To the average governor or state legislator, what matters most is what is happening right now. During economic booms, when revenues are pouring into state coffers, it is politically popular to increase compensation for public employees, hire more teachers to reduce class sizes, expand eligibility for Medicaid and other safety-net programs, or cut taxes. The lobby for setting aside more money in pension and savings accounts, on the other hand, is minuscule. During economic busts, when revenues crash and countercyclical spending soars, it is even more difficult to convince state policymakers to make long-term needs a priority. Forced to choose among cutting personnel (and thereby adding to the jobless rolls), reducing current benefits and services (just when struggling residents are most in need of them), raising taxes (when working families need every bit of their paychecks to make ends meet), or deferring contributions to state savings accounts, the last option — which, in the here and now, seems to have virtually no downsides — is almost irresistible.

This phenomenon is evident not only in the states' management of financial capital, but also in their approach to physical capital. It is far more exciting for politicians to break ground on new buildings and infrastructure than it is to commit state dollars to the maintenance, repair, and renovation of facilities already in use. New construction signifies growth, progress, and expanded access to popular services like education and transportation. Fixing up old facilities is rarely front-page news. Public administrators have thus fallen into the habit of letting facilities problems fester, putting together capital plans that focus on new construction rather than repair or maintenance. The private sector, too, is a party to the scheme: After all, developers, contractors, and tradesmen typically enjoy far higher profit margins from new construction than they receive from maintenance and repair. Members of these professions — and the unions that represent them — simply add pressure in state capitals to build anew rather than maintain the old.

As a result, while the number, size, and market value of state and local buildings and facilities have increased dramatically over the past two decades, budgets for maintenance, repair, and renovation have not kept pace. Many public buildings have thus ceased to become local-government assets, becoming instead additional unfunded liabilities that will consume a great deal of money not currently acknowledged in state budget projections. According to another Pew Center study in 2008, only six states — Florida, Indiana, Nebraska, Texas, Utah, and Vermont — had adequate infrastructure-maintenance policies. Twenty-two states got failing grades for infrastructure, including familiar mismanagement case studies like Illinois and New Jersey.

The combination of vastly unfunded retirement liabilities, poorly maintained physical capital, and general waste and mismanagement has thus left states with budget holes that seem nearly impossible to fill. The states facing the most ominous difficulties, moreover, are in many cases the ones that already have the highest tax burdens—leaving them little room to raise taxes further without driving residents and businesses out of state and thus making matters worse. To propose cuts in spending, jobs, and government services, meanwhile, would be unwise in difficult economic times (and politically painful at any time).

It is therefore not surprising that state policymakers in search of money pursue the path of least resistance: heavy borrowing. But unfortunately for state taxpayers, this borrowing only intensifies the problem—piling enormous and expensive debt onto already wobbly state and local budgets.

### THE CURSE OF PUBLIC DEBT

As of fiscal year 2008, states and localities combined had about $2.6 trillion in outstanding bonded obligations and other formal debts. By the beginning of 2010, the Manhattan Institute's Steven Malanga reports, state and local debt had risen to an all-time high of 22% of GDP, up from 15% a decade ago. But the amount of outstanding government debt attributable to state and local spending is far greater still—because a great deal of the money borrowed by the *federal* government ends up being funneled to the states.

Consider that, since 1967, the federal government has run budget deficits in all but five fiscal years—and that, in the past few years, those federal deficits have been in the neighborhood of a trillion dollars a year. In all of those deficit-spending years, total federal grants to states and localities amounted to at least 40% of the federal deficit; in most years, a majority of federal borrowing went straight to state and local budgets. Over the past decade, the trend grew even more pronounced: In the seven years starting with the return of deficit spending in 2002 (after the brief bipartisan budget-balancing of the late 1990s), *virtually all* of America's federal deficits were consumed by revenue transfers to states and localities, primarily for Medicaid and education. This trend was reversed in 2009, as Washington responded to the recession with a panoply of federal spending programs, driving deficits to unprecedented heights. About 40% of the deficit in the past two years has gone to states and localities.

The consequences of having Washington as a borrower of last resort have been quite severe. Most state constitutions forbid the practice of financing recurring operating costs through borrowing, and rightly so. Access to easy credit is particularly dangerous for teenagers and politicians, for similar reasons: They lack the long-term incentives, and often the knowledge and self-discipline, to make wise decisions. It's best to impose responsibility on them through budget rules. Unfortunately, easy access to federal borrowing subverts the states' well-intentioned balanced-budget requirements. If state politicians can ask Washington for extra Medicaid money, education funds, or other bailouts to fill in holes during recessionary years, they have fewer incentives to control state spending growth when times are good—or to pare back expenses when a recession hits.

The result is a ratchet effect in state spending; through booms and busts, the inexorable trend is higher spending in real terms. Over the past half-century, federal aid to states and localities has grown from about 1% of GDP in the mid 1960s to 3.6% of GDP in 2010. During the same period, total state and local spending rose from about 12% of GDP to nearly 22%. States and localities would likely have increased their spending even without federal borrowing—but access to its proceeds undoubtedly helped make state and local budgets much larger than they otherwise would have been.

Furthermore, because many federally funded services—such as Medicaid, public education, and highway management—require state matching funds, the result of increasing federal "aid" can be calamitous for state taxpayers in the long run. A recent study by economists Russell Sobel and George Crowley for George Mason University's Mercatus Center found that state taxes rise between 33 cents and 42 cents for every dollar a state receives in federal aid. Federal programs that fund state and local spending "create their own new political constituency," Sobel and Crowley observed, "in that the government employees and private recipients whose incomes depend on the program, and their families, will use political pressure to fight against any discontinuation of the program." The end result, Sobel and Crowley wrote, is that federal grants "result in an expansion in state lobbying activity that is successful in gaining influence over future state spending."

Access to the federal credit card isn't the only counterproductive "gift" Washington extends to states and localities. Another is the distortion of capital markets caused by the federal tax policies surrounding state and local bonds. The interest earned by state and local bondholders is exempt from federal income taxes, which inflates the incentive to buy such bonds — in turn making state and local debt artificially cheap (and therefore exaggerating its appeal to state and local policymakers). Indeed, the exemption for state and local bonds — with a fiscal impact of about $27 billion a year — is one of the largest in the federal tax code, after the mortgage-interest deduction (worth about $89 billion) and the state and local tax deduction (worth about $41 billion).

The main justification for exempting state and local bonds from income taxation is that the federal subsidy helps governments afford important capital projects such as schools and roads. Because the return on the bonds is not taxed, governments can offer lower interest rates to investors and still remain competitive with the private bond market. And since this allows governments to borrow at lower rates of interest, governments theoretically save money that can then be passed along to taxpayers.

But in reality, because government bonds have artificially low interest rates, state and local governments end up borrowing more than they otherwise would in order to finance more infrastructure projects than they would otherwise build. In this sense, governments behave like many prospective home buyers: If mortgage rates go down, thereby allowing a person to buy a bigger house with the same monthly payment, he has certainly gained an advantage — but he has also purchased a bigger house, and can't pretend that he has pocketed a savings. State and local officials already have enough perverse incentives to build themselves bigger houses; they do not need additional enticement to spend every last dime they can get their hands on.

An additional danger of the tax exemption for state and local bond interest is that it can crowd private-sector vendors — and, with them, private-sector cost efficiencies — out of large economic ventures. Again and again in debates about building city-owned convention halls, arenas, ballparks, and corporate centers, the case is made that government, not the private sector, should take the lead — because government can do the job cheaper, as its debt costs less to finance. A similar problem emerges with regard to public-private partnerships. In many instances, it would make fiscal sense for private firms to build, maintain, and lease back to public authorities facilities such as schools and toll roads. But opponents often argue that the potential savings — in the form of speedier construction, more economical designs, and better maintenance — are outweighed by the higher cost of servicing taxable private debt. Worse yet, when politicians do recognize this problem, they end up finding ways to give private firms access to the proceeds of taxpayer-backed debt — a "cure" that is often far worse than the disease. There are private companies whose business models consist wholly of cultivating enough political pull in statehouses or city halls to get a piece of the "economic development" pie — an open invitation to influence-peddling and corruption.

There are many other programs and incentives that have helped create enormous, long-term structural divides between the revenues that states can expect to receive and the money they will have to spend just to make good on current promises. And just as these liabilities took many years to accumulate, they will take many years to resolve. They will also require dramatic reforms, which will not be easy to accomplish, either politically or practically. The cruel facts of budget math, however, leave policymakers with no choice but to try — and soon.

### LASTING REFORMS

How, then, should governors and legislators deal with the simultaneous challenges of an immediate fiscal crunch and a long-brewing budget imbalance? As they confront another tough year in 2011, they will be forced to cut their budgets swiftly and significantly. Smart lawmakers, though, will recognize the upside to their situation. Rather than simply enacting indiscriminate, across-the-board cuts — or seeking only the easiest, most immediately achievable savings — they will seize the opportunity to craft budgets that meet their states' long-term policy needs.

Many of these forward-looking budgets will include targeted spending reductions that can accumulate savings over time. These include eliminating optional Medicaid services (like paying for dentures and eyeglasses rather than hospital stays); reducing non-teacher expenditures in public schools (like administration and overhead); consolidating redundant departments and agencies; tightening control of existing contracts with supply vendors and service providers; subjecting more government services to competitive contracting; and selling unproductive or low-priority government assets (such as little-used office buildings, state-owned liquor stores, and some transportation infrastructure) to the private sector.

Other intelligent budget reforms will be designed to save modest amounts of money today, but vastly larger amounts in the future. Of these, the most crucial changes will be to state pension and health-care plans. For older public workers with defined-benefit retirement plans, states need to implement new guidelines that require longer vesting periods, lower cost-of-living adjustments, higher employee-contribution levels, and higher thresholds for disability claims. For younger public employees, states should end the hollow promise of defined retirement benefits — pensions and health care — altogether. Instead, they should pursue (and vigorously promote) the far more sound approach of defined-contribution plans that guarantee annual investments in personally owned, fully portable accounts.

The most important changes, though, will be structural reforms to *processes* of government — reforms that eliminate the perverse incentives that got the states into this mess in the first place, and that privilege the concerns of taxpayers over those of spending lobbies and special interests.

With conservatives poised to exercise more real power in state capitals than they have in generations, now is the time to enact fundamental changes in the rules that govern budgeting and legislation. As they do, lawmakers should keep five broad principles in mind.

First, not all balanced-budget requirements are created equal. While nearly all states have some balanced-budget rules, usually coded into their constitutions, the specifics differ widely (as do the resulting constraints on government growth). In 43 states, for example, the governor must submit a balanced budget to the legislature; in 40 states, the legislature must pass a balanced budget. In some cases, though, the definition of "balanced" is so nebulous that a state can, in effect, fund its operations with debt. Some states' requirements, for instance, apply only to their general funds — meaning that the operating costs for "special funds" and off-budget accounts can be paid for with deficit spending. In 21 states, if unforeseen revenue shortfalls or spending spikes create general-fund holes during the fiscal year, the state can borrow to carry over the deficits into the next year.

Research shows that these differences matter, and that states prohibiting carry-overs mount much stronger and more immediate responses to budget deficits — either through budget cuts or tax hikes — than do states with weaker balanced-budget rules. James Poterba of the Massachusetts Institute of Technology has found that, for every $100 in deficits that arise in a given fiscal year, states with strong anti-deficit rules (rules requiring that the legislature enact a balanced budget and prohibiting the carrying forward of deficits from year to year) reduce state spending by $44. States with weak rules (which require only that governors submit a balanced budget, or allow deficits to be carried forward) cut their budgets by only $17. Moreover, two papers from the late 1990s (one by Alberto Alesina and Tamim Bayoumi, and another by Henning Bohn and Robert Inman) showed that states with strong anti-deficit rules tend to maintain larger financial reserves—suggesting that they are less susceptible to the boom-and-bust fluctuations of our economy.

Second, states should go beyond balanced-budget requirements and impose limits on overall spending. Today, some 30 states have caps on the annual growth of state budgets; Colorado's Taxpayer Bill of Rights (TABOR) is perhaps the best known. Among the rest, the specifics vary widely and make an enormous difference in effectiveness—highlighting how important it is for states to design their spending caps wisely. Indeed, there is scant evidence that states that set loose limits—by, for instance, limiting budget growth to the rate of growth in personal income, while exempting major categories of spending like education and Medicaid—reap any benefits at all. But states that enforce tight limits (Colorado is again the foremost example) tend to perform better: Those that peg budget growth to changes in inflation and population, allow very few exceptions, and crack down on evasive accounting gimmicks succeed in both controlling government growth and mitigating economic booms and busts.

Third, if politicians are given additional revenue, they are sure to spend it. Spending caps therefore work much better if they are coupled with meaningful tax limits. The TABOR amendment in Colorado, for instance, stipulated that any tax increase that would raise government revenue beyond the inflation-plus-population cap had to be approved by voters in a referendum. Fifteen other states require supermajority votes in their legislatures to approve tax hikes. Those with the strictest caps, like Arizona and South Dakota, also have per capita spending levels well below the national average.

A more basic way to limit state taxation is to restrict the *kinds* of taxes the government may impose. While most states employ all three major options—property, sales, and income taxes—some states use only two. (Every state has property taxes, seven have no income tax, and five have no sales tax.) Not surprisingly, the states that use only two kinds of taxes have lower levels of taxation overall. It is crucial, then, for policymakers in these states to protect against the imposition of new taxes. For instance, in states that rely mostly on sales taxes — like Florida, which has no income tax, and Tennessee, which taxes income only from dividends and interest — lawmakers must oppose efforts to introduce an income tax. In states that rely mostly on income taxes — like Oregon, which has no sales tax but the highest income-tax rates in the nation — policymakers need to hold the line against the introduction of a sales tax.

There have also been concerted efforts in state capitals to authorize additional revenue sources and to broaden the bases of existing taxes. These initiatives would, for instance, apply retail sales taxes to cross-border Internet transactions and to major service sectors such as law, finance, advertising, and medical care. (Florida, Massachusetts, Michigan, and Maryland are among the states to have attempted such sales-tax expansions in recent years.) This approach is a shrewd one on the part of policymakers, in that spreading a state's revenue haul across multiple levies makes it harder for voters to grasp the full magnitude of their total tax burden. This, of course, makes it easier to raise taxes over time — meaning that the inevitable result will be greater growth in government. Such taxes must be resisted.

Fourth, debt limits must be strict and enforceable. Naturally, there are proper uses of debt in state and local government — primarily to finance buildings and other infrastructure that will remain in service for many decades. Issuing bonds for these projects admittedly increases their lifetime cost, but it also allows needed projects to come into service sooner — giving state residents immediate benefits like increased mobility or proximity to schools. Plus, it spreads the financial burden over the multiple generations of taxpayers who will receive those benefits.

Still, it is clear that the approach to debt taken by most state and local governments today is well outside the realm of the reasonable. To return to sanity, policymakers should require either a voter referendum or a legislative supermajority to issue bonds of any kind — and there should be a clear enforcement mechanism that ensures taxpayers have standing to sue in court to challenge illegal debt issuances. The current practice of distinguishing between general-obligation debt requiring referenda and special-obligation debt not requiring referenda is too easy to abuse, as governments have demonstrated no qualms about reclassifying general-obligation bonds as, for instance, "revenue bonds" or "tax-increment financing," and so treating them as special-obligation debt. As a result, academic research generally finds no consistent relationship between referendum requirements and overall government indebtedness; it does, however, provide clear evidence that referendum requirements increase the issuance of special-obligation bonds. A 2009 study by K.C. Tydgat of the University of North Carolina found convincing evidence of such patterns of evasion by state governments—confirming similar findings in the 1990s by scholars Beverly Bunch and Jurgen von Hagen. Only by imposing constraints on *all* debt issuance, then, can the problem be tackled.

Fifth, state line-item vetoes can work, but only if they provide governors with the power to reduce as well as eliminate spending items. Governors have the power to strike line items from the budget in all but six of the states (Indiana, Nevada, New Hampshire, North Carolina, Rhode Island, and Vermont are the exceptions), and while this power has been shown to reduce spending on occasion—especially when the governor is of a different party than the majority of the state legislature—its overall effect on state spending has not been great. But in states that give their governors the power to also reduce the amount of money spent on a particular line item without simply striking it—Alaska, Maine, Massachusetts, Missouri, Nebraska, New Jersey, Tennessee, Virginia, West Virginia, and Wisconsin—the use of this power by governors has significantly more effect. As studies by W. Marc Crain, James Miller, and former Congressional Budget Office director Douglas Holtz-Eakin have shown, these effects are, again, more prominent when state government is divided between the parties. But when this is the case, the so-called "item-reduction veto" can significantly reduce spending. In a 2003 book, Crain found that such a power can lower per capita spending by state government by 13%.

People familiar with the history of federal budgeting know how difficult it is to sustain responsible fiscal policy unless the executive branch has meaningful authority over the budgeting process. Logrolling, pork-barrel considerations, and the dynamics of interest-group politics affect all elected officials, but legislators are particularly vulnerable. The same rules apply at the state level: When governors are armed with the most powerful form of the veto—the authority to reduce spending in every line item of the budget, and to gut legislators' earmarks and pet projects — the result is less growth in budgets and taxes.

## IMAGINING THE UNIMAGINABLE

One way or another, 2011 will be a year of reckoning for the states, and for American federalism. As budget gaps persist and pension promises and other obligations come due, several states may confront the possibility of genuine default — a possibility that California briefly toyed with in 2009, and may well face again soon.

If they are to have any hope of avoiding the twin nightmares of default and a federal bailout, governors and legislators must get serious about changing their ways. Guided by the principles outlined above, they need to employ all of their creativity and foresight to avert fiscal collapse, correct budget imbalances, and improve the quality and efficiency of government services.

Even more important, state and local politicians will have to summon uncharacteristic levels of courage and backbone. The policy decisions that this moment calls for — from painful budget cuts to difficult structural reforms — have always seemed politically unachievable. But crises have an odd way of motivating people. And politicians concerned about political fallout should take comfort from the fact that voters, too, are deeply worried. When it comes to rescuing the states, doing what was once politically impossible is quickly becoming absolutely necessary.

*Originally published as "The States in Crisis" in the Winter 2011 issue of* National Affairs.

# How to Dodge the Pension Disaster

## Josh Barro

SPRING 2011

W HEN DAN LILJENQUIST began his first term as a Utah state senator in January 2009, his financial acumen quickly earned him serious legislative responsibilities. A former management consultant for Bain & Company, Liljenquist was appointed by the Utah senate president, Michael Waddoups, to three budget-related committees; he was also made chairman of the Retirement and Independent Entities Committee. As Liljenquist remembers it, Waddoups pre-empted any concerns the freshman might have had about his new responsibilities: "Don't worry," Waddoups said, "nothing ever happens on the retirement committee."

But then, in the early months of 2009, the stock market went into free fall. Worried about the effects the market crash would have on Utah's public-employee pension plan — which, like most states', is invested heavily in equities — Liljenquist asked the plan's actuaries to project how much taxpayers would have to pay into the pension fund in order to compensate for the stock-market losses. The figures that came back were alarming: Utah was about to drown in red ink. Without reform, the state would see its contributions to government workers' pensions rise by about $420 million a year — an amount equivalent to roughly 10% of Utah's spending from its general and education funds. Moreover, those astronomical pension expenses would continue to grow at 4% a year for the next 25 years, just to pay off the losses the fund had incurred in the stock market.

This scenario alarmed lawmakers, and for good reason. It also alarmed public employees, who feared that rising pension costs would limit the state's ability to pay higher wages. Tapping into these concerns during the 2010 legislative session, Liljenquist built consensus around a cost-saving reform plan: Utah will now require all state employees

---

JOSH BARRO is the Walter B. Wriston Fellow at the Manhattan Institute.

hired after June 2011 to choose one of two retirement options — either a 401(k)-style benefit plan, or a sharply modified pension plan with costs to taxpayers capped in advance. The reform isn't perfect, of course, but it will be significantly less expensive for Utah's taxpayers, and will leave more room in the state budget for the real business of government.

Utah, it seems, has thus narrowly escaped catastrophe. But what about the other 49 states? The pension-cost explosion is hitting nearly every one of them, too. And unlike Utah's, these states' efforts at pension reform are not being overseen by management consultants. Rather, in most places, state legislators are overmatched by savvy public-employees' unions and by pension-fund managers wedded to the status quo. Their influence explains why, though 18 states enacted some sort of pension reform in 2010, very few will offer real, long-term relief to taxpayers.

Concern about this impending crisis should extend far beyond state capitals, because its consequences will affect much more than state balance sheets. The staggering burden of paying out retirement benefits is increasingly preventing state and local officials from financing all the other services that citizens expect their governments to perform. For example, Camden, New Jersey — one of the most crime-ridden cities in the country — recently had to lay off nearly half its police force because the state's public-sector unions, including those representing police, were unwilling to cut costly benefits provisions from their contracts. Moreover, should the states prove incapable of getting their pension costs under control, they will put the squeeze on taxpayers across the country — forcing them to pay more in exchange for fewer government services — and could precipitate federal bailouts that would effectively transfer money from fiscally responsible states to profligate ones.

Everyone, then, has a stake in understanding just how the states got into this terrible mess, where many states are going wrong in trying to rectify it, and — perhaps most important — just what principles should animate any reform plan capable of both shoring up state pensions *and* shielding the taxpaying public.

### DEFINED BENEFITS

To understand how the states got into their current sorry predicament, it is essential to examine the structural flaws in the state-pension edifice. There are two fundamental problems with the pension plans offered by state and local governments all across America: One is that, in many

cases, the benefits are excessively costly, insofar as they are more generous than is necessary to attract qualified talent to government work.
The other is that, by guaranteeing annuity-like streams of income in
retirement — regardless of whether the pension funds' assets and market
performance can support those payouts — such plans expose taxpayers
to enormous risk. After all, those taxpayers are the people who will be
responsible for making up any shortages.

Both of these problems are driven by the structure of most
public-employee retirement plans, which follow what is known as a
defined-benefit model. As the name would suggest, a defined-benefit
pension plan guarantees some fixed level of income to workers upon
their retirement; benefits are determined by a formula that is typically
based on the number of years worked and average earnings in several
years leading up to retirement. (Under some defined-benefit plans, retired workers are also entitled to annual cost-of-living adjustments.)

In principle, defined-benefit pensions are designed to be pre-funded.
Employers are supposed to set aside money during a worker's career
to pay for his benefits in retirement; in many cases, the employee is
required to make some portion of the total contributions himself. The
employer — in the case of public workers, the state — then invests these
assets, mostly in equity investments (such as mutual funds or stocks)
with a minority in fixed-income vehicles, such as bonds.

The key to defined-benefit plans, however, is that the employee's
benefit payments are not affected by the market performance of those
assets. In this sense, defined-benefit plans are explicitly designed to shift
investment risk from employees to employers. In the case of public
pensions, if a plan misses its target investment return, state workers
don't see their benefit checks shrink: Instead, taxpayers hand over more
of their earnings to the government, so that it can make good on its
promises to public-sector retirees.

Over the long term, defined-benefit pension plans can pose serious
challenges to an employer's bottom line — as Chrysler and General
Motors (and the American taxpayers who had to bail them out) can attest.
Perhaps this is why defined-benefit pensions have become increasingly
rare in the private sector: As of March 2010, just 30% of private-sector
workers at medium and large firms participated in a defined-benefit
pension program (down from 80% in 1985). Far more common in
today's marketplace is the "defined contribution" plan — such as a

401(k) — through which an employee sets aside earnings in a tax-free account that he can draw from upon his retirement.

But the public sector, characteristically, has been much slower to grasp the problems inherent in the defined-benefit structure — and the model is still used by every state to provide benefits for at least some workers. To be sure, some states are starting to inch away from this approach: Michigan and Alaska abandoned the defined-benefit model for most new state workers in 1997 and 2005, respectively; Alaska's reform also extends to local-government employees. But overall, in 2009, 84% of state and local workers in America were offered defined-benefit plans; today's federal employees also receive relatively small defined-benefit pensions in conjunction with 401(k) plans. (In addition to pensions, many public workers in the United States are eligible for free or heavily subsidized health insurance in retirement — a benefit that states have typically done even less to pre-fund than they have pensions, and one that is rising rapidly in cost.)

Often, taxpayers aren't even fully aware of the degree to which they are on the hook for state workers' generous benefits. Indeed, one of the inherent dangers of defined-benefit pensions is that such schemes allow lawmakers to promise future payments to state workers without having to fund those benefits adequately in the here and now. And because the present costs of state workers' benefits are never transparent to the voting and taxpaying public, politicians enact more expensive benefits provisions than they could get away with otherwise.

## ACCOUNTING DOUBLE STANDARDS

In the past year, think tanks and the press have tried to illuminate the opaque accounting practices of public-pension plans and the vast unfunded liabilities they obscure. Though often presented as impossibly complicated, the problem at the heart of the pension crisis is fairly simple: A pension plan holds a pool of assets and owes a stream of payments to government workers and retirees. If the plan doesn't hold enough of the former to cover the latter, it is said to be "underfunded." And it is this underfunding that presents a severe, long-term challenge to state policymakers. Even accepting the accuracy of the plans' own figures, the funding gap is alarming: As the Pew Center on the States noted in a report released last year, state and local governments were $1 trillion short of funding their pension and retiree health-care commitments. And these calculations were based on figures from the end of fiscal year 2008 — meaning that they included, for the most part, financial statements prepared *before* the stock market took its nosedive.

Yet dire as these figures seem, they are still far too rosy. A consensus has emerged among economists that government plans are fundamentally miscalculating the liabilities they owe, as they understate the cost of benefits to be paid in the future by counting on high investment returns that may not materialize (as discussed below). As a result, these government plans are also understating their funding gaps. Estimates from the Cato Institute and Credit Suisse put states' unfunded liabilities just for health care north of $1 trillion. And economists Robert Novy-Marx (of the University of Chicago) and Joshua Rauh (of Northwestern University) find that pension funds are short by more than $3 trillion.

These numbers are enormous, but their true magnitude becomes more clear when they are placed in fuller context. Consider that the total outstanding bond debt of state and local governments is about $2.4 trillion. If one accounts for pension and health-care debts using the figures supplied by Novy-Marx and Rauh (among others), the total outstanding obligations of the states rises to as much as $6.4 trillion — meaning that our sub-national governments are nearly three times further in the red than they appear to be at first glance.

The difference between these market-value estimates and the official tabulations of pension liabilities has to do with the choice of a discount rate — or rather, the presumptive interest rate one uses to determine precisely how much a sum of money that one will either pay out or receive in the future is worth today. In a sense, discounting works like an interest calculation in reverse: If a person owes $1.05 in one year, is discounting at a 5% rate, and holds $1 today, he can say that his $1.05 payment due in one year is fully funded.

Governmental Accounting Standards Board rules allow public-pension plans to set their liability discount rates equal to the investment returns they expect to achieve on their assets. Among major public-sector pension plans in the United States, that rate ranges from approximately 7.5% to 8.5%, with 8% being the most common choice. These rates reflect the fact that pension funds typically invest most of their assets in equities, which can achieve relatively high returns.

But those higher returns carry a downside: volatility. With the right investment mix, pension funds can, over time, average returns in the neighborhood of these targets; indeed, they have historically achieved such rates, even when one factors in the recent crash. The problem is that they cannot reliably yield such returns in any given year: In some moments, investments will produce windfalls that far exceed expectations; at other times, as in the period from 2008 to 2009, the funds' returns will come in far behind.

State governments expect to exist in perpetuity, which means they tend to take a very long-term view of their pension obligations — longer than, say, a corporation that has to worry about remaining profitable. But that doesn't mean governments can simply wait around for investments to bounce back after a stock-market crash while continuing to pay out benefits at the same level. If they do, they risk allowing a pensionfund balance to run all the way down to zero.

As a result, when pension funds lose money, taxpayers must step in to make up the difference. For example, in a recent report, my Manhattan Institute colleague E. J. McMahon and I estimated that employer — i.e., taxpayer — contributions to the New York State Teachers' Retirement System will more than quadruple over the next five years, principally as a result of recent stock-market declines. In this sense, taxpayers provide valuable insurance to public-employee pension plans, guaranteeing equity-like investments with bond-like certainty.

By contrast, pension plans in the private sector — governed by the separate Financial Accounting Standards Board — are not allowed to choose a discount rate based on expected returns on assets. Instead, they choose a discount rate based on a principle called the "market value of liabilities." Under this principle, a payment due in the future should be discounted at an interest rate consistent with the risk experienced by the creditor (which, in the case of a pension plan, is the worker or retiree). The amount of the liability is unaffected by either the nature or quantity of the assets the pension plan holds. For most private-sector pension plans, the market-value approach produces a discount rate between 5% and 6% — noticeably lower than the 8% presumed by the public sector.

The wisdom of the private-sector approach over that of the public sector is illustrated by an example from Novy-Marx and Rauh. Let's say that a person owns a home that has a mortgage on it, and he also has significant liquid investments that he intends to use to gradually pay off the mortgage. Now imagine that he re-allocates his investment portfolio away from bonds to stocks, increasing his expected return. Would we say that this change in his investment strategy has caused his mortgage balance to fall? Of course not. But that is what public pension plans do, by using expected asset returns as a component of the calculation of liabilities.

## THE TRUE COST OF PUBLIC PENSIONS

The degree to which these GASB-approved accounting tricks have led public pension funds to the brink of insolvency is usually the problem that draws analysts' focus. They are concerned—rightly—that pension plans are claiming to be much better funded than they really are. But this means that a related cash-flow issue often goes overlooked: The same error in discount-rate selection means that pension funds are also far more *expensive* than they claim to be. Clearly, this misrepresentation has major political and fiscal consequences. When lawmakers, and the voters to whom they are accountable, evaluate a state's pension system, the obvious first question is, "What do the benefits cost?" Accounting rules make answering this question less simple than it should be—and that difficulty has allowed lawmakers to hide pensions' true costs to taxpayers.

On the surface, the most obvious way to assess pension costs would be to look at the payments that state and local governments actually make into their pension systems. Every year, pension actuaries essentially send a bill to these governments, telling them what they must pay to cover the accrual of more benefits and to shore up plans that are underfunded. This first component—covering benefits accrued by active employees in the current year—is called "normal cost"; the second part is called "amortization cost." (In the case of an overfunded plan, the amortization cost may be negative.)

The trouble with using pension payments as a stand-in for pension cost—which the Bureau of Labor Statistics does when calculating compensation data—is that the total payment into a pension system in a given year usually does not accurately reflect the cost of paying out that year's benefits. For one thing, amortization cost—a key component of the actuaries' annual bills—is really an assessment to pay for labor that public employees provided in past years. Even if a government had no current workers on the payroll, its pension plan would still have to amortize any unfunded liability.

The complications posed by amortization costs are illustrated through a situation that was common at the peak of the tech bubble. During that period, high investment returns led some pension funds to report that they were significantly overfunded, resulting in large, negative amortization costs. As a result, pension contributions in those years were near zero. But this did not mean that pension benefits in those years were free; by promising pension benefits to workers, governments were still incurring liabilities that they would not otherwise have owed. Rather, the very low fund contributions meant simply that governments were using their investment returns, not tax receipts, to pay for retirement benefits in those years.

Another problem with using annual state contributions to determine a pension fund's cost is that some states disregard their actuaries' recommendations and pay less than they are supposed to when times are tight (Illinois and New Jersey are notable culprits). But failing to properly fund pension benefits does not make them cheaper (indeed, just the opposite); it simply means that the government is delaying the cash payment to a later year.

Rather than looking at annual cash contributions, then, pension cost should be thought of as equivalent to normal cost—the amount by which pension liabilities grow because workers are able to earn pension credits in a particular year.

But while this would be an improvement, there are still problems with a normal-cost approach. And chief among them is yet another issue relating to discount rates. In a pension fund, normal cost represents the present-day expense of promising to make a stream of payments in the future—which means that the cost is calculated using a discount rate. Funds generally use the same rate that they use to calculate their aggregate liabilities—about 8%. Of course, in this case, too, the discount rate is excessively high, leading states to underestimate their annual normal costs.

The effect of using the wrong discount rate is significant. Consider the New York State Teachers' Retirement System, which estimates its normal cost for employees hired in 2009 or earlier at 11.8% of wages and salaries (meaning, on average, that paying out one dollar in wages implies pension benefits that will cost 11.8 cents each year to provide). Adjusting the discount rate from 8% to a more realistic 5% increases that normal cost to approximately 19%—meaning the pension is really about 60% more expensive than its stated normal cost. If lawmakers had to calculate pension funds' normal costs on a market-value basis (as private pension funds do), and also had to increase required taxpayer contributions accordingly, they might think twice about making government workers' pension benefits ever more generous.

Accounting issues like these are but one way in which defined-benefit pensions systematically lead lawmakers to award overly generous pension benefits. Another major flaw is inherent in the very nature of pensions: They allow lawmakers to give valuable benefits to public workers (and to placate unions) without ever having to deal with the ugly future consequences. Handing out a wage increase, after all, generally requires coming up with a significant amount of money in this year's budget, which can pose enormous financial (not to mention political) difficulties. Sweetening pension benefits, on the other hand, achieves much the same political end—and while it does increase a pension system's unfunded liability, that cost is spread across pension payments that will be made for many years. In this way, legislators can please public employees now and leave it to future legislatures to clean up the mess.

This practice was common at the peak of the tech bubble, when many states—particularly New Jersey, New York, California, and Illinois—handed out pension sweeteners that, thanks to the high discount rates permitted under GASB, had the appearance of being "free." Of course, those sweeteners weren't free: They were simply financed with returns on investments that belong to taxpayers—returns that should have been used to reduce taxpayers' contributions to public workers' pensions. Then the stock market performed poorly over the next decade, and those "free" sweeteners ended up being paid for with tax dollars after all. (New York and New Jersey have since taken steps to reverse the increases, but only for newly hired employees.)

Defined-benefit pension plans thus provide lawmakers with both the motive and the means to seriously abuse state finances. All over the country, state lawmakers are tempted to appease government workers now, and let someone else figure out how to pay the bill in the future. At the same time, the complex accounting rules that govern defined-benefit pensions make it easy to cover up the costs of the scheme.

It is not impossible, of course, to construct a defined-benefit plan with reasonable costs. Certain institutional changes—like de-linking liability discount rates from asset returns, or requiring voters to approve any sweetened benefits for government workers (as they must approve the issuance of bonds in many states)—could help make costs somewhat easier to control. But there is another major problem with defined-benefit pensions that is fundamental to their nature — one that cannot be avoided without switching to a defined-contribution system. And that is the excessive risk to which they expose taxpayers.

### RISKY BUSINESS

Defined-benefit plans are, by their very design, intended to shift investment risk away from workers to employers. In most cases, both employees and employers make payments into a pension fund, but the employee payments are fixed — so only employer-contribution rates change with the funds' asset performance. Thus these plans carry the risk that, during economic downturns, the employer will be expected to come up with sharply increased payments for pensions. In the case of public-sector pension plans, this means taxpayers will have to pay much more at precisely the moment when they can least afford to.

To see just how painful this can be for taxpayers, consider the case of the New York State Teachers' Retirement System and the New York State and Local Employee Retirement System. Both were battered by the stock-market decline that followed the 2008 financial crisis; as a result, the funds held $212 billion in assets at their reporting dates in 2010, reflecting no increase since the year 2000. Yet because of growing retiree headcount, rising salaries, and a series of pension sweeteners approved by the state legislature, the funds last year were paying out *twice* as much in annual pension payments as they were a decade earlier. Accordingly, required taxpayer contributions are rising sharply: While employer-contribution rates were near zero a decade ago, and ranged between 6% and 10% of covered payroll over the past several years, rates for both plans are likely to climb above 20% by 2015.

When expressed in dollar terms, the increases appear even more stark. In fiscal year 2011 (which ends June 30), New York state school districts are making $900 million in contributions to the teachers' retirement system. By fiscal year 2016, that annual figure will rise to approximately $4.5 billion — and that's assuming that the fund hits its 8% targeted investment return over the next five years. These figures mean that school property taxes will have to rise 3.5% per year just to pay for the growing expense of providing teachers' pensions — even before addressing cost increases in any other area of the state's education system (including any potential wage increases for current teachers). All of this is the result simply of stock-market declines since 2007.

For this reason, it is incorrect to think of pension-fund assets as "belonging" to retirees. What the pensioners own is a valuable bond-like promise from the government. The taxpayers owe those promised funds to the pensioners—which means they also own the funds' asset pools, and rely on their strong performance to prevent massive tax increases. Essentially, state governments are long in the stock market on taxpayers' behalf.

Placing such a burden on federal taxpayers would be one thing; to limit risk, Washington could just issue Treasury bonds to pay rising costs, and pay them off when times are good (though taxpayers would still eventually be on the hook for interest payments). But almost every state is required to balance its budget each year. This means that swinging pension contributions place added pressure on already strained state budgets during recessions. The result is a harmful de-stimulative effect on the economy—as state program spending must be cut to make up for pension losses, or taxes must be raised on taxpayers who are feeling their own pain from the economic downturn. Both are policies to be avoided during recessions—and yet states' defined-benefit pensions leave lawmakers with few other choices.

Unfortunately, Utah is one of only two states to have seriously attacked the risk problem since the recession hit; Liljenquist's reform plan will shift investment risk away from taxpayers, at least for the retirement benefits of newly hired employees. (Michigan, having moved a large portion of state workers to 401(k) plans in 1997, will start offering new teachers a somewhat less generous defined-benefit pension, plus a 401(k) plan with a 2% match.) Each of the other 24 states that enacted reform plans in the past two years, meanwhile, has worked within the confines of the defined-benefit model. These reforms may provide some cost reductions, but they will not address the enormous risks that today's pension schemes pose to taxpayers.

### PRINCIPLES FOR REFORM

Any successful pension reform, then, should address both problems: excessive cost and excessive risk. Achieving these twin aims will clearly not be easy, and each state will need to consider its own unique problems and circumstances. Even so, there are three general principles that states can follow if they want to enact meaningful reforms that stand some chance of staving off pension disaster.

First, pension reforms should include all benefits that will be accrued in the future, not just benefits that will be accrued by new hires. As mentioned earlier, most states are limiting their pension reforms to new employees only—which means they are likely dooming their reforms to failure.

Admittedly, the political logic of their approach is easy to understand. Workers who might be hired in the future do not belong to unions; they have no voice in the political process. Active workers and retirees, however, are strong political forces in state capitals. Moreover, reforms that apply only to new workers can in fact generate significant savings over time: In the case of Michigan, for instance, thanks to the reform plan enacted in 1997, approximately half of the state's current work force is not eligible for the defined-benefit pension plan. For those employees who remain in the defined-benefit plan, Michigan's pension costs per worker have risen sharply in the past few years—as have those for every other state. But for the majority of the work force now in the defined-contribution plan, the state's costs are flat. As a result, Michigan was saving $210 million per year by 2010, with the savings growing each year.

The problem with this approach, however, is that cost savings in the near term are extremely limited. Last year, New Jersey passed a pension-reform law that rolled back a 9.09% pension sweetener enacted in 2001. But the rollback applies only to workers hired after the enactment of the reform law—meaning that it won't have much effect on the size of pension checks until around 2040. Other large states, including Illinois and New York, have recently enacted similar, purely prospective cutbacks.

Reductions in benefit accruals do enable states to cut back somewhat on pension-contribution payments before they actually flow through as smaller pension checks: A reduction in normal cost for new employees means that less money can be deposited each year to keep the pension system actuarially sound. But even this effect takes years to become substantial, because within the first few years after reform, a large majority of active employees will be accruing under the old rules, with the old (higher) normal cost. This does little to alleviate the cash-flow problem that taxpayers face today. For reform to have any meaningful effect on required contributions in the short term, it must also include current workers.

This does not mean that states should take away workers' already vested benefits. Those payments represent promised compensation for labor provided in the past, and states should honor such contracts unless they lack the overall financial wherewithal to honor their debts. But it does mean that states should act to reduce the benefits that current workers can accrue in future years. Essentially, states should adopt the private-sector model of pension-plan termination: Unless firms go bankrupt, they cannot revise pension benefits already accrued, but they can reduce or eliminate the benefits that workers expect to earn in future years of employment.

A few recent proposals have come close to striking the right balance. The Civic Committee of the Commercial Club of Chicago has suggested such a reform for Illinois, after obtaining a legal opinion stating that cuts to future benefits for current workers are allowable under the pension-guarantee provision in the state's constitution. And New Jersey governor Chris Christie's pension-reform proposal includes some reductions of future accruals by existing workers. But the states that have actually touched the benefits of current workers — Minnesota, Colorado, and South Dakota — have done so in the wrong way, by implementing across-the-board reductions that do not differentiate between benefits already accrued and benefits to be accrued in the future. Not only does this involve the abrogation of real promises to public workers, it has also invited litigation. Clearly, more education needs to take place before state lawmakers have a proper understanding of what to touch, and what not to touch, when it comes to trimming back future benefits.

Second, serious pension-reform plans should abandon the defined-benefit model. Three states — Michigan, Alaska, and Utah — have enacted reforms that will move many employees to defined-contribution retirement plans, or at least to sharply modified defined-benefit plans that shift most investment risk away from taxpayers. In most states, however, pension reform has been a matter of tinkering: increasing employee contributions, adjusting benefit formulas, raising retirement ages, and so on.

The problem with tinkering is that it addresses only the matter of pensions' high costs, doing nothing to shield taxpayers from the investment risks discussed above. Moreover, if states don't seize this moment to do away with defined-benefit models once and for all, they are unlikely to have another chance any time soon. And those small fixes that they do enact will likely be undone in future years. Administrations change, legislative seats turn over, and public-employee unions wax and wane in their power. Given a few years of strong stock-market returns and friendly lawmakers, public-worker interests will likely be able to restore any benefits they lose during the current reform cycle—which will put state finances, and the taxpayers affected by them, in the same tough position during the next downturn.

New York taxpayers have learned about these dangers the hard way. There is a reason that the pension fixes enacted in 2009 were called "Tier V" and not "Tier II": There had been three previous attempts to rein in the excessive cost of New York's public-employee pensions by creating less generous pension "tiers" for newly hired employees. These reforms date back to the fiscal crisis of the 1970s, when unsustainably generous contracts with public-employee unions threatened to throw New York City into bankruptcy. Since then, though, New York's public-worker unions have been highly successful in unwinding previously enacted pension reforms. The new Tier V is nearly identical to Tier IV at the time of its enactment in 1983—but Tier IV has been repeatedly, and retroactively, sweetened through increases in benefit formulas, cuts to employee contributions, and reductions in the retirement age. Similarly, by the time substantial numbers of workers actually start retiring under Tier V around 2040, this plan, too, will probably bear little resemblance to its current form.

Moving to a defined-contribution system would not make such reversals impossible, but it would probably make them much less common. For lawmakers, a key appeal of pension sweeteners in a defined-benefit system is their opacity: The fiscal cost often appears to be financed by windfall returns on pension assets. Similarly sweetening a 401(k) plan, however, would require a direct infusion of cash into workers' accounts, at a significant and immediate cost to taxpayers—making such goodies much more difficult for lawmakers to distribute.

Third, states should consider voluntary buyouts of existing pension benefits. The two reform principles outlined above address only the costs of pension benefits going forward; they do not help resolve the very real problems associated with states' existing pension liabilities—those that were incurred by governments as payment for labor that employees provided in the past. Here, there are no easy policy maneuvers: Short of defaulting on these debts, the only way states can eliminate unfunded pension liabilities is to fund them.

Unless, that is, employees voluntarily agree to sell their pension benefits back to their employers. Even if governments can be trusted to make pension-benefit payments as scheduled—which, given some states' current circumstances, is a big "if"—many employees would probably accept significantly reduced pension payouts if they could get their benefits in one up-front, lump-sum payment. The reason is the difference between cost and value: Part of why pension benefits are so expensive is that it is costly to provide insurance of long-term returns; workers, however, may not place a value on that insurance that is as high as the cost of providing it. Effectively, a pension benefit is similar to a 401(k) plan invested entirely in annuities. And the fact that few individuals choose to invest their retirement accounts entirely in annuities—especially during their working years—suggests that pension benefits may be worth less than they cost to provide.

A working paper by Maria Fitzpatrick, a fellow at the Stanford Institute for Economic Policy Research, attempts to determine just how highly some public employees value their pension benefits. She examined Illinois teachers' choices when, in 1998, they were offered a chance to make a one-time payment up front in exchange for more generous benefits in retirement. The terms of the purchase varied significantly depending on a teacher's salary and years of service. Using reasonable discount rates, the up-front purchase cost was lower than the present value of benefits for nearly all teachers—99% could expect at least a 7% annual return on investment, with no risk so long as the state did not default. But the deal was sweeter for some teachers than for others, a variation that made it possible to estimate the subjective present value that teachers placed on future benefits.

Fitzpatrick's finding is, in a way, depressing: On average, teachers were willing to pay only 17 cents on the dollar to obtain a pension-benefit increase. This suggests that defined-benefit pensions are a highly inefficient form of compensation, costing taxpayers far more than they are worth to public employees.

But it also suggests an appealing policy solution: Governments can offer to buy back promised pension benefits at a discount, and employees may be inclined to take the deal. Admittedly, the proposal presents a political problem to lawmakers, in that it requires them to produce an immense sum of cash up front in order to eliminate a long-term liability. To alleviate some of that pain, however, governments could responsibly issue bonds to raise the money—since this would mean simply substituting explicit debt for a larger amount of implicit pension debt. Governments would incur an obligation to pay interest on the bonds, but in most cases that amount would be more than offset by the reduction in required employer pension contributions.

So just how much would governments have to offer workers to induce them to participate in such a buyback program? There are reasons to suspect the payment would have to be higher than 17% of their benefits' present value. To begin, people tend to irrationally value assets they already own more highly than assets they could buy—a phenomenon known as the "endowment effect." Workers might therefore demand a higher price when selling their benefits than they would have been willing to pay to buy the benefits in the first place (which is what Fitzpatrick measured in her study of Illinois teachers).

There are also negative federal tax implications attached to taking pension benefits as a one-time buyout. In addition to the income tax, workers under 59 and a half years old would have to pay a 10% early-withdrawal penalty. These payments could be avoided by rolling the payout over into an IRA, but the requirement could make the buyout program less appealing to workers seeking flexibility. (Congress should consider waiving the early-withdrawal penalty for buyouts of public-employee pensions as a way to help states shrink their liabilities.)

Finally, union resistance to a voluntary-buyout program would likely be strong—meaning they would probably demand higher payouts for workers in exchange for supporting the plan. Legislators might argue that a voluntary buyout could only make workers better off: If they didn't like the deal, they could keep the benefits they were already entitled to. Historically, however, unions have strongly resisted any moves that have been perceived as weakening the defined-benefit system (such as voluntary 401(k) options for employees).

Obviously, none of these reforms would be easy to implement. The states are in grave trouble, and do not have easy options. Nor are these principles to be mistaken for complete solutions. But they do offer politicians a basic guide for constructing policies that can help rescue seriously ailing pension plans. And they show that the challenges that any reform will inevitably present are not insurmountable. Indeed, the greatest challenge at this moment may be getting lawmakers to realize that whatever unpleasantness reform might bring now would pale in comparison to the pain they invite by doing nothing.

### AGAINST THE CLOCK

Those reformers intent on rescuing states from pension crises will clearly have their work cut out for them. How, then, ought they to get the process moving? To begin, state and local lawmakers will have to borrow a page from Dan Liljenquist's book and clearly explain to their colleagues and voters what will happen to pension plans (and to taxpayers) in the absence of reform. They should get their pension funds' actuaries to disclose the plans' underfunding on a market-value basis, and to reveal the expected trajectory of required taxpayer contributions in upcoming years. Because of the way pension funds delay recognition of abnormal gains and losses, most states can expect a cost explosion similar to the one that is coming in New York state—an increase that is likely to be a powerful motivator for reform.

Congress, too, has a useful role to play. Lawmakers in Washington should mandate, or at least strongly encourage, greater pension transparency by states. For example, the Public Pension Transparency Act—sponsored by Republican congressman Devin Nunes of California—would tie federal subsidies for municipal bonds to states' making certain disclosures about their pension funds, including market valuations and projections.

Even with greater transparency, however, modifying pensions for current employees will remain a tough sell politically; unions especially will fervently resist. In this situation, lawmakers might be well served by a divide-and-conquer approach: They can begin to draw a clear distinction between benefits that have already been earned (and the valid contractual claims held by the people who have earned them) and future benefits to be paid (which, if disbursed, would impose unacceptable and unnecessary costs on future taxpayers). Lawmakers can promise current retirees that their benefits will not be touched at all in any reform plan, emphasizing that those benefits will in fact be safeguarded by changes to benefits not yet accrued—changes that will make the pension system as a whole better funded. Drawing such distinctions might help lawmakers drive a wedge between active and retired government workers, thereby fracturing the anti-reform coalition.

Of course, the best tool reformers have at their disposal is urgency. When Chris Christie talks about why public workers should support reform, he argues that, without meaningful changes, New Jersey's pension funds could run out of money—leaving everyone without benefits in a decade. There are, naturally, some steps short of total default on pension obligations: A state could, for instance, write pension checks on a pay-as-you-go basis once the funds are tapped out. But such a measure would be extremely costly: In the case of New Jersey, it would require a payment of more than $3 billion a year—more than 10% of the state's current general fund, and nearly $400 per resident. The amount would only grow over time, and at a faster clip than the economy. In that event, pensioners would almost certainly end up taking a haircut on their benefits. Lawmakers need to communicate—and public workers and their unions need to understand—that it is much better for everyone to plan and adapt now, in advance, so that cuts are orderly and focus on benefits not yet earned, and thus avoid slashing the fixed incomes of people who are already retired.

Even though we are just starting to recover from the Great Recession, another fiscal crisis lurks around the corner. What we need now are serious reforms—plans that focus on the underlying causes of pensions' excessive costs and excessive risks. The good news is that the looming pension meltdown is still within our power to avert. The question is whether lawmakers and public workers can muster the discipline and political courage to do it.

*Originally published as "Dodging the Pension Disaster" in the Spring 2011 issue of* National Affairs.

# How to Approach Public Sector Unions

## Daniel DiSalvo

FALL 2010

WHEN CHRIS CHRISTIE became New Jersey's governor in January, he wasted no time in identifying the chief perpetrators of his state's fiscal catastrophe. Facing a nearly $11 billion budget gap — as well as voters fed up with the sky-high taxes imposed on them to finance the state government's profligacy — Christie moved swiftly to take on the unions representing New Jersey's roughly 400,000 public employees.

On his first day in office, the governor signed an executive order preventing state-workers' unions from making political contributions — subjecting them to the same limits that had long applied to corporations. More recently, he has waged a protracted battle against state teachers' unions, which are seeking pay increases and free lifetime health care for their members. Recognizing the burden that such benefits would place on New Jersey's long-term finances, Christie has sought instead to impose a one-year wage freeze, to change pension rules to limit future benefits, and to require that teachers contribute a tiny fraction of their salaries to cover the costs of their health insurance — measures that, for private-sector workers, would be mostly uncontroversial.

The firestorm that these proposals have sparked demonstrates the political clout of state-workers' unions. Christie's executive order met with vicious condemnation from union leaders and the politicians aligned with them; his fight with the public-school teachers prompted the New Jersey Education Association to spend $6 million (drawn from members' dues) on anti-Christie attack ads over a two-month period. Clearly, the lesson for reform-minded politicians has been: Confront public-sector unions at your peril.

DANIEL DISALVO *is an assistant professor of political science at the City College of New York.*

Yet confront them policymakers must. As Christie said about the duel with the NJEA, "If we don't win this fight, there's no other fight left." Melodramatic as this may sound, for many states, it is simply reality. The cost of public-sector pay and benefits (which in many cases far exceed what comparable workers earn in the private sector), combined with hundreds of billions of dollars in unfunded pension liabilities for retired government workers, are weighing down state and city budgets. And staggering as these burdens seem now, they are actually poised to grow exponentially in the years ahead. If policymakers fail to rein in this growth, a fiscal crack-up will be the inevitable result.

New Jersey has drawn national attention as a case study, but the same scenario is playing out in state capitals from coast to coast. New York, Michigan, California, Washington, and many other states also find themselves heavily indebted, with public-sector unions at the root of their problems. In exchange, taxpayers in these states are rewarded with larger and more expensive, yet less effective, government, and with elected officials who are afraid to cross the politically powerful unions. As the *Wall Street Journal* put it recently, public-sector unions "may be the single biggest problem...for the U.S. economy and small-d democratic governance." They may also be the biggest challenge facing state and local officials—a challenge that, unless economic conditions dramatically improve, will dominate the politics of the decade to come.

### THE STATE OF THE UNION

Since the middle of the 20th century, organized labor in America has undergone two transformations with major implications for the nation's politics. The first is the dramatic decline in overall union membership. In 1955, organized labor represented one-third of the non-agricultural work force; today, it represents just 12.3%. The second transformation, however, is even more significant: the change in the composition of the unionized work force.

As private-sector unions have withered, public-sector unions have grown dramatically. The Bureau of Labor Statistics reports that, in 2009, for the first time ever, more public-sector employees (7.9 million) than private-sector employees (7.4 million) belonged to unions. Today, unionized workers are more likely to be teachers, librarians, trash collectors, policemen, or firefighters than they are to be carpenters, electricians, plumbers, auto workers, or coal miners.

This shift has produced a noticeable change in the demographic profile of union members; gone is the image of a union man as a beefy laborer in a hard hat and steel-toed boots. According to data from the University of Michigan's American National Election Study, in 1952, about 80% of union members were blue-collar workers, while 20% were white-collar workers; by the mid-1990s, those classified as white-collar workers gained majority status. Nor do men dominate unions any longer: In the 1950s, more than 80% of union members were men, but today there is near gender parity. Union members also have much more schooling than they once did. In 1960, more than 35% of union members had not finished high school and barely 2% had college degrees. Today, almost every union member has completed high school, and more than 25% have college degrees. The typical union member no longer lives in a major city center close to the factory; by the 1990s, union members were more likely to live in suburban than urban areas. Unions have also become multi-racial: Nearly a quarter of union members are now non-white. Unions today represent a vastly different slice of America than they did at the height of the country's manufacturing prowess.

The rise of government-worker unionism has also combined with the broader transformation of the American economy to produce a sharp divergence between public- and private-sector employment. In today's public sector, good pay, generous benefits, and job security make possible a stable middle-class existence for nearly everyone from janitors to jailors. In the private economy, meanwhile, cutthroat competition, increased income inequality, and layoffs squeeze the middle class. This discrepancy indicates how poorly the middle class has fared in recent decades in the private economy, which is home to 80% of American jobs. But it also highlights the increased benefits of government work, and shines a spotlight on the gains public-sector unions have secured for their members. Perhaps this success helps explain why, on average, 39% of state- and local-government employees belong to unions. (Differences in state and local laws of course mean that the percentage varies from state to state; New York tops the chart with roughly 70% of state employees in unions, while many Southern right-to-work states hover in the single digits.)

The emergence of powerful public-sector unions was by no means inevitable. Prior to the 1950s, as labor lawyer Ida Klaus remarked in 1965, "the subject of labor relations in public employment could not have meant less to more people, both in and out of government." To the extent that people thought about it, most politicians, labor leaders, economists, and judges opposed collective bargaining in the public sector. Even President Franklin Roosevelt, a friend of private-sector unionism, drew a line when it came to government workers: "Meticulous attention," the president insisted in 1937, "should be paid to the special relations and obligations of public servants to the public itself and to the Government....The process of collective bargaining, as usually understood, cannot be transplanted into the public service." The reason? F.D.R. believed that "[a] strike of public employees manifests nothing less than an intent on their part to obstruct the operations of government until their demands are satisfied. Such action looking toward the paralysis of government by those who have sworn to support it is unthinkable and intolerable." Roosevelt was hardly alone in holding these views, even among the champions of organized labor. Indeed, the first president of the AFL-CIO, George Meany, believed it was "impossible to bargain collectively with the government."

Courts across the nation also generally held that collective bargaining by government workers should be forbidden on the legal grounds of sovereign immunity and unconstitutional delegation of government powers. In 1943, a New York Supreme Court judge held:

> To tolerate or recognize any combination of civil service employees of the government as a labor organization or union is not only incompatible with the spirit of democracy, but inconsistent with every principle upon which our government is founded. Nothing is more dangerous to public welfare than to admit that hired servants of the State can dictate to the government the hours, the wages and conditions under which they will carry on essential services vital to the welfare, safety, and security of the citizen. To admit as true that government employees have power to halt or check the functions of government unless their demands are satisfied, is to transfer to them all legislative, executive and judicial power. Nothing would be more ridiculous.

The very nature of many public services—such as policing the streets and putting out fires—gives government a monopoly or near monopoly; striking public employees could therefore hold the public hostage. As long-time *New York Times* labor reporter A. H. Raskin wrote in 1968: "The community cannot tolerate the notion that it is defenseless at the hands of organized workers to whom it has entrusted responsibility for essential services."

Another common objection to collective bargaining with public-employee unions was that it would mean taking some of the decision-making authority over government functions away from the people's elected representatives and transferring it to union officials, with whom the public had vested no such authority. In this view, democracy would be compromised when elected officials began sharing with union leaders the power to determine government employees' wages, benefits, and working conditions. Furthermore, collectively bargained work rules could alter what public servants did day to day in ways not condoned by either elected officials or the voting public.

Given the forces and arguments aligned against public-sector unions, what led to their enormous growth? Three conditions prepared the ground for the legal reforms that facilitated collective bargaining in the public sector (and the subsequent swelling of the ranks of unionized government employees).

The first was the weakening of party machines at the state and (especially) local levels. In many of America's large cities, the responsibility for filling government jobs fell to the party machines; turnover in government employment was therefore high, connected as it was to election results. In New York during the 1930s and '40s, for instance, the average tenure of a cop or garbage collector was five years. Another effect of the machines' influence over government hiring was political: People in patronage jobs inevitably devoted a portion of their nominal working hours to party affairs. Because government employment under the machine system was both relatively brief and partisan in nature, a culture of professionalism was never really able to take hold.

Reformers' chief weapon in the war against the machines was the enactment of civil-service laws. Such laws sought to deprive ward bosses of control over patronage, which was their lifeblood. Civic groups, the press, and public-employees' associations believed that greater professionalization of the government work force would draw in talent, increase efficiency, and reduce corruption. In the 1950s, according to historian Leo Kramer, the leadership of the American Federation of State, County, and Municipal Employees (AFSCME) "saw itself as part of a great movement to reform government," one of whose principal aims was "the extension of the merit system to all nonpolicy determining positions in all government jurisdictions."

By the end of the 1950s, reformers had put the old machines on the defensive. And professionalization had had its intended effect: In their 1963 book *City Politics*, Edward Banfield and James Q. Wilson found that, by 1961, 52% of cities with populations over 500,000 had placed nearly all government employees under civil-service protections.

One important consequence of civil-service reform was that, with the end of election-based turnover—and with protections against undue political interference in hiring and firing—public employees gained nearly lifetime job security. This gave workers a long-term interest in their jobs and increased their capacity to express themselves collectively, thereby helping to make the unionization of public employees possible.

The second precondition for public-sector unionization was economic and demographic change. In the post-war period, the number of government jobs grew rapidly: Between 1950 and 1976, state- and local-government employment increased from 9.1% to 15.3% of the non-agricultural work force (an increase from roughly 4 million workers to about 12 million). A large part of this spike was the result of increased demand for government services caused by the Baby Boom. Huge numbers of young people meant a greater need for workers in schools in particular; the number of Americans working as teachers, principals, and administrators thus increased dramatically. It is hardly surprising, then, that some of the first public employees to unionize (and some of the most militant) were teachers. In the 1970s in New York state alone, there were, on average, 20 teacher strikes a year.

Finally, the third precondition was the solidification of the alliance between organized labor and the Democratic Party. Franklin Roosevelt's signing of the Wagner Act (which protected the rights of private-sector workers to organize and bargain collectively) in 1935 fully bonded labor to the Democrats; their partnership was reinforced during the fight over the Taft-Hartley Act of 1947, which was a Republican initiative to rein in union power. By mid-century, Democrats began to rely on labor unions for both funding and on-the-ground campaign organizing. In the 1950s and '60s, according to political scientist J. David Greenstone, "labor functioned as the most important nation-wide electoral organization for the Democratic Party." As a political tag team, both Democrats and labor had an incentive to broaden the base of the labor movement—and they came to see public-sector workers as the most promising new hunting ground, especially as private-sector union membership began to decline.

Democrats began to mobilize this new constituency in the late 1950s. In 1958, New York City mayor Robert Wagner, Jr., issued Executive Order 49, known as "the little Wagner Act." It gave city employees bargaining rights, and provided their unions with exclusive representation (meaning that the unions alone were legally authorized to speak for city workers, regardless of whether those workers belonged to the unions or supported them). And in 1962, President John Kennedy issued Executive Order 10988, reaffirming the right of federal workers to organize and codifying their right to bargain collectively.

From the mid-1960s through the early '70s, states and cities followed with a plethora of laws providing public-employee unions with collective-bargaining rights. In many cases, the consequences were almost immediate. In New York state, one year after the passage of the so-called Taylor Law in 1967, 360,000 state- and local-government employees became unionized; the *New York Times* described the law as having an "almost revolutionary effect." Other states and cities experienced similar expansions in the number of public-sector union members. For example, in 1968, California passed the Meyers-Milias-Brown Act—a law granting local-government workers bargaining rights—and then extended those rights to teachers a few years later; in the 1970s and '80s, both membership in public-sector unions and the number of strikes in California skyrocketed. Nationwide, by 1970, the AFSCME had negotiated more than 1,000 collective-bargaining agreements, nearly twice the number in place in 1964. And by 1972, nearly half of the states had public-employee collective-bargaining laws in place at either the state or local level.

Collective-bargaining laws gave government workers powerful incentives to join unions. Between 1960 and 1980, the portion of full-time unionized public employees jumped from 10% to 36% of the public-sector work force. The AFSCME grew from 99,000 members in 1955 to just under 1 million members in 1980. Over the same period, the American Federation of Teachers grew from 40,000 to more than half a million members. Today, its membership stands at more than 1.5 million—which makes the AFT larger than the largest exclusively private-sector union, the United Food and Commercial Workers (1.3 million members). But even the AFT is dwarfed by the largest labor union in the United States: the National Education Association, which claims 3.2 million members.

Organized labor in America thus increasingly consists of government employees, and government employees increasingly belong to unions. This shift has clearly reshaped the country's labor movement. Far more important to most Americans, though, is the way it has transformed the relationships between public employees, the governments they work for, and the public they serve — often with less than salutary results.

### THE PUBLIC-SECTOR DIFFERENCE

When it comes to advancing their interests, public-sector unions have significant advantages over traditional unions. For one thing, using the political process, they can exert far greater influence over their members' employers — that is, government — than private-sector unions can. Through their extensive political activity, these government-workers' unions help elect the very politicians who will act as "management" in their contract negotiations — in effect handpicking those who will sit across the bargaining table from them, in a way that workers in a private corporation (like, say, American Airlines or the Washington Post Company) cannot. Such power led Victor Gotbaum, the leader of District Council 37 of the AFSCME in New York City, to brag in 1975: "We have the ability, in a sense, to elect our own boss."

Since public-sector unions began to develop in earnest, their importance in political campaigns has grown by leaps and bounds. Starting from almost nothing in the 1960s, government-workers' unions now far exceed private-sector unions in political contributions. According to the Center for Responsive Politics, from 1989 to 2004, the AFSCME was the biggest spender in America, giving nearly $40 million to candidates in federal elections (98.5% of it to Democrats). It is important to stress that this was spending on *federal* elections; the union represents mostly *state and local* workers. But given the magnitude of federal contributions to state budgets, the AFSCME is heavily involved in electioneering to shape Washington's spending in ways that protect public workers and the supply of government services. And so over that 15-year period, the AFSCME was willing and able to outspend any other organization in the country.

The political influence of public-sector unions is probably greatest, however, in low-turnout elections to school boards and state and local offices, and in votes to decide ballot initiatives and referenda. For example, two of the top five biggest spenders in Wisconsin's 2003 and 2004 state elections were the Wisconsin Education Association Council and the AFSCME-affiliated Wisconsin PEOPLE Conference. Only the state Republican Party and two other political action committees—those belonging to the National Association of Realtors and SBC/Ameritech—spent more. The same is true in state after state, as unions work to exert control over the very governments that employs their members.

This political dimension of public-sector unionism also changes the substantive priorities and demands of the unions themselves. Although private-sector unions in the United States have engaged in leftist "social activism," they have mostly concentrated their efforts on securing the best wages, benefits, pensions, and working conditions for their members: "pure and simple unionism," as longtime American Federation of Labor president Samuel Gompers used to call it. Rarely do they demand more hiring, since—given the constant private-sector imperative to keep operating costs minimal—increasing the number of a company's employees can limit wage and benefit increases for the workers already on the company's payroll.

By contrast, as economist Richard Freeman has written, "public sector unions can be viewed as *using their political power to raise demand for public services*, as well as using their bargaining power to fight for higher wages." The millions spent by public-employee unions on ballot measures in states like California and Oregon, for instance, almost always support the options that would lead to higher taxes and more government spending. The California Teachers Association, for example, spent $57 million in 2005 to defeat referenda that would have reduced union power and checked government growth. And the political influence of such massive spending is of course only amplified by the get-out-the-vote efforts of the unions and their members. This power of government-workers' unions to increase (and then sustain) levels of employment through the political process helps explain why, for instance, the city of Buffalo, New York, had the same number of public workers in 2006 as it did in 1950—despite having lost half of its population (and thus a significant amount of the demand for public services).

For a case study in how public-sector unions manipulate both supply and demand, consider the example of the California Correctional Peace Officers Association. Throughout the 1980s and '90s, the CCPOA lobbied the state government to increase California's prison facilities—since more prisons would obviously mean more jobs for corrections officers. And between 1980 and 2000, the Golden State constructed 22 new prisons for adults (before 1980, California had only 12 such facilities). The CCPOA also pushed for the 1994 "three strikes" sentencing law, which imposed stiff penalties on repeat offenders. The prison population exploded—and, as intended, the new prisoners required more guards. The CCPOA has been no less successful in increasing members' compensation: In 2006, the average union member made $70,000 a year, and more than $100,000 with overtime. Corrections officers can also retire with 90% of their salaries as early as age 50. Today, an amazing 11% of the state budget—more than is spent on higher education—goes to the penal system. Governor Arnold Schwarzenegger now proposes privatizing portions of the prison system to escape the unions' grip—though his proposal has so far met with predictable (union supported) political opposition.

A further important advantage that public-sector unions have over their private-sector counterparts is their relative freedom from market forces. In the private sector, the wage demands of union workers cannot exceed a certain threshold: If they do, they can render their employers uncompetitive, threatening workers' long-term job security. In the public sector, though, government is the monopoly provider of many services, eliminating any market pressures that might keep unions' demands in check. Moreover, unlike in the private sector, contract negotiations in the public sector are usually not highly adversarial; most government-agency mangers have little personal stake in such negotiations. Unlike executives accountable to shareholders and corporate boards, government managers generally get paid the same—and have the same likelihood of keeping their jobs—regardless of whether their operations are run efficiently. They therefore rarely play hardball with unions like business owners and managers do; there is little history of "union busting" in government.

Additionally, the rise and fall of businesses in the private sector means that unions must constantly engage in organizing efforts, reaching out to employees of newly created companies. In government agencies, on the other hand, once a union organizes workers, they usually remain organized—because the government doesn't go out of business. Public-employee unions can thus maintain membership levels with much less effort than can private-sector unions.

Finally, public-sector unions enjoy a privileged position in relation not only to their private-sector counterparts but also to other interest groups. Public-sector unions have automatic access to politicians through the collective-bargaining process, while other interest groups must fight for such entrée. Government unions can also more easily mobilize their members for electoral participation than other interest groups can — since they are able to apply pressure at the workplace and, in many cases, can even arrange for time off and other benefits to make members' political activism easier. Furthermore, most interest groups must devote a great deal of time and effort to fundraising; public-sector unions, on the other hand, enjoy a steady, reliable revenue stream, as union dues are deducted directly from members' paychecks (often by government, which drastically reduces the unions' administrative costs).

Taken together, the intrinsic advantages that public-sector unions enjoy over private-sector advocacy groups (including private-sector unions) have given organized government laborers enormous power over government at the local, state, and federal levels; to shape public finances and fiscal policy; and to influence the very spirit of our democracy. The results, unfortunately, have not always been pretty.

## A UNIONIZED GOVERNMENT

The effects of public-sector unionism can be grouped under three broad headings. The first centers on compensation, which includes wages, pensions, health care, and other benefits easily valued in monetary terms — the core issues at stake in collective-bargaining negotiations. The second involves the amount of government employment, or the size of government, as reflected in the number of workers and in public budgets. The third involves the productivity and efficiency of government services. Insofar as unions negotiate detailed work rules, they share the power to shape the day-to-day responsibilities of public servants — which influences what government does, and how well it does it.

These are complex matters that are hard for social scientists to measure, and on which scholars disagree. Nevertheless, the evidence supports a few broad conclusions.

Most economists agree that public-sector unions' political power leads to more government spending. And recently, Chris Edwards of the Cato Institute documented *how* government unionism has abetted growth in public-sector compensation. Generally speaking, the public sector pays more than the private sector for jobs at the low end of the labor market, while the private sector pays more for jobs at the high end. For janitors and secretaries, for instance, the public sector offers an appreciably better deal than the private economy: According to the Bureau of Labor Statistics, the average annual salary for the roughly 330,000 office clerks who work in government was almost $27,000 in 2005, while the 2.7 million in the private sector received an average pay of just under $23,000. Nationwide, among the 108,000 janitors who work in government, the average salary was $23,700; the average salary of the 2 million janitors working in the private sector, meanwhile, was $19,800.

For workers with advanced degrees, however, the public-sector pay scale is likely to be slightly below the private-sector benchmark. Private-sector economists, for instance, earn an average of $99,000 a year, compared to the $69,000 earned by their government colleagues. And accountants in the corporate world earn average annual salaries of $52,000, compared to $48,000 for their public-sector counterparts.

Not as easily captured is the comparable worth of those government workers who lack counterparts in the private sector, such as policemen, firefighters, and corrections officers. But that very monopoly status has given the union representatives of these workers enormous leverage, which they have converted into major gains. For example, in New York state, county police officers were paid an average salary of $121,000 a year in 2006. In that same year, according to the *Boston Globe*, 225 of the 2,338 Massachusetts State Police officers made more than the $140,535 annual salary earned by the state's governor. Four state troopers received more than $200,000, and 123 others were paid more than $150,000. While people whose jobs entail greater risk of life and limb certainly deserve higher pay, union power has clearly added a substantial premium.

When all jobs are considered, state and local public-sector workers today earn, on average, $14 more per hour in total compensation (wages and benefits) than their private-sector counterparts. The *New York Times* has reported that public-sector wages and benefits over the past decade have grown *twice* as fast as those in the private sector. These aggregate pay differentials stem partly from the fact that government work tends to be more white-collar, and that public employees tend to be better educated and more experienced, and to live in urban areas. Another factor is the hollowing out of the middle of the income distribution in the private sector. But union influence still plays a major role.

When unions have not been able to secure increases in wages and salaries, they have turned their attention to benefits. *USA Today* journalist Dennis Cauchon notes that, since 2002, for every $1-an-hour pay increase, public employees have gotten $1.17 in new benefits; private-sector workers, meanwhile, have received just 58 cents in added benefits. Of special interest to the unions has been health care: Across the nation, 86% of state- and local-government workers have access to employer-provided health insurance, while only 45% of private-sector workers do. In many cases, these plans involve meager contributions from employees, or none at all—in New Jersey, for instance, 88% of public-school teachers pay nothing toward their insurance premiums.

The unions' other cherished benefit is public-employee pensions. In California, for example, state workers often retire at 55 years of age with pensions that exceed what they were paid during most of their working years. In New York City, firefighters and police officers may retire after 20 years of service at half pay—which means that, at a time when life expectancy is nearly 80 years, New York City is paying benefits to 10,000 retired cops who are less than 50 years old. Those benefits quickly add up: In 2006, the annual pension benefit for a new retiree averaged just under $73,000 (and the full amount is exempt from state and local taxes).

How, one might ask, were policymakers ever convinced to agree to such generous terms? As it turns out, many lawmakers found that increasing pensions was very good politics. They placated unions with future pension commitments, and then turned around, borrowed the money appropriated for the pensions, and spent it paying for public services in the here and now. Politicians liked this scheme because they could satisfy the unions, provide generous public services without raising taxes to pay for them, and even sometimes get around balanced-budget requirements.

Unfortunately, the hit pension funds took recently in the stock market has exposed the massive underfunding that results from states' and municipalities' not paying for the public services they consume. In Illinois, for example, public-sector unions have helped create a situation in which the state's pension funds report a liability of more than $100 billion, at least 50% of it unfunded. Yet many analysts believe the figure is much higher; without a steep economic recovery, the Prairie State is looking at insolvency. Indeed, Northwestern University finance professor Joshua Rauh puts the date of collapse at 2018; he also predicts that six other states—Connecticut, Indiana, New Jersey, Hawaii, Louisiana, and Oklahoma—will see their pension funds dry up before the end of fiscal year 2020. What's more, according to the Pew Center on the States, 18 states face long-term pension liabilities in excess of $10 billion. In the case of California, like that of Illinois, the unfunded pension liability exceeds $50 billion. In fact, Pew estimates that, when retiree health-care costs are added to pension obligations, the unfunded liabilities of the states total an astounding $1 trillion.

The skyrocketing costs of public employees' pensions now present a huge challenge to state and local governments. If allowed to persist, such massive obligations will inevitably force a fundamental re-ordering of government priorities. After all, if government must spend more on pensions, it cannot spend more on schools, roads, and relief for the poor—in other words, the basic functions people expect their governments to perform. But because many states' pension commitments are constitutionally guaranteed, there is no easy way out of this financial sink hole. Recent court decisions indicate that pension obligations will have to be fulfilled even if governments declare bankruptcy—because while federal law allows bankruptcy judges to change pension and health-care packages in the private sector, it forbids such changes in public employees' agreements.

Yet as skilled as the unions may be in drawing on taxpayer dollars, many observers argue that their greater influence is felt in the quality of the government services taxpayers receive in return. In his book *The Warping of Government Work*, Harvard public-policy scholar John Donahue explains how public-employee unions have reduced government efficiency and responsiveness. With poor prospects in the ultra-competitive private sector, government work is increasingly desirable for those with limited skills; at the opposite end of the spectrum, the wage compression imposed by unions and civil-service rules makes government employment less attractive to those whose abilities are in high demand. Consequently, there is a "brain drain" at the top end of the government work force, as many of the country's most talented people opt for jobs in the private sector where they can be richly rewarded for their skills (and avoid the intricate work rules, and glacial advancement through big bureaucracies, that are part and parcel of government work).

Thus, as New York University professor Paul Light argues, government employment "caters more to the security-craver than the risk-taker." And because government employs more of the former and fewer of the latter, it is less flexible, less responsive, and less innovative. It is also more expensive: Northeastern University economist Barry Bluestone has shown that, between 2000 and 2008, the price of state and local public services has increased by 41% nationally, compared with 27% for private services.

Finally, insofar as government collective-bargaining agreements touch on a wide range of economic decisions, public-sector unions have extraordinary influence over government policies. In the classic model of democratic accountability, citizens vote in competitive elections for candidates offering distinct policy agendas; once in office, the winners implement their programs through public agencies. But when public-employee unions bargain collectively with the government, elected officials partially cede control of public agencies to unelected labor leaders. Many policy choices are then settled in the course of negotiations between office holders and unions, rather than originating with the people's duly elected representatives. Over the long term, these negotiated work rules can drive public policy in directions that neither elected officials nor voters desire. And once enacted, these policies can prove very hard to reverse, even through elections: A new mayor or governor—no matter how hard-charging a reformer—will often find his hands tied by the iron-clad agreements unions managed to extract from his predecessors.

Stanford University political scientist Terry Moe has made exactly this argument with respect to the education sector. "Teachers unions have more influence on the public schools than any other group in American society," Moe argues. "Their massive memberships and awesome resources give them unrivaled power in the politics of education, allowing them to affect which policies are imposed on the schools by government—and to block reforms they don't like." One need only look at the debates over charter-school caps or merit-pay proposals to see Moe's point.

Public-sector unions thus distort the labor market, weaken public finances, and diminish the responsiveness of government and the quality of public services. Many of the concerns that initially led policy-makers to oppose collective bargaining by government employees have, over the years, been vindicated.

As a result, it is difficult for defenders of public-sector unions today to make a convincing case that such unions benefit the public at large.

Their argument has basically been reduced to three assertions. One is that most public employees live modest lives, and so criticizing efforts to improve their lot distracts attention from wealthy CEOs and Wall Street bankers who are the real culprits behind today's economic woes. Another is that the unions defend the dignity of public service, thereby preserving a middle class that would otherwise be plunged — through conservatives' efforts to privatize such work — into the vicious race to the bottom that now plagues the private sector. Finally, government-workers' unions help advance leftist politics by keeping the labor movement hobbling along.

To be sure, there is some merit to each of these arguments, though none is especially convincing. But even if these claims were completely true and obvious, they would not offer sufficient reason to put up with the other, manifestly negative consequences of public-sector unionism.

## GOVERNING IN THE REAL WORLD

"At some point," New Jersey governor Chris Christie said in a February speech to his state's mayors, "there has to be parity between what is happening in the real world and what is happening in the public-sector world."

Achieving such parity will not be easy, as some early attempts to curtail the power of public-sector unions have shown. Some state and local officials (like California governor Arnold Schwarzenegger) have sought to appeal directly to the people through referenda, only to be thwarted by the unions' electoral clout. Others have pursued stop-gap measures like wage freezes and furloughs of public employees, which inevitably draw some public backlash. There have even been calls for some cities to follow the example of Vallejo, California, and declare bankruptcy so that they can renegotiate employment contracts with the unions.

A few places are attempting more serious long-term solutions. As the *Wall Street Journal* reported in June, public-employee unions in Vermont, Iowa, Minnesota, and Wyoming have recently agreed to modest reductions in pension benefits — though none of the cuts is large enough to bring the finances of that state's pension funds fully into balance. In the Garden State, Governor Christie succeeded in getting the state legislature to approve a 2% annual growth cap on property taxes in order to limit local spending — thereby indirectly curtailing the power of teachers' unions to demand more public dollars. Yet even well-designed tax caps can unleash unpleasant consequences, including more crowded classrooms, layoffs of state workers, and increases in pension debt. Few politicians will want to suffer those consequences, and the unions will fiercely oppose all policies that even hint at reform.

All of these efforts are, of course, attempts to deal only with the symptoms of the looming state fiscal crisis — not with its underlying causes. To address those causes, policymakers may even need to re-open the question of whether government workers should enjoy the privilege of collective bargaining.

After all, even without collective bargaining, government workers would still benefit from far-reaching protections under existing civil-service statutes — more protections than most private-sector workers enjoy. And they would retain their full rights as citizens to petition the government for changes in policy. Public-sector workers' ability to unionize is hardly sacrosanct; it is by no means a fundamental civil or constitutional right. It has been permitted by most states and localities for only about half a century, and, so far, it is not clear that this experiment has served the public interest.

It is true that ending government workers' ability to organize is politically inconceivable today in the states where it exists. But if states' and cities' fiscal ills grow painful enough, the unthinkable could someday become political necessity. For all Americans — including public-sector employees — it would of course be better if the situation did not reach that point of catastrophe. We can all hope that a robust economic revival will take the pressure off of states and cities and give policymakers more room to maneuver. If such a rapid recovery is not forthcoming, though, the most appealing solution will be for everyone to re-enter the real world — if only public officials and public-sector unions can be sensible enough to try.

*Originally published as "The Trouble with Public Sector Unions" in the Fall 2010 issue of* National Affairs.

*The editors wish to express their gratitude to the staff, contributors, advisors, supporters, and funders of* National Affairs, *and especially to the magazine's past and present assistant editors — Hillel Ofek, Kevin Vance, Zachary Bennett, and Monica Klem — without whose hard work and dedication neither the magazine nor this book would have been possible.*